Equality, Diversity and Discrimination:

How to comply with the law, promote good practice and achieve a diverse workforce

Lynda A C Macdonald

Lynda Macdonald is a self-em   Ca   writer.
She is a panel member of the   es.

Mar 2004

B629 SS

The Chartered Institute of Personnel and Development is the leading publisher of books and reports for personnel and training professionals, students, and all those concerned with the effective management and development of people at work. For details of all our titles, please contact the publishing department:

Tel: 020-8263 3387
Fax: 020-8263 3850
email publish@cipd.co.uk

The catalogue of all CIPD titles can be viewed on all the CIPD website:
www.cipd.co.uk/bookstore

Equality, Diversity and Discrimination:

How to comply with the law, promote best
practice and achieve a diverse workforce

Lynda A C Macdonald

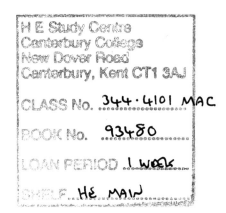
Chartered Institute of Personnel and Development

Published by the Chartered Institute of Personnel and Development,
CIPD House, Camp Road, London, SW19 4UX

First published 2004

Design by Pumpkin House, Cambridge
Typeset by Intype-Libra, Wimbledon, London
Printed in Great Britain by the Cromwell Press, Trowbridge, Wiltshire

British Library Cataloguing in Publication Data
A catalogue of this publication is available from the British Library

ISBN 1 84398 048 7

Chartered Institute of Personnel and Development,
CIPD House, Camp Road, London, SW19 4UX

Tel: 020-8971 9000
Email: cipd@cipd.co.uk
Incorporated by Royal Charter.

Fax: 020-8263 3333
Website: www.cipd.co.uk
Registered Charity No. 1079797

PGEE /LuW

CONTENTS

List of Acts, Regulations and Directives

Anti-Terrorism, Crime and Security Act 2001

Asylum and Immigration Act 1996

Crime and Disorder Act

Criminal Justice and Public Order Act 1994

Data Protection Act 1998

Data Protection Code of Practice

Disability Discrimination Act 1995

Employment Act 1989

Employment Act 2002

Employment Equality (Religion or Belief) Regulations 2003

Employment Equality (Sexual Orientation) Regulations 2003

Employment Rights Act 1996

Equal Pay Act 1970

Equal Pay Directive (Council Directive 75/117)

Equal Treatment Directive (Council Directive 76/207)

European Convention on Human Rights

Fixed-Term Employees (Prevention of Less Favourable Treatment) Regulations 2002

Flexible Working (Procedural Requirements) Regulations 2002

Flexible Working (Eligibility, Complaints and Remedies) Regulations 2002

Framework Directive for Equal Treatment (Council Directive 2000/78)

Human Rights Act 1998

Part-Time Workers (Prevention of Less Favourable Treatment) Regulations 2000

Protection from Harassment Act 1997

Race Directive (Council Directive 2000/43)

Race Relations Act 1976

Race Relations (Amendment) Regulations 2003

Race Relations Amendment Act 2000

Race Relations (Statutory Duties) Order 2001

Sex Discrimination Act 1975

Sex Discrimination (Gender Reassignment) Regulations 1999

Treaty of Rome

Working Time Regulations 1998

List of cases

A v Chief Constable of West Yorkshire Police [2002] EWCA Civ 1584
A v London Borough of Hounslow [2001] EAT 1155/98
Alexander v Home Office [1988] IRLR 190
Allen v H Hargarve & Co EAT 150/99
Aziz v Trinity Street Taxis Ltd & ors [1988] IRLR 204
Baker v Cornwall County Council [1990] ICR 452
Barton v Investec Henderson Crosthwaite Securities Ltd EAT 18/03/MAA
BBC Scotland v Souster [2001] IRLR 150
Bishop v The Cooper Group plc t/a Coopers Thames Ditton ET case number 60910/92
Bower v Shroder Securities Ltd 08 February 2002 case number 3203104/99
Brown v Rentokil [1998] IRLR 445
Burrett v West Birmingham Health Authority [1994] IRLR 7
Burton v Higham t/a Ace Appointments [2003] IRLR 257
Burton and Rhule v De Vere Hotels [1996] IRLR 596
Caisse Nationale d'Assurance Vieillesse des Travailleurs Salariés v Thibault ECJ Case C-136/95
Canniffe v East Riding of Yorkshire Council [2000] IRLR 555
Chaudhary v British Medical Association [2002] case number 2401502/00
Chief Constable of Avon & Somerset Constabulary v Chew EAT [2001] (503/00)
Chief Constable of Bedfordshire Constabulary v Graham [2002] IRLR 239
Chief Constable of the Lincolnshire Police v Stubbs [1998] EAT 145 & 1231/97
Chief Constable of West Yorkshire Police v Khan [2001] IRLR 830
Clark v TDG Ltd (trading as Novacold) [1999] IRLR 318
Commissioners of Inland Revenue & anor v Morgan [2002] IRLR 776
Cosgrove v Caesar & Howie [2001] IRLR 653
Cox v Post Office [1998] case number 1301162/97
Croft v Royal Mail Group plc [2003] EWCA Civ 1045
Dekker v Stichting Vormingscentrum voor Jonge Volwassen [1991] IRLR 27
Diocese of Hallam Trustee v Connaughton EAT/1128/95
Doshoki v Draeger Ltd [2002] IRLR 340
Driskel v Peninsula Business Services Ltd & ors [2000] IRLR 151
D'Souza v London Borough of Lambeth [2003] UKHL 33
Ealing London Borough Council v Race Relations Board [1972] AC 342
Eaton Ltd v Nuttall [1977] ICR 272
Etam plc v Rowan [1989] IRLR 150
Falkirk Council v Whyte and ors [1997] IRLR 560
FME Ltd v Henry EAT 874/86

List of abbreviations

DDA	Disability Discrimination Act 1995
DTI	Department of Trade and Industry
EAT	Employment Appeal Tribunal
ECJ	European Court of Justice
EEA	European Economic Area
EOC	Equal Opportunities Commission
ERA	Employment Rights Act 1996
GOQ	Genuine occupational qualification
GOR	Genuine occupational requirement
HRA	Human Rights Act 1998
RRA	Race Relations Act 1976
RRAA	Race Relations Amendment Act 2000
SDA	Sex Discrimination Act 1975
SOSR	some other substantial reason

Foreword

In a rapidly changing world, traditional approaches to management are no longer effective and successful. New technologies, demographic changes to the workforce, a more demanding and well-informed client base and an increasingly global marketplace challenge organisations to adopt new ways of working. Organisations that value and encourage the diversity of their employees, suppliers and customers will have a competitive and creative advantage over others.

Diversity, therefore, is no longer a nicety – it's a necessity. A willing and committed workforce, where difference is visibly welcomed and where people are actively included so they can use their unique talents to the full, is a key requirement for any organisation wanting to be successful in delivering a diverse range of products and services to a varied client base.

As any workforce evolves to reflect the growing diversity of an organisation's communities and the global marketplace, its efforts to understand, value and incorporate differences become increasingly important. The first stage, as this book illustrates, is for each organisation to define what the terms 'equality' and 'diversity' mean and how they interrelate.

The equal and fair treatment of all employees is central to good people management policies and procedures. The organisational benefits of embracing this outlook is widely acknowledged, and in the CIPD Research Report *Understanding the People and Performance Link: Unlocking the black box* it was demonstrated that:

> Some HR policies and practices were shown to be particularly important in terms of influencing employee outcomes like commitment, job satisfaction and motivation. These were those concerned with career opportunities, job influence, job challenge, training, performance appraisal, teamworking, involvement in decision-making, work-life balance, and having managers who are good at leadership and show respect.

Every single policy listed above will require the concept of equality to be carefully examined and integrated if the policy and associated practice is to have the desired outcomes. And every single one of these activities represents a standard activity that is likely to take place routinely in your organisation – regardless of its sector or size. Equality does not stand alone as a single idea or statement but is integrated in the overall functioning of an organisation.

By valuing diversity and tapping into the unique ideas, opinions, perspectives and talents of all the different people in a workforce, the whole organisation is enriched. An 'inclusive' culture, which respects, values and welcomes difference, is the key: an 'exclusive' mindset, 'If you don't change and become one of us, you won't fit in', for example corporate cloning, has no place in an organisation which embraces diversity.

I was extremely pleased to be asked to write the foreword to this book. In it Lynda Macdonald provides the basis for any organisation taking steps to eliminate all forms of discrimination and develop a workforce that appreciates the value of diversity where people count and the differences between them do not.

The book provides guidance on Great Britain's anti-discrimination and family friendly legislation. Lynda has included some very practical checklists, as well as many useful examples to highlight key principles, in order to help employers comply with the law.

The value of Lynda's endeavour is to try and simplify the law and apply general legal principles to the reality of the workplace. In so doing she has provided a practical understanding of the application of discrimination legislation to the employment cycle. Readers are reminded, however, that discrimination legislation is constantly changing to take account of rulings in the appellate courts and there will be further amendments to the law in the next two years. Specialist legal advice should therefore be taken before embarking upon any course of action and employers must take account of the provisions of the statutory Codes fo Practice which accompany the Sex Discrimination Act 1975, The Race Relations Act 1976 and the Disability Discrimination Act 1995.

Makbool Javaid, Employment Law Partner, DLA
March 2004

Introduction

It is in every employer's interests to promote equality and diversity, and take positive measures to ensure their workplace is free from all forms of discrimination. Implementing equality/diversity policies and outlawing discriminatory practices will help the employer to recruit, motivate and retain the best staff, and will encourage high levels of performance and productivity. This, in turn, will enhance the organisation's reputation and performance.

In contrast, an employer who pays no attention to equality and diversity, or who imagines that no discrimination or harassment ever takes place in their organisation, is likely to face an employment tribunal claim sooner or later. A successful claim for unlawful discrimination can lead to potentially high awards of compensation. Over and above the financial costs, the organisation may face detrimental publicity, loss of reputation, embarrassment in terms of customer relationships and difficulty in motivating their staff.

This book aims to provide guidance to employers of all sizes and in all sectors on what they should do to comply with the anti-discrimination laws and promote equality and diversity in their workplace. The book provides a comprehensive coverage of all types of unlawful discrimination in Britain, ie gender, marital status, gender re-assignment, sexual orientation, race, ethnic origins, religion, disability, age, part-time status and fixed-term status. It provides case examples, checklists and action points, plus many sample policies, procedures, letters and contract clauses. It also includes bullet-pointed 'points to note' and 'action-point' lists at the end of each chapter.

Individual chapters address discrimination during the process of recruitment and selection (Chapter 1), in terms and benefits of employment (Chapter 2), against part-time and fixed-term staff (Chapter 3) and in training and development (Chapter 4), harassment as discrimination (Chapter 5), and discrimination during termination of employment, including redundancy (Chapter 6). Chapter 7 addresses ways of preventing discrimination and of promoting equality and diversity through effective policies, procedures and monitoring. Chapters 8 and 9 address the scope and structure of discrimination legislation and the various grounds for discrimination respectively.

Readers with either no underlying knowledge, or only a little knowledge, of the various laws governing discrimination in employment may prefer to read Chapters 8 and 9 first, as these chapters will provide a solid background for understanding how anti-discrimination law works. For readers who already have a sound understanding of the key principles of anti-discrimination law, Chapters 8 and 9 will provide either a useful refresher or perhaps a more in-depth appreciation of the complexities of the legislation. These two chapters can also be used as a reference where necessary.

Defining equality, diversity and discrimination

Most employers are familiar with the concept of discrimination – that it involves detrimental treatment of someone on grounds connected in some way with gender, race, religion, etc (whether intentional or not). Equality is about treating all workers and job applicants equally, irrespective of gender, race, religion, etc. But what about diversity?

Diversity is about:

- recognising that people are different from one another

- valuing people as individuals, including respecting their differences and their differing needs

- accommodating differences wherever possible, for example making adjustments to working arrangements or practices to accommodate an individual's needs.

The management of diversity develops and complements established approaches to equal opportunities, and broadens them out beyond the issues covered by law. The effective management of diversity encourages people who belong to 'minority groups' to feel comfortable at work and creates an environment in which everyone is empowered to perform at their best. The management of diversity helps to combat prejudice, stereotyping and harassment and thus helps to create an environment of mutual trust and respect and one in which fear is absent. A working environment in which diversity is truly practised will be one in which workers feel comfortable about expressing their views, ideas and their needs, rather than feeling obliged to blend in with the majority.

It is estimated that by the year 2009, ethnic minority people, who at present constitute 9.9 per cent of the UK population, will account for half the growth in the labour force (*Ethnic minorities and the labour market report*). It is also estimated that by the year 2020, more than half the UK population will be over the age of 50, and that there will be two million fewer working people under the age of 50 than at present (*Equal Opportunities Review, No. 115*). These are just two examples of how the make-up of the UK's population is changing to become much more diverse. Employers who make diversity a business priority will be the ones who succeed in the world of tomorrow.

CHAPTER 1

DISCRIMINATION IN RECRUITMENT – THE GENERAL PRINCIPLES

Effective recruitment requires an objective, systematic and planned approach if unlawful discrimination is to be avoided. Both short-listing and selection should be on the basis of candidates' relevant experience, skills, qualifications, knowledge and talent and should be based on factual evidence. Assumptions about individuals should be avoided. Naturally, gender, marital status, race, religion and age (for example) should play no part in the selection process (except where a genuine occupational requirement exists – see below). It is advisable for all organisations to devise and implement recruitment procedures and guidelines for all staff involved in the process of recruitment and to ensure that these incorporate the principles of the organisation's equal opportunities policy. It is also imperative that all those involved in recruitment and selection should be properly trained in recruitment procedures and the principles of equality.

The essential principles of avoiding discrimination in recruitment

The laws prohibiting discrimination on grounds of sex, race, disability, sexual orientation and religion expressly outlaw discrimination in the process of recruitment and selection. Specifically, it is unlawful to discriminate:

- in the arrangements made for deciding who should be offered employment

- in the terms on which employment is offered

- in refusing or deliberately omitting to offer employment.

The word 'arrangements' in the context of recruitment incorporates all aspects of the recruitment process, including the design of job advertisements, the procedures used for short-listing, interview arrangements, the questions asked at interviews, any psychometric testing used as part of the selection process and the final decision as to whom to appoint.

Checklist for equal opportunities in recruitment

- Assess the objectivity of any criteria attached to the post to ensure their application is not indirectly discriminatory, for example against women.

- Avoid using age limits in recruitment, as these will considerably reduce the range of talented people from which the employer can select.

- Review the design and style of all recruitment advertising to ensure that advertisements portray the organisation as one that positively promotes diversity.

- Scrutinise the wording of all advertisements to ensure there is no actual or implied discrimination, no potentially sexist job titles (for example 'storeman') and no possibility of misinterpretation.

- Design or re-design application forms to remove personal information that should not be used as part of the recruitment process to a separate part of the form.

- Select candidates for the short-list by comparing each application to a well-thought-out employee specification.

- Assess candidates' qualifications at a level that is appropriate to the post, rather than assuming that the best-qualified candidate will be the most suitable applicant.

- View overseas qualifications that are comparable with UK qualifications as having equivalent status, rather than assuming that they are inferior.

- Seek information on applicants' nationality and ethnic group only for the purposes of monitoring and verifying whether the successful applicant has the right to work in the UK.

- Avoid making assumptions about individual job applicants – check out any concerns at interview.

- If psychometric testing is to be deployed, check that the chosen tests have been properly verified to ensure that they will not place any applicants at a disadvantage, for example those from certain ethnic groups or those with disabilities.

- Recognise personal opinions, attitudes and prejudices for what they are and do not allow them to influence the interview process or selection decision.

- Carry out interviewing in a planned, structured and objective manner and do not ask intrusive personal questions of any applicant.

- Aim to select the applicant whose experience, skills, qualifications and overall abilities most closely match the employee specification.

- Keep records showing clear and objective reasons for which the successful candidate was selected and why others on the short-list were rejected.

Genuine occupational requirements and qualifications

There are limited exceptions to the general principles that it is unlawful to use gender, race, religion or sexual orientation as criteria in the selection process. In certain limited circumstances that are specified in the relevant legislation an employer may discriminate by expressly setting out to recruit either a woman or a man, a person from a specific racial or religious group, or a person of a particular sexual orientation based on the requirements of the job itself. Essentially this is lawful where being of a particular gender, race, religion or sexual orientation is a genuine occupational requirement (GOR) or genuine occupational qualification (GOQ) for the specific post.

Any potentially applicable GOQ or GOR should be identified at the beginning of the recruitment process. It is important, however, to avoid assuming that one of the exemptions will apply without giving the matter thorough consideration. Jobs can change over time, and just because a particular GOQ applied to the job in the past, this does not automatically mean that it is still legitimate to apply it.

In general, in order for a GOR or GOQ to apply, it must genuinely be necessary, in order to ensure effective performance of the job in question, for the post-holder to be either a man or a woman (as the case may be), a person from a defined racial group, someone who belongs to a specific religion, or someone of a particular sexual orientation. It is not necessary for all the duties of the job to fall within the scope of the stated GOR or GOQ, so long as it can be shown that some aspects of the job create a genuine need for the job to be performed by a person from the specified group.

It should be noted, however, that if sufficient numbers of employees of the 'necessary' group are already employed in the same position as the job into which a new employee is to be hired, and if the existing employees could in practice carry out the particular duties to which the GOR or GOQ applies, then it will not be lawful to apply the GOR to the new post.

Case Example

For example, in *Etam plc v Rowan*, the employer set out to recruit a shop assistant to work in the ladies fashion department of one of its shops. The job involved assisting female customers who could be in a state of undress in the changing rooms. Taking this into account, the employer rejected a man who applied for the job. When the man claimed sex discrimination, the Employment Appeal Tribunal (EAT) held that the decency/privacy requirement (see below) could not apply to the job because the employer already had an adequate number of female shop assistants who could deal with female customers in the changing rooms.

[1989] IRLR 150

The GOR and GOQ provisions in the legislation do not permit employers to take action in order to create an equal balance of the sexes or to increase the number of people in their employment from a minority ethnic group (but see also the section on 'Positive action permitted to encourage minority groups to apply for employment', page 12 below).

When GOQs and GORs can be applied

Where a GOR or GOQ applies, it does not act to compel an employer to limit a job to one gender or racial group (for example), but merely makes it an option for the employer to apply the GOR or GOQ if they believe it is appropriate and necessary to do so.

It is important to note that in the sex discrimination legislation, GOQs apply only during recruitment, including the process of determining who should be promoted or transferred to a different post (but see also the section in Chapter 6 on 'Positive action that is permitted to encourage minority groups to access training', page 105). It is not open to an employer to cite a GOQ in respect of the terms of employment offered to the successful applicant, access to company benefits or perks, or the process of termination of employment.

By contrast, the Race Relations Act 1976 (as amended by the Race Relations Act (Amendment) Regulations 2003), the Employment Equality (Religion or Belief) Regulations 2003 and the Employment Equality (Sexual Orientation) Regulations 2003 also allow a GOR to be applied in dismissal. This could be lawful (ie not discriminatory), where for example an employee changed their religion to one that made them unsuitable in relation to the performance of the job for which they had been employed.

The number and scope of GORs and GOQs that may be used by employers is very limited, and the list in each of the relevant laws is exhaustive. Thus, it is not open to an employer to invent their own reasons for insisting on recruiting a man, for example, no matter how strongly the employer's management may feel about the matter. Reasons that do not accord quite specifically with one of the defined GOQ's or GORs will not be valid.

Gender – GOQs

s7 SDA 1975

The Sex Discrimination Act 1975 contains a list of 'genuine occupational qualifications' (GOQs) that allow employers to seek to recruit either a man or a woman in limited circumstances. The GOQs are as follows:

Authenticity or physiology

A gender GOQ may apply where the essential nature of the job calls for either a man or a woman for reasons of authenticity in entertainment, acting or modelling, or for reasons of physiology (for example in modelling jobs). It is important to note, however, that this GOQ does not incorporate a requirement for strength or stamina. It is therefore not open to employers to restrict employment to men (thus excluding all women who may apply for the job) for reasons of strength or stamina.

Decency or privacy

It is lawful to restrict employment to only one of the sexes where it is necessary for a job to be filled by either a man or a woman for reasons of decency or privacy. It is important to note that this GOQ will apply only if it can be shown that it is necessary for the post to be filled by either a man or a woman. A preference for either a man or a woman will not suffice. Thus, for example, a health authority would not be permitted to insist on recruiting a female gynaecologist for a hospital job just because a number of female patients at the hospital had expressed a preference or desire to be treated by a woman.

The decency/privacy GOQ may arise for one of three reasons:

- because the job involves physical contact with either men or women
- where the job has to be performed in a place where individuals are likely to be in a state of undress or using sanitary facilities
- where the job involves the person working or living in a private home.

In all three cases it must be shown that men or women might reasonably object to the job being carried out by a person of the opposite sex. Thus, jobs such as security officer (where the job duties involved conducting physical searches of men or women), lavatory cleaner and nursing assistant in a private home could be covered.

Live-in jobs with single-sex accommodation

If the nature of the job is such that the employee has to live in premises provided by the employer, and there are no separate sleeping quarters or toilet/washroom facilities for men and women, and where it is not reasonable for the employer to provide separate facilities, it will be lawful to seek to recruit only a man or a woman. An example of this GOQ could be a job on an oil-rig that has communal sleeping and shower facilities and where the people already employed there are exclusively or predominantly men.

Single-sex establishments

It may be permissible to insist on recruiting either a man or a woman where the job is in a single-sex establishment for people requiring special care, such as a hospital, prison, children's home or old-people's home. One key point to note is that the residents in the single-sex establishment must be people who require special care. Thus the job of school teacher in a single-sex infants' school would not fall within the remit of this GOQ unless it could be shown that the infants had special needs, for example if the school specifically catered for children with disabilities. By contrast, the job of care assistant in a residential home for geriatric women might potentially be covered by the single-sex establishment GOQ, depending on all the circumstances.

The provision of personal services

This GOQ may apply where the job involves the provision of personal services promoting welfare or education, and these services can best be provided by a member of one sex. It is easy to imagine, for example, that a woman might respond more favourably to a female rape counsellor than to a man doing the same job. However, the services to be provided must be personal services for the GOQ to apply. Thus a managerial post in social work that does not involve personal contact with individual clients would not be covered.

Jobs outside the UK

It will be permissible to insist on recruiting a man where the job to be filled involves working in a country other than the UK and the laws or customs of that country are such that the duties cannot be performed effectively by a woman. The most likely example of this would be a job in a country where women are forbidden to drive in circumstances where the ability to drive was a necessary component of the job.

Jobs for married couples

This GOQ allows an employer to seek to employ a husband and wife team (rather than two single people) where the job is 'one of two to be held by a married couple'.

Gender re-assignment

As the law stands at present, there are two situations in which it may be lawful to refuse employment to a trans-gender person. Specifically, an individual who has announced an intention to undergo a sex change, is part-way through the process of gender re-assignment or has completed a sex change may be refused employment in a job that involves:

- working and/or living in a private home in circumstances where objection might reasonably be taken to a trans-sexual

- conducting intimate physical searches.

Even in circumstances where the job involves conducting personal physical searches, however, the employer should consider whether the applicant could be employed and exempted from the requirement to conduct such searches.

> In *A v Chief Constable of West Yorkshire Police*, a male-to-female trans-sexual who had applied to join the police was rejected on the grounds that she would be unable to carry out personal searches of people in custody. In considering the applicant's claim for sex discrimination, the Court ruled that the police force's assertion that the GOQ applied could not be upheld. This was because it would have been possible to exempt the applicant from the need to conduct searches, particularly in view of the fact that she had made it clear that she had no objection to her trans-sexuality being disclosed to colleagues if necessary.

[2002] EWCA Civ 1584

Please refer also to Chapter 11 under 'The UK's position on trans-gender status' for further information (page 201). The law is set to change in the near future so that people who have completed the process of sex change will have the legal right to be regarded as belonging to their acquired sex in every respect. This will alter the position with regard to the GOQ described above, which will no longer be capable of application to people who have completed the trans-gender process.

Race – GOQs and GORs

Like the Sex Discrimination Act 1975, the Race Relations Act 1976 contains some GOQs that allow employers to restrict employment in certain posts to people of a particular colour or nationality. The GOQs are as follows:

s5 RRA 1976

Authenticity

The authenticity GOQ applies where the essential nature of the job calls for someone of a particular racial group for reasons of authenticity in entertainment or modelling. This GOQ expressly includes front-of-house jobs in public restaurants, cafés or bars. For example, the owners of a Chinese restaurant would be permitted to seek to recruit Chinese waiting staff in order to create an authentic atmosphere. This principle cannot, however, be lawfully applied to behind-the-scenes jobs such as that of kitchen porter, or to jobs in private clubs or staff canteens.

The provision of personal services

It is permissible to seek to recruit someone from a defined colour or nationality where the job involves the provision of personal services promoting welfare to people of that racial group, and there is evidence that these services can best be provided in this way. The services to be provided must be personal services if the GOQ is to be relied on. It might, for example, be legitimate to seek to recruit someone from Bangladesh into the post of social worker if the people in the community in which the post-holder is to be working are predominantly Bangladeshi and it is reasonably believed that they would respond more favourably to someone from their own country than to a British person doing the same job.

The race GOR

Over and above the permitted GOQs that apply to the concepts of colour and nationality, the Race Relations Act 1976 contains a general provision that, if it is genuinely necessary for the holder of a particular post to be of a particular race, ethnic origin or national origin, the prospective employer may lawfully discriminate in favour of someone from that race, ethnic or national origin, provided also that the race-related requirement is proportionate in the particular case. This genuine occupational requirement (GOR) was added to the Race Relations Act in July 2003 following the implementation of the Race Relations (Amendment) Regulations 2003.

Religion – GORs

The Employment Equality (Religion or Belief) Regulations 2003 contain two provisions that allow employers to discriminate in favour of those who belong to a specific religion when recruiting or when considering individuals for promotion or transfer, or (in the event that an individual changes their religion) in dismissal.

The first GOR can be applied where being of a particular religion or belief can be shown to be a genuine and determining occupational requirement for the post in question. Thus recruitment into the job of minister in the Church of Scotland may be restricted to applicants who uphold the religious principles of the Church of Scotland. The job of cleaner in the church would not, however, fall within this GOR, since there would no logical need for the cleaner to uphold a particular faith in order to be able to perform cleaning duties effectively. This exception is therefore narrow and applies only where there is a very clear connection between the work to be done and the characteristics required to perform it. The GOR will only be valid where it is necessary for particular job duties to be carried out by someone of a specific religion and not merely because someone of that religion would be preferred.

The second provision relates to organisations that have an ethos based on a particular religion or belief, such as churches or religious schools. In this case, the GOR based on religion or belief may be applied to any post so long as it can be shown to be a genuine requirement. The difference between this GOR and the general GOR described in the preceding paragraph is the word 'determining'. In other words, where the employer is an ethos-based organisation, being of a particular religion or belief need not be a decisive requirement for the post in question, although it must still be a genuine requirement that is broadly relevant to the organisation. Under the religious ethos GOR, a Catholic school (for example) may be able to justify requiring all its teachers to be Catholic on the grounds that teaching the principles of the Catholic faith to pupils is part of every teacher's responsibility. Even this GOR, however, would be unlikely to justify insisting that the school cleaners must be Catholic. Although the ethos-based organisation GOR is broader than the general GOR, this does not mean that it can be applied universally within the organisation.

In both cases, the employer must be able to demonstrate that it is proportionate to apply the religion or belief requirement in the particular case.

Sexual orientation – GORs

The Employment Equality (Sexual Orientation) Regulations 2003 also contain a general GOR and a specific GOR. The general GOR can be applied where being of a particular sexual orientation can be shown to be a genuine and determining occupational requirement for the post in question, and the employer can demonstrate that it is proportionate to apply the requirement in the particular case. This is parallel to the general GOR in the Employment Equality (Religion or Belief) Regulations 2003 (see above). A possible example could be a job whose main function was the provision of counselling to young people who are gay or lesbian.

The second GOR in relation to sexual orientation is available where the employment is 'for the purposes of an organised religion'. However, the sexual orientation GOR can only be relied on if it is being applied either to comply with the doctrines of the particular religion or to avoid conflicting with the strongly held religious convictions of a significant number of the religion's followers.

The range of jobs that can be said to be 'for the purposes of an organised religion' is very narrow and is likely to include only such jobs as ministers of religion involving work for a church, synagogue or mosque where the religion in question disapproves of homosexuality or where many of the religion's followers find it unacceptable. This GOR will not therefore apply to all jobs in an organisation that has an ethos based on a particular religion. This is because the wording in the statute makes it clear that, in order for the sexual orientation GOR to apply, the job itself must exist for the purposes of an organised religion rather than just be a job in an ethos-based organisation. For example, it could be argued that the job of nurse in a religious hospice is not 'for the purposes of an organised religion' but rather that the job exists for the purpose of health care.

Positive action permitted to encourage minority groups to apply for employment

Positive discrimination (sometimes termed 'reverse discrimination') in employment is not permitted by UK law (unless one of the specific exceptions applies – see 'Genuine occupational requirements and qualifications', page 5). In other words it is not lawful to recruit a black candidate in preference to a white candidate, or a woman in preference to a man, if the white candidate or the man is better suited to the job in terms of qualifications, experience and skills (but see also 'Positive action in relation to disabled job applicants', page 15). This principle stands firm even if the motivation for appointing a particular person is based on a genuine desire to promote diversity, to increase the numbers of people from a disadvantaged group in employment, or to create a more balanced workforce. At the point of selection for the job, the principle of equality must always prevail, and gender, race, religion and sexual orientation must never be taken into account as a criterion for selection.

[1976] IRLR 283

Case Example

One example of an employer who misinterpreted the law in this area was in the case of *Roadburg v Lothian Regional Council*. In this case, two men and one woman were short-listed for the post of voluntary services officer. The Council wished to maintain a balance between the sexes in the team of officers and therefore decided initially to appoint one of the men. The female applicant was offered a different job elsewhere in the Council. Subsequently neither post was filled as a result of financial cuts. The woman nevertheless succeeded in a claim for direct sex discrimination on the grounds that the arrangements for filling the first post had been discriminatory.

Quotas and targets

In line with the principle that positive discrimination is unlawful, setting a quota, for example for the recruitment of people from a minority racial group, would not be permissible because a quota would inevitably lead to positive discrimination. Conversely, establishing targets is allowable. The difference is that a target is something to aspire to and will encourage positive measures to be taken within the ambit of the law, whilst a quota would be a figure that would have to be achieved at all costs, irrespective of the merit of the individuals who applied for employment.

When positive action is permitted

Within the above general framework, certain forms of positive action (sometimes known as affirmative action) are permitted by the legislation, provided they take the form of encouragement to members of an under-represented or disadvantaged group to take up opportunities for employment or training. In effect, positive action will widen the pool for selection, promotion or development and increase the chances that people from a minority group can be legitimately employed or promoted.

However, where positive action is being planned or carried out, this will not entitle the employer automatically to exclude people from consideration who do not belong to the under-represented group. At the point where any decision is being made as to whom to short-list or appoint, the principle of equality must prevail, and the gender, race, religion or sexual orientation of the applicants under consideration must play no part.

It will also be vital to make sure that the steps taken to encourage members of the minority group to come forward for employment do not overstep the mark of what is permissible in law.

Positive action in relation to gender and race may be undertaken only when either men or women, or people from a particular racial group, are under-represented. There will be an under-representation of a particular group if the number of people employed from that group in a particular type of work has, at any time during the previous 12 months, been disproportionately low when compared with the group's proportion in the workforce as a whole, or with the population from which the employer normally recruits.

The equivalent provisions related to religion and sexual orientation permit employers to take steps to encourage people of a particular religion (or sexual orientation) to take advantage of employment opportunities, provided such action is carried out to prevent or compensate for disadvantages linked to religion (or sexual orientation) suffered by those of that religion (or sexual orientation). Positive action is therefore a lawful means of attempting to redress an existing imbalance.

Despite the limitations, positive action may be a useful tool for employers who wish to promote diversity within their workforce. Employers may, however, wish to consider the possible negative effects of positive action, namely that applicants who are not from the under-represented group may feel that their prospects are diminished, and may be discouraged from applying for employment. There may even be resentment from within the organisation from those who perceive (perhaps mistakenly) that women or people from minority racial groups (for example) are being given priority in recruitment or are receiving extra-favourable treatment.

It is important to note that positive action is not compelled by law but instead is an option that allows employers to choose to take certain steps to increase the number of people from under-represented or disadvantaged groups that they employ.

Checklist for positive action

Positive action, where it is permitted, can include such actions as the following:

- targeting the advertising of a vacant post, for example placing advertisements in publications that are known to be popular with Asian or Chinese people, advertising in a different geographical area, or using a business journal read predominantly by women

- stating in a job advertisement that applications from women or from people from a minority racial or religious group will be particularly welcome – although if this is done there should also be a statement in the advertisement that the job is open to both sexes and all racial (or religious) groups

- publishing a booklet promoting employment opportunities that exist within the organisation and targeting it at female undergraduates

- setting up a careers fair or promotional event targeted at overseas nationals to encourage them to learn about the organisation and apply for employment

- developing links with community groups that work to promote the interests of people from minority or disadvantaged groups

- stating in a job advertisement that focused training will be provided for new recruits from the under-represented group, for example to increase the opportunities for women to be developed into supervisory or management posts

- promoting flexible working practices (which, arguably, benefit everyone).

See also Chapter 6 under 'Positive action that is permitted to encourage minority groups to access training', page 105.

Positive action in relation to disabled job applicants

The Disability Discrimination Act (DDA) 1995, although similar in many ways to the other anti-discrimination legislation, has some features that are distinct and different from the other laws. One difference is that the Act is structured so that it technically allows a disabled candidate to be selected for a job in preference to an able-bodied person simply because they are disabled. In other words, the Act does not contain any provision that prohibits discrimination against someone because they are not disabled, although such favouritism in recruitment is not, of course, compulsory. Furthermore, the duty to make reasonable adjustments under the Act could, arguably, be viewed as a form of positive discrimination (see Chapter 3 for a discussion on the duty to make reasonable adjustments under the Disability Discrimination Act, pages 65–67).

Ensuring any criteria or conditions attached to the job are not indirectly discriminatory

The meaning of indirect discrimination is discussed in Chapter 10 (pages 181–184). In the early stages of the recruitment process, management will wish to draw up an employee specification that will describe the type of person the employer seeks to appoint in terms of qualifications, experience and skills etc. Such criteria may, however (if the employer is not alert to the possible difficulties), be potentially indirectly discriminatory on grounds of sex, sexual orientation, race or religion (the Disability Discrimination Act 1995 does not incorporate the concept of indirect discrimination). Specifically, the imposition of inappropriate or unnecessarily high standards or criteria may indirectly discriminate against people of one sex compared with the other, or against people from a particular minority racial group or religion. It is therefore very important that the requirements and standards specified for job candidates' qualifications, experience and skills etc should be objectively and sensibly matched to the needs of the job without allowing personal opinions to play any part. Two examples of potentially discriminatory criteria could be:

DDA 1995

- a requirement for the post-holder to work unsocial or very long hours, which would discriminate indirectly against women. Unless the requirement could be justified on objective grounds related to the job or to the business, it would be unlawful.

- a condition that whoever is appointed must speak fluent English, which would discriminate indirectly against anyone brought up in a country whose first language is one other than English. Unless the requirement was relevant to the job and proportionate, it could be judged unlawful.

Guidelines for avoiding indirectly discriminatory criteria

Managers who are responsible for preparing employee specifications should therefore:

- write the employee specification objectively and in accordance with the needs of the job, excluding any subjective views or personal opinions

- scrutinise the proposed criteria for the job in order to ensure they are genuinely relevant, rather than being based on convenience, personal preference or somebody's whim

- review, even if a requirement is relevant to the job, whether it is proportionate (ie not excessive) and whether the aim to be achieved could be attained in a different (non-discriminatory) way

- take care not to overstate the qualifications and level of experience required to perform the job

- pay special attention to any personal qualities ascribed to the prospective job-holder (eg 'outgoing personality'), as they may be the result of somebody's personal opinion and may not actually be necessary

- avoid using age limits

- avoid stipulating that a candidate must be physically fit, unless this is necessary for the job (since this requirement could place disabled candidates at a disadvantage)

- avoid making general statements that are prone to subjectivity, for example requiring candidates to be 'outgoing', 'enthusiastic' or 'energetic'. Since most people believe that they have these qualities anyway, they will not assist the recruitment process and may inadvertently discriminate.

Distinguishing between 'necessary' and 'desirable' criteria

It will be helpful, in preparing an employee specification, to identify which criteria are necessary for the job to be done effectively and which are merely desirable. Having made these distinctions, it is advisable to stick to them. In other words, if a criterion has been stated as 'desirable' it should not subsequently be the sole reason for the rejection of a particular candidate unless there are two or more candidates who match the 'necessary' criteria equally in every respect. It is suggested that this is unlikely in practice except (possibly) in the case of school leavers with no work experience and the same qualifications. Individuals, if interviewed well, will nearly always reveal differences between themselves in talents, achievements and skills. Managers involved in recruitment should take care, therefore, not to automatically exclude candidates based on criteria that are only desirable and not actually necessary for the job.

Stating the job duties

It is important that all candidates for the job are fully informed of all the duties of the job at an early stage in the recruitment process. Doing this will ensure that applicants have an opportunity to consider fully whether any aspect of the job conflicts with their religion or belief. It may be, for example, that an applicant who is a vegetarian (and who believes strongly that it is morally wrong to use animals for human consumption or gain) would not wish to work in a job where animals were used for experimentation purposes, or in a job that involved preparing or serving meat in a restaurant. There is no obligation on an employer to offer employment to someone who, as a result of their religion or belief, is unable or unwilling to undertake key parts of the job (but see also 'Time off for religious holidays and when a refusal may be discriminatory or in breach of the individual's human rights' in Chapter 3, page 52). It is clearly in the interests of both the employer and the prospective employee that any such conflicts are identified earlier in the recruitment process rather than later.

Designing application forms

Employers who seek to promote equality and diversity may wish to consider reviewing, and where necessary redesigning, their application forms. It is considered good practice to exclude questions about gender, marital status, number and ages of children, nationality, age and disability from the main part of the application form. Although some of this information will be needed in respect of the person who is appointed, it is hard to envisage how any of it could be relevant to the short-listing process. Arguably the exclusion of such information from the application form ensures that all job applicants are treated fairly and equally, and any conscious or subconscious bias in the minds of those responsible for short-listing will be avoided.

Questions to ask on application forms

Apart from requesting information about candidates' experience, qualifications and training, the main part of the application form could include some or all of the following questions:

Please state any experience, skills and talents you have gained as a result of activities outside of paid employment

Please state why you think you are suited to the job for which you are applying

Please state what you believe you could contribute to this organisation if you are employed

Please state what you believe to be your main strengths

Continued

Continued

Please state what you believe to be your weaknesses

What steps have you taken to overcome any recognised weaknesses?

Please state what you feel is your greatest achievement(s) in your career to date

Which aspect(s) of your work interest you most?

Which interest you least?

How would you like to see your career develop over the next three to five years?

How do you think this job would fit in with your career aspirations?

What notice period do you have give to your current employer?

What has prompted you to seek new employment?

Applicants' personal details

One way of obtaining the required personal information about applicants without compromising the objectivity of the recruitment process is to design the application form with a tear-off page. The tear-off page can contain any necessary personal questions about gender, marital status, nationality, age and disability, and can be removed by the employer's HR department before the application form is passed to the line manager responsible for the vacancy. In this way, the risk of discrimination is minimised whilst at the same time HR staff have information to hand that they may need during the recruitment process. The model 'personal details and equal opportunities monitoring form' suggested below could be used for this purpose.

The personal details form should encourage applicants to disclose any disability that they may have, whilst also making a statement about the employer's commitment to a positive approach towards the employment of disabled people. It is also a sound idea to make the application form available in alternative formats, for example in Braille or extra-large print, and also electronically.

Job application forms should not contain questions that require applicants to reveal their religion or belief, or their sexual orientation.

Recommendations in the Data Protection Code of Practice

It may be advantageous in any event to scrutinise the application form thoroughly to ensure it asks only questions that are relevant to the job. The Data Protection Code of Practice (Part 1) (which provides guidance on how to comply with the Data Protection Act 1998 in the context of recruitment) recommends that employers should:

- use different application forms for different jobs

- aim to seek information from job applicants that is proportionate to their business needs

- not request information about applicants' private lives

- remove or amend any questions on application forms that are not directly relevant or necessary to the selection decision.

The Code of Practice is not legally binding on employers, but an employer who does not adhere to its principles may find, in the event of a legal claim against them, that the court or tribunal will use the Code as a measure of assessing the appropriateness of the employer's actions. In other words, any evidence of non-compliance is likely to operate to the employer's detriment.

Obtaining information for monitoring purposes

It is generally considered to be good practice for employers to monitor their recruitment processes in order to promote equality. Indeed, public authorities are under a positive duty to conduct racial monitoring of job applicants as a result of the implementation of the Race Relations Amendment Act 2000.

Where an employer is planning or reviewing how it should monitor job applicants, they may wish to consider monitoring not only candidates' racial origins, but also their gender, age and whether they have a disability, since a comprehensive exercise is likely to produce maximum benefit. It is important, however, to distinguish between information that is needed for the purpose of monitoring, and information required for recruitment and selection. It will be equally important to communicate to job applicants that any personal information provided will not be used as part of the process of short-listing or selection, and that the information will be used to assist the organisation to review and improve its equality and diversity practices.

The objectives of monitoring in recruitment would generally be to:

- establish whether the proportions of men and women and people of different racial groups who apply for employment are proportionate to the numbers in each of these groups within the general community

- identify whether a higher proportion of applicants of one sex or racial group than another is rejected for employment, and at what stage in the recruitment process they tend to be rejected

- review the age profile of those who apply for jobs, and establish whether or not the correlation between this and the age profile of those who are appointed is the same

- review how many disabled people apply for employment and, of those who do apply, what proportion are subsequently employed

- take action to establish the reasons for any evidence that suggests that a disproportionate number of women, men, members of minority racial groups, people in different age bands or disabled people do not apply for employment or are rejected for employment, and to devise means of remedying this situation.

Model personal details and equal opportunities monitoring form

We would be grateful if you would assist us in our aim of promoting equal opportunities and diversity in employment by completing the questions on this form.

The information you provide on this form will be treated in strictest confidence and will not be seen by staff involved in the recruitment decision. The information will be used principally to assist the organisation to review and improve its equality and diversity practices.

In the event that you are employed by the organisation, relevant information from this form will be transferred to a personnel file and retained during your employment with the company.

Your name   Date form completed

Your address

Telephone number   E-mail

Job applied for   Location

Please tick the appropriate box for each question below

Gender   ☐ Male   ☐ Female

Please state your date of birth

Marital status   ☐ Married   ☐ Single   ☐ Divorced/separated   ☐ Other

Do you have responsibility for dependants, ie children, or elderly or other persons for whom you are the main carer?   ☐ Yes   ☐ No

If you have children under 18, please state their ages

Do any of your children under 18 have a disability?   ☐ Yes   ☐ No

The company promotes flexible working and will consider every employee's personal, family and religious needs when designating hours of work. It would be helpful if you could indicate whether there are any dates, days, or times of day that you would prefer not to work

....

....

....

....

....

....

Please state your nationality

Please describe your ethnic origin by placing a tick in the appropriate box

☐ White EU

☐ White other (please specify)

☐ Black EU

☐ Black-African

☐ Black-Caribbean

☐ Black-Other (please specify)

☐ Indian

☐ Pakistani

☐ Bangladeshi

☐ Chinese

☐ Other

Do you have a disability?　　☐ Yes　　☐ No

If 'yes', please describe briefly the nature of your disability

....

The organisation is committed to a positive approach towards the employment of disabled people and will seek to make reasonable adjustments to its working arrangements wherever possible to accommodate the needs of a disabled job applicant or employee

Have you ever been convicted of a criminal offence?　　☐ Yes　　☐ No

If 'yes', please give brief details of the nature of the conviction and state the date when it occurred

....

The information you provide on this form will be held and processed [manually or electronically] by [HR department or nominated job titles(s)] and will be treated in strictest confidence. The aim of the organisation is to comply fully with the *Data Protection Act 1998.*

Would you please sign below to consent to the information contained in this application form being collected and processed by the organisation.

I consent to all the information contained in this application form being gathered and processed by the organisation.

Signed ....

Name ....

Date ....

Thank you for your assistance.

Data protection and monitoring

The Data Protection Act 1998 contains restrictions on the type of information that employers are allowed to gather about job applicants (and existing employees). In particular, the Act prevents employers from collecting certain information that is classed as 'sensitive data' unless one of a list of conditions is met. 'Sensitive data' is defined under the Act as information about an individual's racial or ethnic origins, religious or philosophical beliefs, sexuality, physical or mental health, trade union membership and the commission of any criminal offence. Essentially, the employer should ensure that they have clear, express consent from all job applicants to authorise the holding of any such data and that job applicants are informed about the purpose for which the information is being gathered.

The easiest way to achieve compliance with the law in this area is to place a clause in the application form stating that the employer wishes to process certain information (which should be defined, eg information on ethnic origins), the purpose for which the information will be processed, and how and by whom it will be processed. The job applicant's signature should be requested against the clause to indicate their consent to the information being gathered and processed under the Data Protection Act 1998.

Ensuring short-listing is done against objective criteria

The key aim in short-listing should be to draw up a manageable list of candidates for interview for a specified post, all of whom could potentially do the job in terms of the qualifications and experience outlined in their job application form or CV. Short-listing is best done methodically by comparing each application with a previously prepared employee specification. Such an approach should ensure objectivity and minimise the risk of bias on sex, racial grounds or age influencing the choice of candidates. Obviously, factors such as gender, race etc should play no part in the short-listing process.

The criteria for appointment should be decided in advance (see above under 'Ensuring any criteria or conditions attached to the job are not indirectly discriminatory', page 15) rather than attempting at a later time to justify the selection of a particular applicant by 'post-hoc rationalisation' (as the tribunal put it in the case of *Bishop v The Cooper Group plc t/a Coopers Thames Ditton).* ET Case No 60910/92 In this case two male applicants were successful in their applications for work as car technicians whilst a highly qualified female applicant was unlawfully rejected.

If a disabled candidate appears to have the requisite experience and qualifications for the post in question, but there is some concern in the mind of the person responsible for short-listing about the person's abilities, the best approach is to invite the candidate to interview and explore their abilities in relation to the post through an open and fair questioning process. Negative attitudes towards disabilities are common in recruitment and should be strongly resisted. Rejection for employment for a reason related to the person's disability would constitute disability discrimination, which will be unlawful unless the employer can justify their actions. Rejection prior to interview of a candidate who appears to meet the essential criteria for the job would generally be hard to justify. Some employers adopt a policy of automatically inviting for interview any disabled applicant who meets the essential criteria for the post, and this approach is to be recommended.

The key to ensuring equality and diversity in short-listing is to ensure that decisions are based on an assessment of the facts provided on each candidate's application form or CV as measured against the requirements stated on the employee specification. Allowing personal opinions or attitudes to influence decisions may lead to discriminatory practices that could be unlawful.

Care should also be taken to avoid assumptions about individual candidates and the type of work they would want to do, or be capable of doing.

Avoiding making assumptions

Some classic examples of discriminatory assumptions, invalid generalisations and stereotypes are:

- women are not suitable for jobs that involve heavy or dirty work

- a young female applicant is unlikely to remain in employment for long because she's bound to decide to start a family

- a woman with young children will be unable to work long hours or travel away from home on business

- a woman with children cannot be fully committed to her job

- part-time employees do not take their job responsibilities seriously

- problems of authority and effectiveness will arise if a young person is appointed to a supervisory post

- an older person, if recruited, will not stay long with the organisation

- older people take a lot of time off work due to sickness

- disabled people take a lot of time off work due to sickness

Continued

Continued

- disabled people are trouble because they will need all sorts of special arrangements made for them

- problems might arise if a woman is recruited into a post where she will be working alone with a man much of the time

- a candidate from a particular racial or cultural background will not fit in to the team

- a candidate of foreign nationality will need a work permit, and that will inevitably cause an inordinate amount of hassle for the organisation

- someone from a particular religion will cause disruption because they will demand frequent time off work to pray

- it wouldn't be a good idea to recruit a gay or lesbian individual because they might be harassed by their colleagues.

It would be inherently unfair and unprofessional to allow any of the above spurious assumptions to affect the decision as to whom to short-list. Blanket assumptions of this nature carry with them the risk that a job applicant who is highly suitable for the job could be rejected. Furthermore, in some cases, non-selection for the short-list based on this type of false reasoning could lead to a successful complaint of unlawful discrimination at an employment tribunal.

Points to note

- The laws prohibiting discrimination on grounds of sex, race, disability, sexual orientation and religion expressly outlaw discrimination throughout the process of recruitment and selection.

- There are limited exceptions to the general principles that it is unlawful to use gender, race, religion or sexual orientation as a criterion in the selection process; these are known as genuine occupational requirements or genuine occupational qualifications.

- Certain forms of positive action are permitted in UK law provided they take the form of encouragement to members of an under-represented group to take up opportunities for employment or training.

- The Data Protection Code of Practice (Part 1) recommends that employers should use different application forms for different jobs, seek only information that is proportionate to their business needs and refrain from requesting information about applicants' private lives.

Action points

- Devise and implement recruitment procedures and guidelines for all staff involved in the process of recruitment, and ensure that these incorporate the principles of the organisation's equal opportunities policy.

- Ensure that the requirements and standards specified for job applicants' qualifications, experience and skills etc are objectively and sensibly matched to the needs of the job without allowing personal opinions to play any part.

- Identify, when preparing an employee specification, which criteria are necessary for the job to be done effectively, and which are merely desirable.

- Review, and where necessary re-design, application forms so that they exclude questions about gender, marital status, number and ages of children, nationality, age and disability from the main part of the form.

- Make a statement encouraging applicants to disclose any disability that they may have, whilst at the same time making clear the employer's commitment to a positive approach towards the employment of disabled people.

- Distinguish between information that is needed for the purpose of monitoring, and information required for recruitment and selection when requesting information about candidates' gender, race, age and whether they have a disability.

- Place a clause in application forms stating that the employer wishes to process certain information about the job applicant and requesting the job applicant's signature to indicate their consent to the information being gathered and processed under the Data Protection Act 1998.

- Short-list methodically by comparing each application with a previously prepared employee specification ensuring that such factors as gender, race etc play no part in the process.

2

RECRUITMENT INTERVIEWING AND SELECTION

Managers and others involved in recruitment interviewing and selection need to be constantly aware of the need to be objective in the way they assess candidates. Selection should be on the basis of candidates' relevant experience, skills, qualifications, knowledge and talent, and should be based on factual evidence rather than personal opinions or assumptions. This chapter aims to provide guidance on the processes of interviewing and selection with a view to promoting equality and diversity.

Conducting selection interviewing without discrimination

Selection interviewing is a notoriously unreliable process. Whilst a job applicant's qualifications, experience and knowledge can usually be assessed objectively, it can be challenging (to say the least) to assess accurately such factors as personal motivation, attitude and flexibility in approach. To achieve maximum effectiveness from the interview process, whilst also promoting equality and diversity, the interviewer should:

- focus on the job and the skills needed to perform it effectively

- deploy open questions (ie questions beginning with 'what', 'which', 'why', 'how', 'who', 'where' and 'when')

- be prepared to probe for more information where appropriate

- listen actively and with an open mind to everything the candidate has to say

- ask specific questions about the candidate's actual experiences – for example, 'Tell me about a time when you experienced conflict with a colleague, and how you handled it'

- recognise subjective views, opinions, biases and prejudices, and learn to put them to one side when interviewing – lack of awareness of these can have a negative effect on the objectivity of the interview process

- not assume but assess

- aim to select the candidate whose experience, skills, qualifications and abilities most closely match a previously prepared employee specification.

Questions at interview

In order to ensure equality during the interview process, it is important to ask only questions that relate to the needs of the job and not to stray over into personal or intrusive questions that may inadvertently discriminate against, for example, women. Another danger is that certain questions may inadvertently indicate a biased view on the interviewer's part, or may be motivated by the interviewer's personal attitudes towards people of a particular ethnic background. A tribunal may draw adverse inferences from the fact that certain questions were asked if they were such that they could place (for example) women at a disadvantage.

Nevertheless, interviewers will naturally and quite rightly wish to establish whether the candidate being interviewed could, if recruited, fulfil all the requirements of the job under review. To achieve this, direct (and possibly challenging) questions will need to be asked, but it is important that these are framed in an appropriate and fair way. It is likely to be viewed as discriminatory, for example, if a female applicant is asked personal questions concerning marriage plans, child-care arrangements or her husband's employment. Tribunals tend to perceive such questions as having a discriminatory undertone and interpret them as an intention in the mind of the interviewer (whether conscious or unconscious) to discriminate.

There will be rare exceptions, where direct questions about family circumstances may be appropriate in order to establish whether applicants have fully thought through the implications of a job that has special demands, but such occasions will be uncommon. In any event, it is better to re-frame such questions to make them job-related rather than family-related (see page 30, 'Checklist of questions to ask/avoid during recruitment interviewing').

The Code of Practice published by the Equal Opportunities Commission (its full title is the 'Code of Practice for the elimination of discrimination on grounds of sex and marriage and the promotion of equality of opportunity in employment') emphasises that questions should be based on the requirements of the job, and that relevant issues should be discussed objectively without any assumptions being made by the interviewer about whether a candidate's personal circumstances could affect their ability to meet the requirements of the job.

In posing questions about candidates' availability for work at particular times, care should be taken not to ask questions in such a way that requires the applicant to disclose their religion, or whether they will require time off work at particular times on account of their religion or belief. This could be perceived as unlawful discrimination under the Employment Equality (Religion or Belief) Regulations 2003, in the same way as questions to female candidates about time off to look after their children could be perceived as sex discrimination. It would be equally inappropriate to ask questions about the job applicant's religious affiliation, place of worship or which religious customs they observe.

It is also possible that a gay or lesbian job applicant may feel disadvantaged if asked questions about their marital status or whether they have any children. As gay men and lesbian women are less likely than heterosexual people to be married or have children, they may perceive a requirement to disclose their single and/or childless status as a detriment.

The merits and demerits of asking all candidates the same questions

It may be tempting, in order to avoid the problems identified in the preceding section, to decide simply to ask all candidates exactly the same questions. Whilst ensuring consistency, this approach will be unnecessarily restrictive and will not allow a full or satisfactory exploration of all the issues relevant to each candidate. Certain questions may be relevant to only one applicant, for example based on something the person has stated on their application form that needs to be clarified. In addition, the interviewer will wish to respond to some of the answers a candidate gives, and they should not be limited on following up a particular topic just because previous candidates have not been asked similar questions.

In any event, asking the same questions of all candidates will not be sufficient on its own to protect the employer from a claim for unlawful discrimination. This is because it is not only the questions themselves that may be discriminatory, but also the purpose for which they are asked, the context within which they are asked and the use to which the candidate's answers are put. The overall test of whether questions at interview were discriminatory will be (for example) whether a female applicant was treated less favourably on grounds of sex than a male applicant was or would have been treated, or whether someone from a minority ethnic group was treated less favourably than a British candidate was or would have been treated.

Nevertheless, there are considerable advantages in starting the interview programme with a planned list of questions that are relevant to every candidate for the job under consideration. Provided the list of questions is not viewed as a means of restricting the interview, it will provide a useful and consistent framework for the interviewer and can help to ensure that no key issues are overlooked.

All the necessary and relevant information required to assess whether someone is suitable for the job in hand can be obtained by designing questions so that they relate to the requirements of the job rather than to the applicant's personal circumstances. The following checklist provides some ideas.

Checklist of questions to ask/avoid during recruitment interviewing

Whilst it is legitimate to ask direct questions relating to a candidate's ability and willingness to meet the genuine needs of the particular job, care should be taken to avoid discriminatory questions, especially when interviewing women.

Ask	*Avoid*
To what extent would you be available to work overtime at short notice?	Who would look after your children if your manager asked you to work overtime at short notice?
The job involves travelling away on business on average two or three days a month. How would you feel about that?	How would your husband feel about you being away from home two or three days every month?
How frequently have you worked at weekends during the past year?	How would weekend working affect your family life?
What would you like to be doing in five years' time?	Do you have any plans to start a family in the next five years?
How many days sickness absence have you had in the past two years?	How many days absence have you had in the past two years due to child-care problems?
How do you cope with pressure of work?	How does pressure of work affect your relationship with your children?
How would you feel about working extra hours during the company's busiest periods?	Would you require any special time off due to your religion or beliefs?
What steps would you take to build a successful relationship with a new manager?	How do you feel about working for a male (female/black/gay) manager?
How would you deal with someone at work whose views were strongly opposed to your own views?	How would you deal with a difficult male colleague if his views were strongly opposed to your own views?
What do you think makes a good supervisor/manager?	What difficulties do you think you might have supervising men/women/white staff/black staff?
What do you think is the best approach to handling minor disciplinary matters?	How would you handle a disciplinary matter if the employee concerned was black?

Interviewing disabled job applicants

The short-listing of disabled candidates was considered above in the section 'Ensuring short-listing is done against objective criteria' (see Chapter 1, page 23).

Where a job applicant on the short-list has stated that they have a disability, the employer will need to consider whether it is appropriate to make any different or special arrangements for the interview. As explained in Chapter 11 (pages 221–229), the Disability Discrimination Act 1995 places a duty on employers to make 'reasonable adjustments' to their arrangements and practices in order to accommodate the specific needs of a disabled job applicant (or employee). The principle behind this requirement as it applies to recruitment is to ensure that a disabled candidate does not suffer any disadvantage in terms of their likely success in being appointed to the job.

Making reasonable adjustments for disabled job applicants at interview

Where a job applicant has indicated that they have a disability, the person responsible for arranging interviews should ask the person to indicate what (if any) special arrangements might be helpful for them in relation to the interview. Special arrangements could, for example, involve moving the location of the interview to somewhere with easier access, rescheduling the timing of the interview to suit someone whose movements depend on the availability of a carer, or permitting a deaf applicant to bring a sign language interpreter with them to the interview. Employers should aim to be flexible in their approach. One way of dealing with this is to write a letter along the following lines to the disabled job applicant prior to the interview.

Model letter to a job applicant who has disclosed a disability prior to interview

Dear . . .

XYZ organisation welcomes job applications from disabled people. Before we finalise the arrangements for your interview, could you please let us know (by telephoning . . .) if there are any specific adjustments that you would like us to make, or any special arrangements you will need during the interview itself.

At the interview, we will ask you some questions about your condition and its possible effects on your ability to perform the job for which you have applied. We will want to do this in order to ensure that we treat you fairly and consider fully what steps might be appropriate or necessary for us to take in order to accommodate your needs, if we appoint you to the post.

Continued

> *Continued*
>
> You will be given a full opportunity to suggest or discuss any potential adjustments to the arrangements for the job or to the workplace itself that may help you to carry out your duties effectively if you are appointed.
>
> I look forward to hearing from you, and to meeting you at your interview.
>
> Yours sincerely

Asking questions of a disabled candidate

The Disability Discrimination Act 1995 does not place any duty on disabled job applicants (or existing employees) to volunteer information about any disability they have (although, clearly, all job applicants are under an implied general duty to tell the truth if asked direct questions). In interviewing, therefore, it will be up to the employer to seek relevant information from a disabled job applicant about their abilities in relation to the job in question. It is clear from case law that the responsibility lies with the employer to ask the necessary questions to establish the applicant's suitability for the job. Furthermore, the Employment Appeal Tribunal (EAT) emphasised in *Cosgrove v Caesar & Howie* that the responsibility is on the employer (and not the disabled person) to take the initiative in reviewing what reasonable adjustments could be made to facilitate the person's employment.

[2001] IRLR 653

Questions should, of course, be asked in a sensitive way and only for the purpose of gaining a proper understanding of the employee's condition and its likely effect on their ability to do the job for which they are applying. It will also be helpful if the interviewer makes it clear that the reason the questions are being asked is to allow the employer to treat the applicant fairly and consider what steps might be appropriate or necessary to accommodate their needs if they were appointed.

Disabled people frequently face negative and discriminatory attitudes in seeking employment. Naturally, many interviewers will have little or no knowledge about a particular impairment or condition and will not be in a position to objectively assess the person's suitability for the job unless they discuss the relevant issues with the applicant directly. It is very important that interviewers avoid making any negative assumptions about a disabled candidate's abilities or forming premature judgements that there might be problems if someone with a particular disability was recruited. Negative assumptions or a failure to explore the relevant issues in a reasonable way could lead to the unfair rejection of a disabled candidate who was suitably qualified and capable of performing the job. This in turn could lead to a claim of disability discrimination being taken to an employment tribunal.

Instead of making assumptions or forming negative views, therefore, interviewers should discuss the requirements of the job fully with the disabled candidate and ask the candidate to comment both on their abilities in relation to the job duties, and on what adjustments, if any, would help them perform the job satisfactorily. It is important that interview questions are framed in such a way that they neither display nor imply a negative attitude to the person's disability. Whilst it is wholly appropriate for those conducting interviews to seek to establish whether the applicant being interviewed could, if recruited, fulfil the requirements of the job to a satisfactory degree, a positive approach should be taken to the questioning process. A good maxim in this context is the familiar adage that one should look for solutions, not for problems.

Checklist for equal opportunities in recruitment

- In relation to the job description that we have discussed, what would be the range of tasks that you would be able to perform with no difficulty or minimum difficulty?

- This organisation is committed to supporting and assisting disabled people in employment. With that in mind, may I ask in what ways you think your disability might have an effect on your ability to carry out any of the duties of the job?

- What help and support could the organisation give you in relation to the performance of the job?

- Would it help you if we were able to offer different hours of work/the option of doing some of the work from your home?

- Are there any special aids, equipment or tools that are easier, or particularly difficult, for you to use?

- What adjustments, if any, did your previous employer make for you? How did these adjustments help you to do your job?

- What types of adjustment to the job itself or to our working arrangements do you think might help you overcome any disadvantage that your disability might otherwise cause?

- If we appoint you, is there any specific training that we could offer you that might assist you to settle in to the job?

- Is there anything else that you can think of that would assist you to perform the job if we appoint you?

Past disabilities

In enquiring generally about a job applicant's state of health, care needs to be taken to avoid discrimination on account of an applicant's past disability. The Disability Discrimination Act 1995 protects job applicants from discrimination on account of a past impairment (no matter when it occurred) if, at the time, it would have been judged to be a disability under the Act.

What to do if a pre-employment medical examination reveals that a job applicant has a disability

It may be that a job applicant's disability is disclosed as a result of a pre-employment medical examination. In these circumstances, the employer should not unquestioningly accept any conclusion put forward by an occupational doctor, but instead consider making further enquiries of the job applicant in order to establish their suitability for the job.

[2000] IRLR 691

Case Example

In *London Borough of Hammersmith & Fulham v Farnsworth*, for example, the EAT held that an employer had subjected a job applicant to unlawful disability discrimination when they withdrew a provisional offer of employment following their acceptance of a medical report indicating that the applicant's medical condition could affect her performance and attendance at work. The EAT judged that the employer, instead of rejecting the applicant on these grounds, should have sought her views about the report and in particular about the impact of her illness on her employment in recent years. If they had done so, they would have discovered that in recent years she had enjoyed relatively good health and that her attendance at work had not been adversely affected by her condition.

Weighing up the abilities of a disabled applicant

In making the final decision as to whom to select for employment, the interviewer should weigh up the skills and abilities of any disabled applicant after taking into account the likely effect of any adjustments to working arrangements or premises that the employer could reasonably make. By adopting this approach, the employer will ensure that disabled and non-disabled candidates are considered on a level playing field. A disabled candidate who meets the essential criteria for the job must not be rejected on grounds related to their disability unless the employer has first given proper consideration to the question of reasonable adjustments. Even then, any decision to reject a job applicant on grounds related to their disability will need to be capable of justification on grounds that are material and substantial.

A range of financial assistance and support is available to employers who decide to recruit someone with a disability. This is done primarily through the Access to Work Scheme and a programme called Workstep, which specifically takes into account the fact that an employee with a disability may not always be capable of undertaking the full range of duties appertaining to the job, or may have a lower output than other employees doing the same job. Both schemes are administered by the Employment Service, whose head office telephone number is 0870 001 0171.

The dangers of allowing first impressions or personal factors to influence the selection decision

It is well known that an interviewer's first impression of a job applicant can influence the outcome of the interview, and various pieces of research suggest that many interviewers make their minds up about a candidate's suitability for a job within about 90 seconds of meeting the candidate for the first time. Factors such as the candidate's dress, appearance, manner and accent can create a powerful positive or negative first impression on the interviewer for reasons that are often completely irrelevant to the candidate's suitability for the job. Apart from the obvious disadvantage of causing a potentially suitable applicant to be rejected, taking some of these factors into account could lead to a discriminatory decision. If, for example, the interviewer allows a negative reaction to a candidate's accent to influence the selection decision, this could be racially discriminatory if the person is of foreign nationality.

The so-called 'halo-effect' occurs when something about the candidate creates such a favourable impression on the interviewer in the early stages of the interview that it is as if the candidate thereafter has a halo around their head and can say nothing wrong. The result can be that everything that the candidate does say passes through a 'favourable filter', and any negative aspects of the candidate are overlooked or minimised. The opposite effect (known as the 'reverse halo' or 'horns effect') can occur if the interviewer's first impression of the candidate is unfavourable in some respect. It is important for interviewers to recognise the dangers inherent in first impressions, which are inevitably based on personal views and attitudes. If not recognised, these can create a barrier to equality and diversity because they can prevent a truly objective assessment of the candidate's suitability for the job from taking place.

Discrimination during recruitment interviewing is often perpetrated uncon-
sciously as a result of the interviewer's personal views, attitudes, assumptions or
acquired stereotyped views. As the House of Lords said in their judgment in the
case of *Nagarajan v London Regional Transport*:

[1999] IRLR 572

> all human beings have pre-conceptions, beliefs, attitudes and prejudices
> on many subjects and it is part of our make-up. People do not always
> recognise their own prejudices . . . An employer might genuinely believe
> that the reason why he rejected an applicant had nothing to do with the
> applicant's race, but it could nevertheless be the case, whether the
> employer realised it at the time or not, that race was a reason why he acted
> as he did.

An interviewer may assume, for example, that a woman (or a man) would be
unsuitable for a particular type of work based on a deep-seated stereotyped view
of what constitutes 'men's work' and 'women's work', or they may hold a
generalised view that older people are not likely to be fit or flexible enough to
perform a particular job effectively. Generalised assumptions of this nature based
on gender, race or age should be recognised as personal (and often stereotypical)
views that are not necessarily true of individuals, so that they can be put to one
side whilst interviewing.

Assessing whether a candidate would fit in with the team

One common and difficult issue is the assessment of whether a particular
candidate will fit in to an existing team. A job applicant's general attitude and
likely degree of team effectiveness is of course very difficult to assess at
interview, as most candidates will strive to put forward their best side and will do
their utmost to avoid disclosing any negative attitudes or weaknesses. Questions
such as 'Do you like working with people?' are less than useless – after all, how
many candidates are likely to answer 'No'?

Sometimes an interviewer may develop a 'gut feeling' that a particular applicant
would or would not fit in to the team, but it can be dangerous to make a decision
based on this alone, as such a gut feeling often occurs as a result of the perceived
degree of 'sameness' between the interviewer and the candidate. For example, if
the interviewer is a white, 35-year-old male, who has been born, brought up and
educated in England, then it would be natural for him to feel comfortable in the
presence of a candidate with a similar background. If, however, one of the
candidates is (for example) a black, 55-year-old female who has been born,
brought up and educated in Kenya, there will be many differences (both visible
and invisible) between the interviewer and the candidate. The interviewer may
feel less comfortable with this candidate than with the English applicant, and if
he has not received awareness training in racial and cultural issues, may conclude
that the Kenyan candidate will simply not fit in to the department, or to the

organisation as a whole. The racial and cultural differences between the two people may be enough to create a degree of unease (which may be at a subconscious level) which, if allowed to affect the outcome of the interview, could lead to race discrimination. This is the most likely criterion of all to result in a failure to practise diversity in recruitment.

In the case of *Baker v Cornwall County Council*, one of the Court of Appeal judges summed up this issue by saying 'An excuse such as "we wanted someone who would fit in" is often a danger signal that the choice was influenced not by the qualifications of the successful candidate, but by the sex or race of that candidate'. [1990] ICR 452

Instead of making assumptions about a candidate's likely degree of success in fitting in to a team, the interviewer should ask specific questions about the person's past working relationships, when they have been successful or unsuccessful, what made them successful or unsuccessful, what kind of person they find it difficult to work with, why this is so, and how they have dealt in practice with conflict or disagreement in a team. In this way, the interviewer can gain information about how the applicant tends to behave in real situations, rather than make assumptions about their attitudes or behaviour. Thus, any conclusion at the end of the interview that the candidate would not fit in to a team will be based on factual evidence and not gut feeling. Interviewers should always be prepared to challenge their own thought processes and question whether there are facts to back up any view they may have formed that a particular candidate will or will not fit in.

The possible effects of racial, cultural and religious differences in interviewing

Racial, cultural and religious differences between people can lead interviewers astray in other respects. For example, in Britain and in many other Western countries, eye contact is viewed as an indication that the person is honest and sincere. In some countries, however, lowering the eyes so as to avoid eye contact is a mark of respect when dealing with someone in a position of seniority or authority. The interviewer should take care therefore not to view lack of eye contact as a negative factor if the interviewee is from a country outside Europe, America or Australasia. Another point is that people of certain religions may not wish to shake hands. When starting and finishing the interview, therefore, the interviewer should take their cue from the applicant rather than automatically expecting the interviewee to shake hands.

EAT 67/94

> *Case Example*
>
> An example of unlawful race discrimination based on gut feeling and lack of eye contact occurred in *Staffordshire County Council v Bennett*. A black Afro-Caribbean candidate with excellent qualifications was rejected for the job of temporary assistant in a school in favour of an unqualified white woman. One of the interviewers had formed a view that the black candidate's personality was 'wrong' for the job and that she would 'not get on' with other staff members. This view was based partly on the fact that she had not made good eye contact with the interviewers during the interview. In light of evidence that people of Afro-Caribbean origin often avoid eye contact with people in authority, as such eye contact is viewed as impolite, the tribunal concluded that the black applicant's 'face did not fit' because she had a different racial background from those who conducted the interview.

Another feature of recruitment interviewing that can inadvertently lead to race discrimination is if candidates are assessed on the basis of their physical presence, in other words where the selection decision is influenced by the degree of confidence, assertiveness and fluency with which the candidate communicates during the interview. Physical presence is a factor that often sways interviewers, despite the fact that it is, in many jobs, not a key element on which effective performance depends. Interviewers should therefore assess the information they are receiving from the candidate and the mode of presentation as separate factors, and resist the temptation to be swayed by personal presence if it is not relevant to the job.

This is particularly important from a race point of view because candidates from certain racial groups may, for a variety of reasons, be less adept at selling themselves. For example, an applicant may come from a racial group in which boasting of one's achievements is culturally unacceptable, whereas modesty is highly valued. An interviewer who is unaware of such cultural issues may not be favourably predisposed towards an applicant who displays such modesty. Conversely, a candidate from a different part of the world may have been brought up in a culture in which it is viewed as admirable to sell one's achievements in an assertive manner, and this candidate's forthcoming and direct manner may create an irrelevantly favourable impression. Furthermore, if English is not the candidate's first language, this could adversely affect the interviewer's perception of the candidate's degree of confidence or ability to communicate.

Ensuring fair treatment of an applicant who is pregnant

As already discussed, it is unlawful to refuse employment to a job applicant on the grounds of gender. Normally, for a claim for sex discrimination to be well-founded, it must be structured around the argument that the applicant was treated less favourably than another candidate of the opposite sex was or would have been treated in similar circumstances. The one exception to this general principle is in a case where discriminatory treatment is on the grounds that a woman is pregnant.

Case Example

The European Court of Justice (ECJ) ruled as early as 1991 in *Dekker v Stichting Vormingscentrum voor Jonge Volwassen* (a Dutch case) that a refusal to appoint a pregnant job applicant who was undisputedly the most suitable candidate for the job under review amounted to direct sex discrimination.

The ECJ further held that in such a case there is no need for the woman to compare her treatment with that of a man. The judges pointed out the rather obvious fact that only women, and not men, can be pregnant and there cannot logically be a valid male comparator. They deduced from this that any discrimination based on pregnancy or on the consequences of pregnancy (eg the employee's inevitable absence from work on maternity leave) will be 'gender-specific'.

[1991] IRLR 27

It will also be discriminatory and unlawful to refuse employment to a pregnant job applicant for a reason that is based indirectly on the fact she is pregnant.

[2000] ECJ Case
No C-207/98

> ### Case Example
>
> In the German case of *Mahlburg v Land Mecklenburg-Vorpommern*, a health authority had declined to appoint a nurse who had worked in one of their hospitals on a fixed-term contract to a permanent post that involved working in operating theatres. The decision was based on the fact that the nurse, who was eight weeks pregnant at the time, would have been unable to take up her duties immediately owing to a health and safety law that prevented pregnant women from working in operating theatres.
>
> The ECJ held ultimately that the refusal to appoint the nurse in these circumstances was direct sex discrimination, and the fact that she would have been unable to take up the duties of the job initially had no impact on the key principle that a refusal to employ a woman owing to reasons associated with pregnancy is unlawful.

What an employer is obliged to do in circumstances like the ones that arose in the *Mahlburg* case is to recruit the woman (assuming she is the most suitable candidate for the post) and then, in accordance with the relevant health and safety legislation, treat her in the same way as they would treat an existing employee who becomes pregnant. Normally this will involve offering the applicant suitable alternative work until the commencement of her maternity leave.

A more recent case dealt with the question of whether the general principles established in relation to unfavourable treatment of a woman for reasons connected with pregnancy should still be enforced in relation to work on a fixed-term contract.

[2001] IRLR 853

> ### Case Example
>
> In *Tele Danmark A/S v Handels-og-Kontorfunktionaererernes Forbund i Danmark on behalf of Brandt-Nielsen* (a Danish case), the applicant had applied for, and been successful in being appointed to, a job on a six-month fixed-term contract. A few weeks into the contract she informed her employer that she was pregnant and that her baby was due some two months before the date the job was due to come to an end. She was consequently dismissed on the grounds that she had failed to inform the employer of her pregnancy when she was recruited (the evidence was that she had known, at the time of her recruitment interview, that she was pregnant).
>
> *Continued*

Continued

Facing a claim for sex discrimination, the employer contended that the reason for their treatment of the employee was not her pregnancy as such, but rather the fact that she would be unable to fulfil a substantial and important part of the contract. They also asserted that the employee had been in breach of the implied duty of good faith in not informing them at her interview that she was pregnant and that she would thus be unavailable to work the full six-month term of the contract. The ECJ, however, threw these arguments out and ruled that the employee had been the victim of unlawful direct sex discrimination. This would be the outcome, they stated, whether or not the employee's presence at work at a particular time was essential to the employer's business and whether or not the employer would suffer a financial loss as a result of the employee's absence due to pregnancy. Furthermore, it was irrelevant to sex discrimination law whether the contract was a fixed-term contract or a permanent contract.

This area of employment law at least has the advantage of being clearly defined. The principle is simple. The employer must disregard a job applicant's pregnancy during every stage of the recruitment process, and especially when making the selection decision. To do otherwise will constitute direct sex discrimination, no matter what degree of inconvenience, or cost, might be created for the employer.

It should be noted that decisions of the ECJ such as those cited above are binding on all EU member states, including the UK.

Age discrimination in recruitment

At present there is no age discrimination legislation in the UK. As a result of the EU Framework Directive, however, the UK will be obliged to implement age discrimination legislation by 2006, and the Government has pledged to do so by October that year.

Council Directive 2000/78

The Code of Practice on age diversity in employment (which is not legally binding) recommends that employers should not use age as a criterion in the recruitment process (nor in any other employment decisions). The Code recommends (among other things) that employers should:

- not specify age limits or age ranges in job advertisements

- avoid including age as a question on their application forms

- try wherever possible to structure interview panels dealing with recruitment and promotion to consist of people of a variety of ages

• ensure that age is not a barrier to training.

It is logical to conclude that the application of age limits or preferences in recruitment will severely restrict the pool from which selection can be made, and will often result in the most suitable person for the job being excluded from applying, being screened out during the early stages of recruitment, or being rejected after interview.

Further information on age discrimination appears in Chapter 11, page 229.

When an upper age limit in recruitment can amount to indirect sex discrimination

Although age discrimination is not at present unlawful, using an upper age limit as a criterion for selection for employment can in certain circumstances constitute indirect sex discrimination. This is particularly likely if the upper age limit is combined with a requirement for the successful applicant to have a specified minimum number of years' experience in a particular type of work. The discriminatory effect comes about because more women than men take career breaks in order to have children. Thus, the combination of an upper age limit and a requirement to have several years' experience will have a disproportionately adverse impact on women (see also Chapter 10, 'Indirect discrimination', page 181). This principle was first established in the case of *Price v Civil Service*

[1977] IRLR 291

Commission, in which the EAT held that an upper age limit of 28 applied to the job of executive officer was indirectly discriminatory against women and could not be justified by the Civil Service (who subsequently changed their policy).

It is therefore advisable to follow the guidelines set out in the Code of Practice and refrain from applying age limits in recruitment. Often, age limits are dreamed up by people based on their personal opinions or stereotypes, such as the notion that an older person will not fit in or will be inflexible. There is no evidence for these propositions, and the application of an arbitrary age limit may in practice have negative consequences for the organisation both from a legal and practical standpoint.

Making the selection decision

Although there is nothing in any of the anti-discrimination legislation that obliges employers to appoint the best-qualified candidate for a particular job, they will place themselves at risk of discrimination complaints if they do not do so. If a candidate is rejected in favour of someone who, on the face of it, appears to have qualifications, experience and/or skills that are less suited to the requirements of the job, and if there is a difference in sex, race, religion or sexual orientation between the successful and the unsuccessful candidates, then a claim for unlawful discrimination may well succeed. The onus will be on the employer to show, to the tribunal's satisfaction, that the criteria for selection were not discriminatory or applied in a discriminatory way (see Chapter 10, 'The burden of proof in discrimination cases', page 192, for further information).

Scoring systems

One effective and fair method of selection is to use a scoring system based on the skills, competencies, experience and training required for the job. It may help to give weightings to each individual element so that the assessment of candidates is made relevant to the specific job duties. This approach, if properly designed, can provide an objective aid to the evaluation of the candidates.

Keeping records

It is strongly recommended that employers should always keep a record of the interview process and the outcome of the recruitment exercise. In particular, it is essential to keep a record of the reason(s) for which the successful candidate was selected and why others on the short-list were rejected. In this way, if a claim for unlawful discrimination is brought to tribunal by one of the unsuccessful applicants, the employer will have some concrete evidence with which to defend themselves, ie show that the selection was based on merit and not influenced by sex, sexual orientation, race or religion. Conversely, an employer who is facing a tribunal hearing without any documentary evidence of the recruitment programme or the reasons for the selection decision will be in a very weak position when trying to persuade the tribunal that the recruitment procedure was carried out in an objective manner without any discrimination.

Employers should bear in mind that any documentation held on file may be the subject of an access request from the individual to whom the file relates (under the Data Protection Act 1998) and also that a court or tribunal may order the disclosure of documentation if it is considered necessary in the interests of justice.

The questionnaire procedure

There is no legal duty on an employer to inform an unsuccessful job applicant why their application was rejected. If, however, a job applicant is considering bringing a complaint of discrimination to an employment tribunal, they may serve a questionnaire on the employer which may ask (among other things) for the reasons the candidate was rejected. Printed forms are available under the various statutes for such an exercise, and the applicant may add their own questions, such as a question about the criteria used to select the successful candidate. Where an employer receives such a questionnaire, it is advisable to complete it accurately and fully, although there is no statutory obligation to do so. However, if no response is provided, or if the response given is evasive or equivocal, this may lead the tribunal to infer that the selection decision was discriminatory.

Observing the requirements of the Asylum and Immigration Act without perpetrating race discrimination

Employers are under a legal duty, since the implementation of the Asylum and Immigration Act 1996, not to appoint anyone who is subject to immigration control and does not have permission to live and work in the UK. To do so is a criminal offence subject to a fine of up to £5,000 per employee illegally employed. Employers therefore need to verify, before any offer of employment is confirmed, that the prospective employee has permission to work in the UK and that their permission is current and valid in respect of the job in question.

The Asylum and Immigration Act 1996 applies only to new appointments and does not impose any requirement on employers to check up on their existing staff in relation to their ongoing right to reside or work in the UK.

The Asylum and Immigration Act 1996 does not apply to the employment of British citizens, Commonwealth citizens with the right of abode in the UK and citizens of any country in the European Economic Area (EEA) and their spouses and dependant children under the age of 21. The EEA consists of the following countries: Austria, Belgium, Denmark, Finland, France, Germany, Greece, Holland, Iceland, Ireland, Italy, Liechtenstein, Luxembourg, Norway, Portugal, Spain, Sweden and the UK.

Ten further countries join the EEA in May 2004, namely Cyprus, Czech Republic, Estonia, Hungary, Latvia, Lithuania, Malta, Poland, Slovakia and Slovenia.

In order to comply with the Asylum and Immigration Act 1996, employers should take the following steps in relation to anyone whom they are seriously considering employing:

- inspect the original of any document relating to the job applicant indicating that they have the right to work in the UK

- retain a copy of such documents on record (throughout employment and for six months after employment has ended).

The law does not require employers to develop the expertise to verify the authenticity of any document produced by a job applicant. Responsibility extends only to viewing the original of the document, checking that it appears to relate to the individual in question, and retaining a copy of it. If, however, the employer knows, or has grounds to suspect, that the employment of a particular person would be illegal, or that the document produced is a forgery, then further checks should of course be carried out.

The Home Office issues a list of documents (reproduced below) that may be used as evidence of a job applicant's right to work in the UK. Only one document from the list need be produced by the applicant, and all the documents on the list have equal status. The documents used most often in practice are those that show the individual's name and national insurance number (eg a P45), birth certificates and passports. The Home Office guidance and the Code of Practice are available at www.ind.homeoffice.gov.uk/default.asp?pageid=17 or from the employers' help-line on 020 8649 7878.

Checklist of documents that may be used to verify a job applicant's right to work in the UK

- A document issued by a previous employer, the Inland Revenue, the Benefits Agency, the Contributions Agency or the Employment Service which states the national insurance number of the person named.

- A passport describing the person as a British citizen, or having the right of abode in, or entitlement to re-admission to, the UK.

- A passport containing a certificate of entitlement certifying that the holder has the right of abode in the UK.

- A certificate of registration or naturalisation as a British citizen.

- A birth certificate issued in the UK, the Republic of Ireland, the Channel Islands or the Isle of Man.

- A passport or national identity card issued by an EEA State describing the holder as a national of that State.

- A passport or other travel document endorsed to show that the person named is exempt from immigration control, has indefinite leave to enter or remain in the UK, or has no time limit on their stay, or a letter issued by the Home Office confirming that the person named has such status.

- A passport or other travel document endorsed to show that the person has current leave to enter or remain in the UK, and is not precluded from taking the employment in question, or a letter from the Home Office confirming that this is the case.

- A UK residence permit issued to an EEA national.

Continued

Continued

- A passport or other travel document endorsed to show that the holder has a current right of residence in the UK as the family member of a named individual who is an EEA national and who is resident in the U.K.

- A letter issued by the Immigration and Nationality Directorate of the Home Office indicating that the person named in the letter is a British citizen or has permission to take employment.

- A work permit or other approval to take employment issued by the Department for Education and Employment.

- A passport describing the holder as a British Dependent Territories Citizen, and which indicates that that status derives from a connection with Gibraltar.

At the time of writing, proposals are being considered that may change the statutory list of documents that act to prove an individual's right to work in the UK. There is evidence of an increased number of forged documents being used to seek employment illegally, and the Government wishes to curb this trend. The main proposed change is that a document that states the individual's national insurance number will in future not suffice on its own. The employer will have to gain sight of either a passport showing the individual's right to work in the UK or an equivalent document. Alternatively, the employer will be under a duty to see and copy two documents, one of which may be a document bearing the individual's national insurance number, and the other a birth certificate, a certificate of naturalisation or an official letter indicating that the individual has leave to remain in the UK.

There is a further proposal that employers will be obliged to satisfy themselves that each of the documents produced actually relates to the person presenting them. This will include a duty on the employer to scrutinise any photograph contained in a document to verify that it is in fact a photograph of the job applicant and, where a document contains the individual's date of birth, to review whether this 'is consistent with the appearance' of the individual. This rather controversial proposal may cause some rather difficult moments for the unwary employer!

Reconciling the requirements of the Asylum and Immigration Act 1996 with the duty not to discriminate under the Race Relations Act 1976

The main difficulty in complying with the Asylum and Immigration Act 1996 is reconciling its requirements with the important requirement under the Race Relations Act 1976 not to discriminate against job applicants on grounds of nationality. The key point is to ensure that no foreign candidate is singled out for unfavourable treatment as a result of the employer's legitimate desire to check whether that applicant has the right to work in the UK.

The best way to avoid discrimination whilst meeting the requirements of the Asylum and Immigration Act 1996 is to adopt a policy of asking all candidates (whatever their actual or perceived nationality) to produce documentary evidence of their right to work in the UK at a specified stage in the recruitment process. This can conveniently be done at the time candidates are being invited to interview (or second interview) and can, for example, be combined with a request to produce documentary evidence of qualifications. In this way, no candidate can claim that they were treated differently from or less favourably than another candidate on grounds of race or nationality. Adopting a practice of demanding evidence of the right to work in the UK from one job applicant (for example, someone with a foreign surname) in circumstances where other applicants were not asked to provide such evidence would give the applicant required to produce such evidence solid ammunition to bring a complaint of race discrimination to an employment tribunal.

If a job applicant is unable to produce a document that confirms their right to work in the UK, the employer should not assume that the person is seeking to work illegally. Instead, the person should be referred to a Citizens Advice Bureau or other agency for advice. It is, however, legitimate to refuse to employ someone who is unable or unwilling to produce documentary evidence of their right to work in the UK.

Code of Practice

The Home Office has issued a statutory Code of Practice entitled 'Immigration and Asylum Act 1999 – Section 22: Code of Practice for all employers on the avoidance of race discrimination in recruitment practice while seeking to prevent illegal working'. The Code, although not legally binding, may be taken into account in any employment tribunal proceedings under the RRA 1976. The Code essentially offers helpful advice to employers to assist them in reconciling the requirements of the Act with the Asylum and Immigration Act 1996. It stresses the importance of treating all job applicants in the same way at every stage of the recruitment process in relation to any request to produce documentary evidence of the right to work in the UK. The Code also states that employers should guard against making assumptions about any particular applicant's right to work in the UK based on colour, race, nationality or ethnic or national origins, or the length of time the person has been in the UK.

Checklist for reconciling the requirements of the Asylum and Immigration Act with the Race Relations Act

- Establish a clear, written procedure to be used as part of the recruitment process that covers the requesting, checking and copying of documents.

- Ensure that all employees who are involved in recruitment are familiar with the procedure and, where appropriate, provide training in how to apply it.

- Make it a routine part of the recruitment process to ask all applicants invited for either a first or second interview (including British citizens) to bring with them a document that establishes that they have the right to work in the UK.

- Treat all job applicants in exactly the same way at every stage of the recruitment process with regard to any request to produce documentary evidence of their right to work in the UK.

- Train staff responsible for recruitment decisions not to draw adverse inferences on account of a job applicant's delay in producing documentary evidence of their right to work in the UK.

- Make sure that no job applicant is discouraged from applying for employment or rejected for employment on account of their colour, race, nationality, ethnic origins or national origins.

- Make sure that those involved in recruitment have received equality/diversity training that covers the risk of subconscious assumptions being made or discriminatory treatment occurring on such grounds as name, colour, accent, mode of dress or appearance.

Work permits

The UK operates a work permit scheme, the objectives of which are to enable employers to recruit key people from outside the EEA to work in the UK whilst safeguarding the interests of UK nationals. Work permits are administered and issued on behalf of the UK Government by Work Permits (UK), part of the Home Office's Immigration and Nationality Directorate. A detailed account of the work permits scheme is beyond the scope of this book; however, the following represents a summary of some of the key provisions of the scheme.

If the person whom the employer wishes to appoint is not a UK national, a national of one of the EEA countries, a citizen of Switzerland, or a Commonwealth citizen who had a grandparent born in the UK, they may need a work permit. It is important to note that the criteria necessary for an individual to be granted a work permit are quite distinct from the criteria for permission to enter or remain in the UK.

Work permits are not issued directly to individuals but instead must be applied for by the employer who wishes to recruit the overseas national into a specific job. In most cases a fee is payable. A work permit is normally issued only if the job is one in which there is a known or proven skills shortage. Employers may not allow an overseas national who requires a work permit to commence work until a work permit has been obtained. The work permit will be issued for a specified, limited period (normally a maximum of five years).

Work permits are not transferable between employers or jobs. If an individual already holds a work permit in respect of a particular employment and wishes to move to a new job with a different organisation, the prospective new employer must apply for a new work permit for the individual.

Points to note

- The responsibility lies with the employer when interviewing a disabled candidate to ask appropriate questions to establish the applicant's suitability for the job, and whether there are any reasonable adjustments to working arrangements, working practices or premises that they could reasonably make in order to facilitate the person's employment.

- The European Court of Justice has consistently held that it is discriminatory and unlawful to refuse employment to a pregnant job applicant for a reason based directly or indirectly on the fact she is pregnant.

- At present there is no age discrimination legislation in the UK, but there is a (non-legally binding) Code of Practice on age diversity in employment which recommends that employers should not use age as a criterion in the recruitment process.

- If a candidate is rejected in favour of someone who, on the face of it, appears to have qualifications, experience and/or skills that are less suited to the requirements of the job, and if there is a difference in sex or race between the successful and the unsuccessful candidates, then a claim for unlawful discrimination may well succeed.

- Employers are under a legal duty, under the Asylum and Immigration Act 1996, not to appoint anyone who is subject to immigration control and does not have permission to live and work in the UK.

Action points

- When interviewing, focus on the job and the skills needed to perform it, and recognise and put to one side any subjective views, opinions, biases and prejudices.

- Consider whether to make any different or special arrangements for the interview of a disabled job applicant, in order to ensure that the applicant does not suffer any disadvantage in terms of their likely success in being appointed to the job.

- Beware of allowing first impressions about such factors as the candidate's dress, appearance, manner or accent to determine the outcome of the interview, as these are often irrelevant to the candidate's suitability for the job and could in some cases lead to a discriminatory decision.

- Do not ask questions of female applicants about their marriage plans or child-care arrangements, because these are likely to be viewed by an employment tribunal as having a discriminatory undertone and may be interpreted as an intention in the mind of the interviewer (whether conscious or unconscious) to discriminate.

- Keep a record of all selection interviews held and the outcome of the recruitment exercise; in particular, keep a record of the reason(s) the successful candidate was selected and why others on the short-list were rejected.

- Disregard a job applicant's pregnancy during every stage of the recruitment process, and especially when making the selection decision, since to do otherwise will constitute direct sex discrimination.

- Avoid using age limits in recruitment, as they will severely restrict the pool from which selection can be made and may discriminate indirectly against women.

- Adopt a policy of asking all candidates to produce documentary evidence of their right to work in the UK at a specified stage in the recruitment process, so that there is no risk of one candidate claiming they were treated less favourably than another on grounds of race or nationality.

CHAPTER 3

DISCRIMINATION IN TERMS AND BENEFITS OF EMPLOYMENT

This chapter addresses a number of important equality issues that employers may frequently have to deal with during the course of employing people. The aim is to alert employers to ways of promoting equality and avoiding discrimination and, in the event that a problem nevertheless arises, provide guidance on what to do.

Time off for dependants

The Employment Rights Act 1996 entitles all employees to a reasonable amount of time off work (on an unpaid basis) in order to take care of, or arrange for the care of, a dependant who has been taken ill or been injured or assaulted. It also entitles employees to take time off in the event of the death of a dependant or the birth of a child to a dependant, or in the event of unexpected disruption to a dependant's care arrangements, for example child-care.

s57A ERA 1996

'Dependant' is defined as an employee's:

- spouse

- child

- parent

- any person living in the same household as the employee (other than lodgers).

In light of the Employment Equality (Sexual Orientation) Regulations 2003, which require equality of treatment for gay and lesbian employees, employers may wish to review their policies and procedures on bereavement leave and other forms of compassionate leave to ensure that these allow for employees to take appropriate time off in the event of the death, illness or injury of a same-sex partner.

Time off for religious holidays and when a refusal may be discriminatory or in breach of the individual's human rights

Following the implementation of the Employment Equality (Religion or Belief) Regulations 2003 in December 2003, employees are entitled not to be treated unfavourably on grounds of 'any religion, religious belief or similar philosophical belief' (see Chapter 11, 'Religion or belief' for information about the Regulations, pages 197, 217). The Regulations do not expressly require employers to provide time off or special facilities for religious purposes, and no employer is obliged to accept unreasonable disruption to their business activities on account of employees' religious needs. However, if an employer unreasonably refuses to accommodate an individual's needs where doing so would be feasible, this could be in breach of the Regulations.

The extent to which employees may have the right to time off for religious reasons

An employee's religious belief may involve practices associated with not working on a particular day of the week or on specified dates during the year. It follows that (for example) requiring a practising Christian employee to work on a Sunday where that employee held strong religious views that Sunday working was unacceptable would constitute indirect religious discrimination (see Chapter 10, 'Indirect discrimination', page 181). Even though the employer might well apply the Sunday working requirement equally to all employees, it would nevertheless place people who shared the particular employee's religious beliefs at a disadvantage, thus constituting indirect discrimination. In order to be lawful, therefore, the employer would have to show that the requirement was proportionate to the achievement of a legitimate aim, taking into account all the relevant circumstances.

Employers may also face requests from Jewish employees or Seventh Day Adventists (for example) to be exempted from working on Saturdays (or requests from Jews to be permitted to leave work in time to be home one hour before sunset on Fridays, which is when their Sabbath begins). If not working on a particular day is genuinely a key facet of an employee's religious beliefs, then a refusal to accommodate the individual's request will be discriminatory. Similarly the dismissal of an employee for refusing to work on Saturdays, where the refusal was on grounds of the person's religious beliefs, could constitute unlawful religious discrimination. Once again, the key question is whether a refusal to grant an employee's request was proportionate to the achievement of a legitimate aim (see also Chapter 10 under 'Indirect discrimination', page 181).

Another potential problem is the payment of overtime premiums for Sunday working. Paying premium rates of pay for Sunday work could be challenged as discriminatory if the employer did not also pay the same premium rates for work performed on other religious Sabbath days, for example Saturday. Employers who have not already done so may wish to review this matter and take steps to harmonise overtime premiums payable for work done on different days of the week.

Sunday working

The Employment Rights Act 1996 affords protection to shop workers and betting workers against detrimental treatment and dismissal on the grounds that they refuse to work on Sundays. This provision is not, however, connected with religion or religious beliefs, but is in place to protect people who do particular jobs.

ss45, 101 ERA 1996

Time off on special religious days

Another conundrum for employers is how to deal with employees who wish to celebrate special religious days during the year and seek time off on those days instead of (for example) time off at Christmas or Easter. It could be argued that if a Muslim employee (for example) was refused paid time off on an important Islamic festival in circumstances where the employer gave (Christian) employees paid time off on Christmas Day, this would constitute indirect and possibly direct religious discrimination. It could be indirect discrimination because a refusal to grant time off on the religious day in question would disproportionately affect Muslim employees compared with others, and direct discrimination on the grounds that the Muslim employee was refused a perk enjoyed by a Christian employee. Whilst indirect religious discrimination can (potentially) be justified, direct discrimination cannot. Because the legislation in this area is relatively new, it will be necessary to wait until an appeal court or tribunal rules on this particular point in order to be certain whether such actions would be regarded as direct, or indirect, discrimination.

In view of these difficulties, it would be advisable for employers to review their programme of public holidays and if necessary take steps to make their policies or practices more flexible, so that employees who are not Christians are not denied the right to paid time off on the days or dates of the year that have special religious significance for them.

One option would be to introduce a policy under which there are no prescribed public holidays, but instead grant staff a predetermined number of floating holiday days each year (for example eight days' paid leave over and above annual leave). The policy could provide that these days be taken either on traditional public holidays or (by agreement with management) on other days. This approach would benefit those who, as a result of their religion, do not celebrate Christmas or Easter and who might prefer time off at a time of the year that coincides with a date that is important to their faith.

Another option for employers who wish to promote diversity is to grant all employees who adhere to a religion or belief a set number of days holiday per year specifically for the purpose of celebrating religious holidays or festivals. Below is a suggested clause for use in employment contracts or staff handbooks regarding employees' entitlement to take paid leave for the observance of religious holidays.

Model clause for entitlement to paid leave for the observance of religious holidays

The company promotes religious diversity and operates a policy of granting all employees, whatever their faith, up to [ ] days' paid leave in each calendar year for the observance of religious holidays or festivals.

An employee who wishes to take advantage of this policy should put in a written request to their line manager that specifies the particular religious holiday for which they wish to seek leave.

Employees will be granted paid leave under this policy only for religious holidays that they genuinely wish to celebrate as a result of their faith.

Time off to pray

Employees of certain religions may wish to pray at set times or at regular intervals during the day.

Muslims, for example, are required to pray five times a day for about 10 minutes each time, Jains are obliged to worship three times a day and Zoroastrians must pray five times during the day.

Whilst there is no obligation in the Employment Equality (Religion or Belief) Regulations 2003 on employers to provide time off work or special facilities for employees for religious observance, employers may nevertheless wish to adopt a flexible approach towards the timings of rest breaks. Often the time off requested will be no longer than what is needed for a cup of coffee or a cigarette.

In order to promote equality and good will, the employer may also wish to set aside for employees a room in a quiet part of the workplace in which to pray or engage in private contemplation. The best way forward when considering this is to consult staff (or their representatives) to seek agreement on the room and its facilities, so as to ensure that employees of all denominations are equally catered for, and that the facilities provided are appropriate. During consultation, the following matters may have to be considered (the list is not exhaustive):

- the location of the room (some faiths need a facility to point in a particular direction)

- the amount of space required

- the storage and display of religious symbols

- the provision of washing facilities

- the removal of shoes in the room

- whether both sexes are to use the room at the same time (which would not be allowed in some faiths).

Checklist

In light of the complexity of the subject of time off for religious reasons, employers should also:

- engage in dialogue with practising faith employees to increase understanding of their religious needs and endeavour to reach agreement to any adjustments they may seek

- devise training programmes to increase employees' awareness (in particular managers' awareness) of religious diversity

- be sensitive to the particular needs of any individual for whom a particular day or date has special religious significance

- aim to be flexible with individual employees and accommodate religious holidays and restrictions on days or hours of work whenever possible, for example allowing flexibility in arrival and departure times, in the length and timing of lunch breaks and by permitting employees to swap hours or shifts

- be willing to compromise, for example where the employee offers to work additional hours at another time

- adopt a flexible attitude towards lunch breaks, especially during Ramadan when Muslim employees are likely to be fasting until the end of the normal working day

- if a request for time off for religious needs is refused, ensure the refusal can be justified in line with a legitimate aim of the business.

Time off for religious holidays – human rights implications

The Human Rights Act 1998 gives individuals the right to freedom of thought, conscience and religion, and any breach of that right by a public authority could

Art 9 HRA 1998

give rise to a further legal claim. Where the employer is a public authority, a breach of the Human Rights Act can form the basis of a stand-alone claim to a court or tribunal.

Art 9 HRA 1998 Although it does not overtly give employees the right to time off work to attend religious events or time off to pray, any refusal to grant such time off by a public-sector employer may nevertheless lead to a legal challenge under the Human Rights Act. To succeed in defending such a claim, the employer would have to show either that the employee had agreed contractually to work on the particular day or at the particular time (and had thus waived their 'right' to time off for religious reasons) or that the refusal was justified when balanced against the 'rights and freedoms' of the employer or the employees' colleagues. The employer could, for example, argue that they had the right to expect their employees to perform their contracts or to be available during peak periods of work. An employer would in no way be obliged under human rights law to grant excessive time off if this had an adverse effect on the business.

Dress codes and when they may discriminate or breach human rights

Another sensitive subject for employers and employees alike is the subject of dress codes. Employers should be aware that if they impose company rules on dress and appearance (including any restrictions on hair length, jewellery, tattoos and body piercings), they will inevitably displease some, alienate others and run the risk of spawning claims for direct or indirect sex, race or religious discrimination. Nevertheless, employers may quite legitimately wish to introduce and maintain rules and standards of dress and appearance in order to ensure:

• health and safety

• hygiene (for example in food-handling jobs)

• smartness (in order that the organisation can project a professional corporate image to clients, customers or the public at large)

• conventionality (in order to maintain good relations amongst staff and customers and avoid the possibility of causing offence).

Rules on dress or appearance (whether formal or applied on an ad hoc basis) should never be imposed on account of management preferences, nor be based on the personal opinions of an individual manager. This approach would be likely to cause resentment and could lead to tribunal claims if the standards applied adversely affected some people on grounds related to gender, race or religion. After all, there is little value in having a smartly dressed, but demotivated, workforce!

Employers should also be willing to consider any legitimate objections raised by an employee in relation to a particular aspect of the dress code and, where appropriate, make exceptions. In *FME Ltd v Henry*, for example, an employee succeeded in a claim for unfair constructive dismissal when he was told that he would be sent home if he reported for work unshaven. The employee had objected to the rule that required men to shave on a daily basis because he developed a rash if he shaved every day.

EAT 874/86

Checklist of factors to consider before introducing a dress code

Here are some general principles for employers who wish to impose rules or standards in relation to their employees' dress and/or appearance:

- Ensure there is a sound business objective that justifies any rule or code that will restrict employees' dress or appearance at work.

- Make sure the proposed rules are proportionate to the achievement of the stated business objective, and not excessive when viewed against it.

- Consider whether it is necessary to apply a dress policy to all staff, or whether only those who meet clients or customers should be covered by the policy.

- Consult trade unions and/or employees widely to maximise the possibility of achieving a policy that the majority of employees finds acceptable.

- Endeavour to make any rules flexible.

- Make sure that none of the proposed rules reinforces stereotypical prejudices or assumptions – for example a ban on women wearing trousers to work.

- Present the rules and standards in an unambiguous and meaningful way. For example, just requiring employees to dress 'smartly' could give rise to many different interpretations!

- Ensure that company policies and rules on dress and appearance are clearly communicated in writing to all employees and job applicants.

- Put a system in place to ensure the rules will be enforced fairly and consistently for all staff, including management.

- Structure the policy and rules so that they can be varied for an individual if there is a special reason justifying an exception.

The risk of sex discrimination claims arising from dress codes

There are two specific issues that may give rise to difficulties for employers who wish to implement or enforce a code on dress and/or appearance and at the same time avoid sex discrimination. The first is the fact that men and women traditionally do not dress in the same manner or fashion, and rules on dress and appearance cannot therefore (logically) be identical for men and women. For example, it might be viewed as absurd for an employer to require female employees to wear a collar and tie to work. The second issue is that fashions, and what is acceptable to society at large, change over time and what was socially unconventional and possibly unacceptable 20 years ago may nowadays may regarded by the majority of people as 'normal'. For example, it is widely regarded as acceptable and 'normal' nowadays for a woman to wear a trouser suit to work, whilst this would have been unusual (and possibly frowned upon) 30 or 40 years ago (which is within the working lifetime of many people employed today).

The general principle developed by courts and tribunals is that it is an employer's dress code as a whole that stands to be judged, rather than the individual elements of the dress policy. There is no need for an exact item-by-item comparison, but it will be necessary to apply equal standards to men and women.

[1994] IRLR 7

> *Case Examples*
>
> In *Burrett v West Birmingham Health Authority*, a nurse claimed indirect sex discrimination when she was disciplined for refusing to wear a cap as part of the prescribed female nurses' uniform. Male nurses were not required to wear a cap. The employment tribunal held that the existence of differing uniform requirements for men and women did not in itself amount to sex discrimination. The nurse had not been subjected to a detriment when compared with male staff because both male and female nurses were required to conform to a similar standard, and a male nurse would have been equally disciplined for refusing to comply with the rules.

To avoid sex discrimination, therefore, the employer should adopt an even-handed approach as between men and women and:

- ensure any dress code is applied fairly to both men and women

- apply the same general standards of smartness and/or conventionality to men and women

- ensure any rules are enforced to the same degree for both men and women

- take care when applying different rules to men and women (for example on hair length or jewellery) that there is a proper business reason for each rule and that no rule is based on stereotypical gender assumptions.

The risk of racial or religious discrimination claims arising from dress codes

Some racial and religious groups have rules, standards and customs that affect their dress and appearance. It follows that an employer's dress code may discriminate indirectly against people from a particular racial or religious group if the code prevents or restricts them from following their customs. Sikhs, Muslims, Hindus and Rastafarians are just some of the groups that may be adversely affected by employers' rules on dress and appearance. For example:

- Sikhs are required by their religion to wear turbans and have uncut hair and beards. It follows that a ban on beards at work would discriminate indirectly against Sikhs. Such a rule might be capable of justification on hygiene grounds if the job involves handling food (although a better solution would be for the employer to permit men to wear beards provided they cover them with a snood whilst at work).

- Orthodox Sikh men may wear a metal bangle called a Kora, which has a deep religious significance for them. Any rule that requires the removal of jewellery would have to be justified, for example on safety grounds if the job involved working with machinery.

- Women from certain ethnic groups and some religions may be required to dress modestly, for example to have their legs and/or arms covered at all times. Employers' dress codes should of course accommodate any need (or preference) for women to wear trousers.

- Women from some religious groups may wish to have their heads covered at all times, and a failure or refusal to accommodate this in a dress code may be indirectly discriminatory on grounds of race or religion.

- Orthodox married Hindu women may wear a nose stud to mark their married status. Any employer that imposes a blanket ban on facial piercings may find that this constitutes indirect religious discrimination. No employer would (presumably) ban women from wearing their wedding ring to work, unless there was a safety reason for such a rule.

- Some Hindu men wear neck-beads as a symbol of their faith.

- Some Hindu men wear a small, knotted tuft of hair tied at the back of their head like a ponytail as a symbol of their belief. A blanket ban on male employees having ponytails could thus be indirectly discriminatory on grounds of religion unless it can be justified.

- Orthodox Jewish men need to keep their heads covered at all times and may therefore require to wear a 'skull cap' to work.

Rules on dress and appearance – whether formal or informal, or specified by an individual manager or department – should be flexible enough to accommodate individuals' racial, religious or cultural customs, and employers should:

- avoid imposing rules rigidly without regard for individual employees' objections

- be willing to vary or adapt dress codes where possible to accommodate employees whose racial or religious backgrounds might prevent them from complying with the rules.

Employers may also wish specifically to consider:

- modifying health and safety gear to permit an employee to wear an item of religious dress safely

- providing beard bags or snoods if hygiene is an issue, rather than requiring a man to shave off his beard

- (where there is a company uniform) introducing specially designed outfits, for example saris, turbans and hijabs.

Sikhs and turbans

Generally, Sikhs are subject to the same employment laws as any other racial or religious group, but with one major exception. The Employment Act 1989 contained a provision that permitted male Sikhs to be exempted from the requirement to wear safety helmets on construction sites, provided a turban was worn instead. It is important to bear in mind that this dispensation applies only to Sikhs and only on construction sites. In other types of workplace, it will normally be lawful for an employer to insist that all employees, including Sikhs, wear protective headgear for safety reasons.

If a Sikh suffers an accident or injury on a construction site, any damages awarded against the employer will be limited to compensation for the injury that would have been sustained if the Sikh had been wearing a safety helmet.

In line with the Employment Act 1989, the Employment Equality (Religion or Belief) Regulations 2003 state that it can never be lawful to require a Sikh to wear a helmet on a construction site. The Regulations also state that the exemption for Sikhs contained in the Employment Act 1989 cannot give rise to a claim for unlawful discrimination by anyone else.

Dress codes – human rights implications

Art 10 HRA 1998

Article 10 of the Human Rights Act 1998 (the right to freedom of expression) will be another element affecting public-sector employers who decide to impose restrictions on what employees wear to work. The Act provides, however, that an individual's right to freedom of expression can be restricted by a public authority 'for the protection of the reputation or rights of others'. 'Others' in this context includes the employer, the employee's colleagues and potentially members of the public with whom the employee might come into contact. So, for example, an employer who denied an employee the 'right' to wear a t-shirt sporting an animal rights slogan to work would not necessarily be in breach of Article 10, provided the employer had a proper reason for the restriction. Valid reasons might include a desire to ensure the employee projected a smart image to members of the public or a concern that colleagues might be offended by the slogan or image on the t-shirt.

So long as a dress code is reasonable, not unnecessarily restrictive, and designed to achieve a legitimate business aim, it should not breach employees' rights to freedom of expression under the Human Rights Act.

Model contractual clause governing the employer's dress code

The following statement could be used as part of employees' contracts of employment:

'It is a condition of your employment that whilst at work you maintain an appearance that is clean, tidy and appropriate to the work you undertake in relation to health and safety. If your job takes you into contact with customers, clients or members of the public, you are required to dress smartly and in a manner that reflects the professional standing of the organisation.

Employees are not permitted to wear casual or sports clothing in the office, for example jeans, trainers, t-shirts with slogans, football shirts and similar attire. Hair should be neat and tidy and not dyed an unconventional colour. Any jewellery worn, including facial piercings, should not be excessive.

(Optional clause) Men and women who work in the food-handling area must, if they have hair that falls on or below shoulder length, wear it either tied up or clipped back. This rule is in place for reasons of food hygiene.

Failure or refusal to abide by the employer's dress code without good reason will render the employee liable to disciplinary action.'

Partners' benefits

Many employers offer benefits to their employees' partners, for example inclusion in a company private medical plan, provision of a widows'/widowers' pension under an occupational pension scheme, free or subsidised access to sports and social facilities, or travel concessions. In some cases, employers offer such benefits only to employees' married partners, but in others to unmarried partners as well, subject usually to the proviso that the employee must live with the partner in a stable, long-term relationship.

Since the implementation of the Employment Equality (Sexual Orientation) Regulations 2003, employers who offer benefits to their employees' unmarried heterosexual partners will have to provide equivalent benefits to employees with same-sex partners. To do otherwise would constitute direct and/or indirect discrimination against lesbian and gay employees. However, the Regulations contain a clause that expressly permits employers to offer benefits by reference to marital status. In other words, schemes that offer benefits only to married (and thus not to unmarried) partners continue to be lawful, even though on the face of it this type of arrangement discriminates indirectly against gay and lesbian people, who of course cannot marry their same-sex partners.

Social events

When organising social events for staff and their partners, the employer should make it clear when communicating the event that employees may bring either an opposite-sex partner or same-sex partner. Another factor to take into account is catering. It will be important to ensure that the special dietary requirements of people from different religious groups are fully catered for, and that soft drinks are readily available for those whose religion may prevent them from drinking alcohol or cause them to object to alcohol.

Sickness absence on account of a pregnancy-related condition

There has been a long line of cases both in Britain and at the European Court of Justice (ECJ) that have ruled that any less favourable treatment of a female employee on grounds of pregnancy, or the consequences of pregnancy, will amount to direct sex discrimination. For example, in the case of *Webb v EMO Air Cargo (UK) Ltd*, the ECJ held that the dismissal of a woman for reasons connected with pregnancy will always amount to direct sex discrimination simply because only women (and not men) can be pregnant.

[1994] IRLR 482

If a woman is absent from work during pregnancy, then, whether her illness is pregnancy-related or not, the employer should under no circumstances place her at any disadvantage as a result of her illness, for example by paying her less occupational sick pay than she would otherwise be entitled to receive, or by dismissing her. The employer will not succeed in defending a claim for sex discrimination by arguing that they treated the woman no less favourably than a man absent for an equivalent period of time. This is because the ECJ has held that unfavourable treatment of a woman on grounds related to pregnancy is gender-specific and a comparison with a male employee is not relevant or appropriate.

Case Example

In *Brown v Rentokil*, for example, the employee (a service driver) was absent from work continuously after she became pregnant. The employer operated a contractual policy under which any employee who exceeded 26 weeks' continuous sickness absence would be dismissed automatically. The employee in this case was dismissed in accordance with the policy once her sickness absence reached 26 weeks (at which time she was still pregnant). The ECJ held that the treatment of the employee amounted to direct sex discrimination despite the existence of the policy, which, the ECJ held, was largely irrelevant because no comparison with a man off sick could legitimately be drawn. The ECJ did not criticise the employer's policy in a general sense, but their judgment made it clear that the employer should have disapplied the policy in the case of an employee who was absent for a pregnancy-related reason.

[1998] IRLR 445

Special rules during the last four weeks of pregnancy

There are special rules in place in respect of sickness absence that occurs within the last four weeks of an employee's pregnancy. If the employee is off sick with a pregnancy-related condition at any time during these final four weeks (even for a day), the employer may trigger the commencement of her maternity leave automatically. In this case, statutory sick pay and occupational sick pay (if either or both of these were being paid) would stop and statutory maternity pay would become payable if the employee was eligible to receive it.

If, however, a pregnant employee is off sick during this four-week period on account of a condition that has nothing to do with pregnancy (for example a cold or flu) then this rule does not apply and the employee would continue to be eligible to receive contractual and statutory sick pay in the normal way.

Up until the fourth week before the employee's expected date of childbirth (unless maternity leave has already started), payment of sick pay should be made according to the company's normal rules and conditions, with statutory sick pay and/or contractual sick pay being paid depending on the normal eligibility rules.

Making reasonable adjustments for disabled employees

Under the Disability Discrimination Act 1995 there is a duty on employers who employ 15 or more staff to make reasonable adjustments to working arrangements, working practices and/or premises whenever they employ (or consider employing) a disabled person. This provision in effect places the responsibility on the employer to identify and take appropriate steps to prevent or reduce any substantial disadvantage that the disabled employee might face at work on account of their disability. Further details of the scope of the Act are contained in Chapter 11, pages 221–227. It should be noted that the threshold of 15 staff is to be abolished (set for 1 October 2004).

It is important to bear in mind that it is the employer, and not the disabled employee, who is responsible for taking the initiative in determining whether there are any reasonable adjustments that can be made for the employee. In *Cosgrove v Caesar & Howie [2001]*, the Employment Appeal Tribunal (EAT) ruled in a case where neither the employee (who suffered from clinical depression) nor her doctor were able to suggest any possible reasonable adjustments that the employer had breached the law by failing to address whether there were any reasonable adjustments that they might nevertheless be able to make. The EAT commented in this case that it was wrong to regard the employee's views and those of her doctor as 'decisive on the issue of adjustments, where the employer himself had given no thought to the matter whatsoever'.

[2001] EAT 1432/00

In another case, *Mid-Staffordshire General Hospitals NHS Trust v Cambridge*, the EAT judged that the employer had breached the duty to make reasonable adjustments because they had failed to conduct a full assessment of the employee's position, which would have allowed them to decide properly what adjustments it would be reasonable for them to make.

EAT 0755/02

The legislation itself provides some headings under which employers must consider making adjustments. These are considered below.

Making adjustments to premises

Physical adjustments to premises need not always involve high costs. Actions such as moving furniture around to make space for someone who uses a wheelchair, relocating shelves for an employee who has difficulty reaching up, redesigning a work station for someone with an upper limb disorder or installing a hand-rail to support a person with mobility problems may be relatively inexpensive and simple to carry out.

Allocating some of the disabled employee's duties to someone else

Where a particular job duty is only a minor element of the job, or if the need to perform it occurs only occasionally, it may be reasonable for the employer to allocate that part of the job to another employee. Examples could include re-assigning lifting and carrying duties where the employee has a heart condition or mobility impairment, exempting an employee with a hearing impairment from the need to attend meetings, or re-allocating driving duties for an employee whose disability means that they cannot hold a driving licence.

Transferring the disabled employee to a different job

The duty to make reasonable adjustments does not impose an obligation on an employer to create a new or special job for an employee who becomes disabled or whose disability worsens. If, however, the disabled employee is unable to continue to perform their normal job, and if an alternative post exists within the organisation which they could reasonably do, then the employer would in effect be obliged to offer it.

There is, however, no obligation on the employer under the Act to maintain the disabled employee's previous terms and conditions in these circumstances (for example if the alternative job was on a lower grade or salary), but of course any change to the employee's contract could only be implemented with the consent of the employee. It would therefore be important for the employer in these circumstances to hold detailed discussions with the disabled employee about the possible alternative job, any training required, the terms on which the job would be offered and whether or not any other options were available.

Altering the disabled employee's working hours

An employee with a mobility impairment may find travelling during peak periods difficult and a reasonable adjustment may be to agree to allow the employee to start and finish work at different times of the day so that they can travel during quieter periods. A reduction in hours (whether permanently or temporarily) may be another option to help an employee; for example, someone who is recovering from a serious illness may be content to agree to work part-time for a while. A further example could be an agreement to exempt a disabled employee from a requirement to work night shifts or overtime.

Assigning the disabled employee to a different place of work

Where an employee has limited mobility or uses a wheelchair, the employer should consider, if appropriate, whether it would be feasible to move the employee's job to a different location with easier access. Allowing the disabled employee to do some of their work from home may help in circumstances where the employee lives in a location where there is infrequent public transport and they are not able to drive.

Permitting the disabled employee to be absent from work for the purposes of rehabilitation, assessment or treatment

The employer should be willing to offer flexibility in relation to the employee's attendance at the workplace, for example by allowing time off work for medical appointments, therapy and other treatment. Alternatively, altering an employee's working hours to fit in with the availability of a carer may be appropriate.

Providing the disabled employee with training

An employee with a mental impairment, for example someone with learning difficulties, may be able to perform a job to a satisfactory standard provided they receive extra training. In some cases, it may be appropriate for the employer to develop and use different types of training material, or design and deliver a different type of training, for example for an employee who is blind. Providing an induction loop for an employee with a hearing aid during a training course might be another reasonable adjustment.

Acquiring or modifying equipment

Many disabled employees will be able to perform the duties required of them if they are provided with tools and equipment suited to their needs. For example, an employee with a back impairment may require a special chair or stool, an employee with arthritis in their hands may benefit from a specially designed keyboard, and an employee with a hearing impairment may need a different type of telephone handset. Whether or not it is reasonable for the employer to provide adjustments such as these will depend on the cost as measured against the employer's resources. Often grants are available, particularly in the case of newly recruited employees.

Modifying instructions or reference manuals

It is unlikely to cause an employer very much inconvenience or extra cost to provide instructions or procedures in Braille or on audiocassette for an employee with a visual impairment. Similarly, reference manuals could be provided in different formats.

Modifying procedures for testing or assessment

When recruiting or considering employees for promotion, the employer should reflect on whether any selection tests they propose to use might discriminate against a disabled candidate, and if so, review whether the test can be adjusted in some way. It may, for example, be appropriate to allow a candidate with dyslexia longer than the normal permitted time to complete a test, or exempt them from taking the test altogether. Similarly, it may be appropriate to allow a candidate with a physical disability in their hands to do a test orally rather than in writing.

Providing a reader or interpreter

In some cases, the employer may consider it appropriate to recruit a reader or interpreter to work alongside a disabled employee, or to train an existing employee to offer the necessary support to the disabled employee.

Providing supervision

Additional supervision or closer supervision may be necessary for an employee with a mental impairment or a physical condition that is likely (for example) to cause blackouts or fits. If it is reasonable for the employer to provide such supervision, then they should do so. Additional supervision during training may be another reasonable adjustment that the employer could make if it helped a disabled employee overcome a disadvantage arising from their disability.

The list of possible adjustments is infinite, and since no two disabled people are exactly alike in terms of how their condition affects them, the employer should treat each case individually and take a pro-active approach towards the question of adjustments.

The best way forward for the manager of an employee who is, or becomes, disabled is to discuss possible adjustments with the employee directly in order to explore what possibilities exist and whether these are likely to be reasonable from the employer's perspective and effective in supporting the employee. The disabled employee will be likely to have a much clearer and more in-depth knowledge and understanding than the manager of what changes to working practices would help them.

If an employer fails or refuses to make a reasonable adjustment for a disabled employee, this will be in breach of the Disability Discrimination Act. At tribunal the onus will be on the employer to provide evidence to show why a particular adjustment was not reasonable for them to make (see also Chapter 11 under 'The duty to make reasonable adjustments', page 226).

Managing sickness absence in respect of a disabled employee

The majority of disabled people are fit and healthy and do not require any more time off work than employees who do not have disabilities. Assumptions are often made (wrongly) that disabled people are likely to require frequent periods of absence from work or be prone to frequent illnesses affecting attendance at work.

Nevertheless, if an employee's disability is an illness, they may require time off work on an occasional basis, for example for medical treatment, or be absent from work for lengthy periods owing to incapacity.

In these circumstances, the employer will be under a duty to make reasonable adjustments to working arrangements and practices in relation to the disabled employee. Depending on the nature of the person's disability, a reasonable adjustment might be to:

- allow the person more time off work than would normally be considered acceptable

- allow the employee to take longer or more frequent rest breaks if their condition causes them to tire easily

- (if the payment of occupational sick pay is at management's discretion) exercise discretion in the employee's favour

- adjust sickness absence procedures so that absences that are caused by the person's disability are discounted or recorded separately.

[1998] Case No.
1301162/97

An employment tribunal in the case of *Cox v Post Office* provided some useful guidance for employers. The tribunal suggested that, in relation to a disabled employee who has had extensive sickness absence, the employer should:

- review their sickness and attendance procedures to ensure these identify any absences that are due to the employee's disability

- provide adequate training for all managers who are responsible for dealing with employees' attendance and absences in order to promote understanding of the Disability Discrimination Act

- ensure that any adjustments that would help the employee to improve attendance are considered and, where reasonable, implemented

- distinguish in record-keeping between absences that are related to disability and those that are for other reasons, if necessary by seeking medical advice and consulting the employee

- refrain from penalising the employee on account of disability-related absences when implementing any absence or attendance policy

- refrain from dismissing an employee unless their absences, including the disability-related absences, are having a substantial and material effect on the business even after any reasonable adjustments have been made.

Dismissing a disabled employee on grounds of ill-health absence

If an employee who is on long-term sickness absence is dismissed on grounds of lack of capability, the employer's actions may constitute disability discrimination. This will be irrespective of whether the dismissal is fair under the Employment Rights Act 1996, since unfair dismissal law requires an analysis of entirely separate criteria. In order to justify their actions, the employer would have to be certain that before taking the decision to dismiss they had considered all possible reasonable adjustments that might allow the disabled employee to return to work. Reasonable adjustments in this context might include transferring the employee to lighter duties, reducing their workload, allowing part-time working or home-working, or modifying some of their policies, for example accepting a lower standard of work or slower pace of work from the disabled employee than would normally be acceptable. Chapter 8 contains more detailed information about the implications of dismissing disabled employees (pages 142–145).

Case Example

In *London Borough of Hillingdon v Morgan*, the EAT upheld an employment tribunal decision that the employer had unlawfully discriminated against the employee by refusing to allow her to work part-time from home for a temporary period. The employee, a service information officer, had been absent from work for eight months on account of myalgic encephalomyelitis (ME), and her doctors (including an occupational doctor) had recommended that this type of arrangement would help her to ease back into full-time employment. Despite the doctors' recommendations, the employer refused to agree to the home-working arrangement and, when the employee did return to work, took no steps to support her. As a result, she was unable to cope with the stresses of the job and consequently resigned.

The EAT found that there was no objective reason the employer could not have permitted the employee to work on a part-time basis from home initially. The employer had thus failed to fulfil their duty to make reasonable adjustments.

[1999] EAT 1493/98

Points to note

- The law does not expressly require employers to provide time off or special facilities for religious purposes, and no employer is obliged to accept unreasonable disruption to its business activities on account of employees' religious needs.

- An employee whose religious beliefs involve practices associated with not working on a particular day of the week or on specified dates during the year is protected in law against any unjustified refusal to allow time off on such days or dates.

- Employers may quite legitimately wish to introduce and maintain rules and standards of dress and appearance in order to ensure health and safety, hygiene, smartness or conventionality, but such rules and standards run the risk of generating claims for direct or indirect sex, race or religious discrimination unless they are proportionate to the achievement of a stated aim and applied even-handedly to both men and women.

- Any less favourable treatment of a female employee on grounds of pregnancy, or the consequences of pregnancy, will amount to direct sex discrimination.

- The duty to make reasonable adjustments to working arrangements, working practices and/or premises for disabled workers places a responsibility on employers to identify and take appropriate steps to prevent or reduce any substantial disadvantage that a disabled employee might face at work on account of their disability.

Action points

- Review any policy on public holidays and if necessary take steps to make it more flexible, so that employees who are not Christians can be granted paid time off on the days or dates of the year that have special religious significance for them.

- Consider setting aside a room in a quiet part of the workplace for employees to pray or engage in private contemplation.

- Engage in dialogue with practising faith employees to increase management's understanding of their religious needs and endeavour to reach agreement to any adjustments that employees may seek.

- Ensure there is a sound business aim that justifies any rule or code that will restrict the way employees dress at work, and that the proposed rules are proportionate to the achievement of the aim and not excessive when viewed against it.

- Devise rules on dress and appearance to be flexible enough to accommodate racial, religious or cultural customs and be willing to vary the rules to accommodate individuals whose racial or religious backgrounds might prevent them from complying with them.

- Make sure that any scheme under which the employer confers benefits on employees' unmarried partners is applied equally to employees with same-sex partners.

- Ensure that an employee who is absent from work during pregnancy is not placed at any disadvantage, for example by being paid less occupational sick pay than she would otherwise be entitled to receive.

- Bear in mind that it is the employer, and not a disabled employee, who is responsible for taking the initiative in terms of determining whether there are any reasonable adjustments that can be made for the employee.

- Discuss possible adjustments with a disabled employee directly in order to explore what possibilities exist and whether these are likely to be reasonable from the employer's perspective and effective in supporting the employee.

- Seek to make all possible reasonable adjustments to allow a disabled employee who has been off sick to return to work, for example transferring the employee to lighter duties, reducing their workload or allowing part-time working or home-working, whether permanently or temporarily.

CHAPTER 4

EQUAL PAY

This chapter aims to provide a basic framework of the law on equal pay and to provide guidance on what employers can do to ensure their pay practices are free from sex discrimination.

Equal pay and terms of employment for women

The Equal Pay Act 1970 requires equality of treatment in pay and contractual terms (including pension benefits) as between men and women doing 'like work', work rated as equivalent, or work of equal value (see Chapter 10 for more information about the structure of the Equal Pay Act, page 188). The Act cannot be used to found claims of unequal pay based on comparisons between employees of the same sex.

The comparator

In order to succeed in a claim for equal pay, the complainant must identify a comparator of the opposite sex who is 'in the same employment' (hypothetical comparisons are not permitted). Normally, that will mean a comparator who works for the same employer or an associated employer at the same 'establishment' (ie the same unit or workplace), but the comparator may also be someone at another of the employer's workplaces, if substantially common terms and conditions of employment apply there. The comparator does not have to give consent to being named.

Recent case law has shown that an employee can make a comparison with someone beyond their own organisation in certain circumstances. A key example was a female primary school head-teacher in one education authority who compared herself with a male secondary school head-teacher in a different authority (*South Ayrshire Council v Morton*). The key criterion for such a claim to succeed is the requirement for the pay of the claimant and that of the comparator to be attributable to a single source (which in the Morton case was the Scottish Joint

[2002] IRLR 256

[2002] IRLR 822

Negotiating Committee). By contrast, in *Lawrence & ors v Regent Office Care Ltd*, former employees of a county council who had been transferred to a private firm following a competitive tendering exercise claimed equal pay with employees of the council whose work had previously been rated as having equal value to theirs. The European Court of Justice (ECJ) ruled that the claim was invalid because, even though the employees were still performing the same work as before, their pay and that of their comparators were each determined separately and were not governed by a single source.

[2002] IRLR 693;

EAT/1128/95

Claims for equal pay can also be brought by using either a predecessor or a successor as the comparator. In *Kells v Pilkington plc*, for example, the claimant succeeded in a claim for equal pay with a comparator who had performed equal work to her more than six years earlier, whilst in *Diocese of Hallam Trustee v Connaughton*, the female claimant (who had resigned from her post) won her case by comparing herself to her male replacement, who was recruited on a higher salary than she had been receiving.

The genuine material factor defence

An employer can defend a claim for equal pay by showing that there was a reason for the difference between the pay package of the man and the woman that represented a 'genuine material factor' unconnected with sex. The word 'material' in this context has been held to mean 'significant and relevant'. Factors such as qualifications, experience, performance and in some instances market forces may justify pay differences between a male and female employee. An employer will not, however, be able to defend an equal pay claim solely on the grounds that they cannot afford to pay the complainant more.

If the reason for an employee's lower level of pay is that they have shorter service than their chosen comparator, the employer must be in a position to justify operating a pay scheme based on length of service. To do this, they will need to demonstrate that length of experience in the particular job under review actually enables the employee to do the job more effectively.

Even if an employee expressly agrees to accept a lower rate of pay than someone else performing the same job or work of equal value, this will not prevent that employee from succeeding in an equal pay claim. It is not open to an employer to seek to contract out of their statutory responsibilities!

It is also worth bearing in mind that any female employee whose pay is dependent on length of service could claim under the Sex Discrimination Act 1975 that this practice was indirectly discriminatory against women. This would be based on the well-established argument that women generally have shorter service than men because more women than men take career breaks to raise a family. In the event of such a claim, the employer would have to satisfy a tribunal that the practice of basing pay on length of service was objectively justified.

The box below summarises a range of factors that may or may not justify differences in pay.

Examples of genuine material factors

Potentially valid	*Unlikely to be valid*
Higher level of qualifications, enabling better or different job performance	Formal qualifications that do not affect job performance
More relevant experience, enabling better job performance	More experience where the type of experience is not directly relevant
Special skills relevant to the job	Special skills where these are not used in the job
Longer service, where this leads to enhanced job performance	Longer service that does not affect job performance
Significantly higher level of responsibility	Different job titles
Superior job performance as measured in an objective appraisal scheme	Alleged superior performance where this cannot be evidenced, for example where no objective appraisal scheme is in operation
The terms of a collective agreement that are gender-neutral	Historical practices that may themselves have been based on discriminatory assumptions
Time of work, eg a clearly defined premium paid for night shift working	Differences between the pay of men on night shift and women on day shift for traditional reasons
Place of work, for example an allowance paid to compensate for higher living costs in London	Different rates of pay in different branches of the same company because of separate collective bargaining procedures
Market forces where it is genuinely necessary to pay more to attract the 'right' person into the job	Argument that the organisation cannot afford to pay more to the claimant
Red-circling (ie temporarily maintaining an employee's higher salary upon transfer to a lower-graded job)	Continuing indefinitely to pay an employee transferred to a lower-graded job a higher rate of pay

Where an equal pay claim reaches a tribunal hearing, the onus will be on the employer to establish that there was a genuine material factor that justified the difference in pay between the claimant and the comparator. An employer will be in a much stronger position to succeed in doing this if they operate a pay system that is transparent, ie a system in which the basis for determining pay rates is known and clearly understood by both managers and their employees. In the high-profile case of *Barton v Investec Henderson Crosthwaite Securities Ltd*, the EAT declared that it was unacceptable for an organisation to operate a bonus culture involving secrecy and/or lack of transparency.

EAT 18/03/MAA

Employers who wish to overhaul their pay schemes, and hence minimise the risk of equal pay claims, would do well therefore to start out with the prime objective of creating a pay system that is transparent and capable of being clearly understood by all.

Job evaluation

Where an employer elects to implement a job evaluation scheme and base employees' pay on the results of the scheme, it will be very important to make sure that the process of job evaluation is analytical, objective and based on factors that are not in any way discriminatory.

The overall purpose of job evaluation will be to establish a fair structure of job gradings on which the employer's pay system can be based. The key preliminary point to bear in mind is that a job evaluation scheme should be designed to evaluate jobs, and not the people doing the jobs. It is therefore advisable to assess and grade jobs on an anonymous basis whenever possible.

[1977] ICR 272

If a job evaluation scheme is to protect the employer against equal pay claims, it must be based on an analytical study, ie a detailed analysis of jobs that has been conducted in a structured, rational and objective way. The Employment Appeal Tribunal in *Eaton Ltd v Nuttall* provided some useful guidance in the methods of job evaluation that can be viewed as analytical. These fall broadly into two categories:

- A scheme based on a points assessment system. Different numbers of points are attributed to different factors within each job according to a predetermined scale, and each job is then graded according to its total number of points. Different factors may be weighted differently according to their importance.

- A factor comparison system, in which several benchmark jobs are selected on the basis that their existing rates of pay are considered to be fair. These jobs are then analysed in order to split them up into different factors, each of which is allocated a proportion of the total rate of pay for the job. Other jobs can subsequently be assessed by identifying which factors they contain, and adding together the rates of pay for each factor.

The EAT went on in the *Eaton* case to say that certain types of job evaluation study, such as job-ranking, paired comparisons and job classification systems, cannot be regarded as sufficiently analytical to justify a defence against equal pay claims. The key difference between an analytical and non-analytical scheme is that an analytical scheme breaks down each job, or at least representative benchmark jobs, into individual components, whilst non-analytical systems focus on comparing whole jobs that are then ranked in order of priority.

The specific factors that are usually used to evaluate jobs include:

- the knowledge required for effective performance of the job

- the interpersonal and communication skills required for effective performance of the job

- any physical skills relevant to the job (but employers should guard against attributing too much importance to such factors as physical strength, as this could discriminate indirectly against women)

- the physical, emotional and mental demands inherent in the job

- the amount of effort required to perform the job in terms of concentration, attention to detail, etc

- the level of decision-making and problem-solving required in the job

- the job's overall level of responsibility, for example responsibility for people, resources, finance, development and safety

- the amount of initiative, innovation and independence required for the job

- the working environment and conditions in which the job is performed.

Once jobs are evaluated, pay is usually determined by creating job grades or pay bands based on a points system, so that each job grade/pay band encompasses all jobs that score between a defined lower number and a defined upper number of points. This produces the inevitable consequence that each grade or band will contain a number of jobs with a range of points scores, some at the lower end of the scale and some at the higher. This may result in some practical difficulties, because an individual whose job falls at the top end of one grade may feel disadvantaged on account of not being placed in the next grade up. Nevertheless, it is reasonable to conclude that dividing lines have to be drawn somewhere, and the key requirement is to ensure that the exercise to draw the lines does not produce a discriminatory or perverse outcome.

Checklist to ensure fair job evaluation

Employers should ensure that they take account of the following in conducting job evaluation:

- ensure all job descriptions are written to reflect accurately the nature of the job as it is done

- eliminate any personal factors when evaluating jobs, eg disregard the employee's actual level of performance

- ensure the factors and weightings chosen for the job evaluation scheme contain no gender bias, for example placing an inordinately high weighting on physical strength and a very low weighting on interpersonal skills

- endeavour to create a job evaluation panel that contains an equal mix of men and women

- ensure that the method of job evaluation is applied impartially and fairly to all jobs irrespective of who is performing them

- ensure job descriptions are regularly updated, and that any changes to the job are then reviewed to establish whether the job needs to be regraded (up or down)

- introduce an objective and fair procedure for dealing with complaints about job grading.

Equal pay questionnaires

An employee who is considering bringing an equal pay claim may serve an equal pay questionnaire on the employer. The key purpose of the questionnaire is to help employees obtain relevant information in order to establish whether they are receiving equal pay, and if not, the reasons for any differences or discrepancies.

Although there is no statutory obligation on the employer to respond to an equal pay questionnaire served on them, it is important to bear in mind that replies given are admissible in evidence. The legal effect of the questionnaire is that a failure to reply or the provision of a reply that is incomplete, evasive or equivocal may lead an employment tribunal hearing a claim for equal pay to draw inferences that are unfavourable to the employer. It is therefore advisable to provide a carefully worded and detailed response to all the employee's questions. The time limit for doing so is eight weeks.

One obvious problem for employers is that there will inevitably be confidentiality and/or data protection issues to take into account in providing answers to the employee's questions. It may, for example, be thought inappropriate to disclose how much another employee is earning, unless that employee's consent to the disclosure is first obtained. Arguably, the employer should take appropriate steps to obtain such consent rather than simply refusing to disclose the information. It should also be possible in most circumstances to provide general information about the organisation's pay structures, job grades, the average of a group of employees' salaries, criteria for pay rises, how skills and experience are reflected in the pay system, and the like. Employers should bear in mind that tribunals have the authority in any event to order an employer to disclose relevant information if they believe that it is necessary to do so in the interests of justice.

The Code of Practice on Equal Pay

The Equal Opportunities Commission (EOC) produced a revised Code of Practice on Equal Pay, which was implemented on 1 December 2003. Like other Codes of Practice, the Code is not legally binding on employers, although any failure to act on its provisions may be taken into account by a court or employment tribunal in the event of a claim for equal pay or sex discrimination taken against an employer.

The Code of Practice on Equal Pay provides useful practical guidance on how employers can ensure their pay practices are free from sex discrimination. The Code also recommends that employers should conduct equal pay reviews, and asserts that these are the most appropriate method for ensuring delivery of pay systems free from sex bias. The Code contains a section summarising the essential features of an equal pay review, including a five-step model for carrying one out. Further information on conducting equal pay reviews, and the Code of Practice itself, can be accessed on the EOC's website at www.eoc.org.uk.

Checklist for ensuring equal pay

The following represents a checklist for best practice:

- Conduct a pay review throughout the organisation or corporate group to identify and tackle any inequalities in pay and conditions as between men and women at all levels in the organisation.

- Aim to make the organisation's pay system, including the criteria for the award of any bonuses, transparent.

- Ensure there is a structured process in place, clearly understood by all, to determine pay increases.

- Ensure decisions about pay are based on objective criteria and are not dependent on the opinions of only one manager.

- If a job evaluation scheme is in place, audit it to ensure that it does not place too much weight on 'hard skills' such as physical effort and undervalue 'soft skills' such as interpersonal ones.

[2002] IRLR 822

- If a particular pay practice is likely to have a greater impact on women than on men (or vice versa), ensure the reason for the pay practice corresponds to a real business need, and is appropriate and necessary for the achievement of that need.

- Ensure that the criteria for the payment of bonuses are objective and fair, and that they are applied rationally and consistently.

- Refrain from offering new starts a pay package that reflects their package in a previous job if this would lead to an inconsistency in relation to what others performing similar work are paid.

[2002] IRLR 693;

- When offering a new start a pay package that is different in value from that of the person who previously occupied the job, take care that the difference in pay is justified by objective factors.

EAT/1128/95

- Check that part-time staff are not being paid at lower rates than full-time staff performing the same or similar work, as this type of arrangement may breach not only the Equal Pay Act 1970 but also the Sex Discrimination Act (SDA) 1975 (if the majority of part-timers are women) and the Part-Time Workers (Prevention of Less Favourable Treatment) Regulations 2000 (see Chapter 5).

Points to note

- The Equal Pay Act 1970 requires equality of treatment in pay and contractual terms as between men and women doing 'like work', work rated as equivalent, or work of equal value.

- In certain circumstances, an employee may be able to make a comparison for equal pay purposes with someone beyond their own organisation if their pay and that of the comparator can be shown to be attributable to a single source.

Action points

- Seek to operate a pay system that is transparent, ie a system in which the basis for determining pay rates (including bonuses) is capable of being understood clearly by all.

- Take care, if a man and woman are doing similar work but are paid differently, that there is a genuine material factor that justifies the difference in pay.

- Respond as fully and honestly as possible to any equal pay questionnaire served by an employee, as any failure to respond or a response that is incomplete, evasive or equivocal may lead an employment tribunal to draw inferences that are unfavourable to the employer.

- Conduct a pay review throughout the organisation or corporate group to identify and tackle any inequalities in pay and conditions as between men and women at all levels in the organisation.

CHAPTER 5

DISCRIMINATION AGAINST PART-TIME AND FIXED-TERM STAFF

Specific laws exist to protect the interests of part-time workers and fixed-term employees, and to prevent discriminatory treatment against them both in contractual terms and non-contractual benefits. Over and above these provisions, the Sex Discrimination Act (SDA) 1975 affords considerable protection to women against employers' policies or practices that impose long or unsocial hours of work, or even full-time hours. This chapter aims to explore all these provisions.

Equivalent contractual terms for part-time workers

A part-time worker is someone who works fewer hours per week or month than the organisation's standard full-time hours. Interestingly, there is no legal definition of full-time working or full-time hours, and each employer is therefore entitled to make their own decision as to the number of hours per week that they regard as full-time hours.

Equality of treatment for part-timers in employment

Statutory rights

Part-time employees have the same statutory employment rights as full-time employees, irrespective of the number of hours they work. Thus, for example, an employee who worked two days a week would have the same entitlement as a full-time employee (on a pro-rata basis) to statutory paid annual leave under the Working Time Regulations 1998, and the same entitlement to take maternity or paternity leave under the Employment Rights Act 1996. Where, in order to qualify for a particular statutory right, an employee must have a defined minimum length of service, the same length of service is required of a part-timer. Thus, the part-timer who works two days per week would need to have gained six months' continuous service in order to qualify for additional maternity leave, as is the case for a full-time employee.

Contractual rights

When the Part-Time Workers (Prevention of Less Favourable Treatment) Regulations 2000 were implemented in July 2000, part-timers gained the right to equality of treatment in relation to contractual terms and also non-contractual benefits. The Regulations provide that employers must not treat their part-time workers less favourably than comparable full-timers just because they work part-time, unless there is an objective reason justifying different treatment in the particular case. It is important to note that the Part-Time Workers Regulations apply to all workers, and not just to employees engaged directly by the organisation.

In order to ensure that the provisions of the Part-Time Workers Regulations are being complied with, employers should conduct a review of the work done by part-time staff and check whether the part-timers are receiving pay and benefits on a par with full-timers performing similar work (on a pro-rata basis). If discrepancies are identified, these should be removed as soon as possible – unless, of course, they exist for a reason that has nothing to do with the fact that the workers in question work part-time.

Drawing the correct comparison

When reviewing the pay and benefits package of part-time workers, the employer should take care to make the right comparisons. The 'comparator' in the context of part-time working is a full-time worker engaged by the same employer and performing the same or broadly similar work on the same type of contract. Comparisons may not be made on a hypothetical basis, unlike comparisons for the purposes of sex, sexual orientation, race or religious discrimination legislation. It is important to note, however, that no distinction is made in this context between work on a permanent contract and work on a fixed-term contract, ie a part-time employee working on a fixed-term contract could compare their treatment with either a full-time employee working on a permanent contract, or a full-time employee engaged on a fixed-term contract. If, however, the part-timer was working for the employer via a contract with an employment agency, the person would be unable to compare their treatment with a full-time employee engaged directly by the employer.

One further criterion is that the comparator must work at the same establishment (but can be someone working at a different establishment if there is no full-time comparator at the same establishment).

The scope of the Part-Time Workers (Prevention of Less Favourable Treatment) Regulations 2000

The Part-Time Workers (Prevention of Less Favourable Treatment) Regulations 2000 cover:

- rates of pay (ie a part-time employee must not be paid at an hourly rate that is less than the rate payable to a full-time employee performing the same or similar work just because the person works part-time)

- premium overtime rates (but these need only be paid once the part-timer has exceeded the employer's standard full-time hours)

- contractual holiday entitlement, including entitlement to paid public holidays

- contractual sick pay (ie equal access to occupational sick pay and equivalent rates of sick pay)

- contractual maternity, paternity, adoption and parental leave schemes (equal access to and benefits under any contractual scheme that offers benefits in excess of the statutory minimum)

- access to and benefits from an occupational pension scheme (unless different treatment can be justified on objective grounds)

- access to career breaks unless the exclusion of part-timers can be objectively justified on grounds other than their part-time status.

In relation to non-contractual terms, the employer should ensure that no part-timer is excluded from training or appraisal, or from opportunities for promotion or transfer on account of their part-time status (see also Chapter 6, 'Including part-time and fixed-term employees within the scope of training and development', page 102).

Holidays and holiday pay for part-timers

Part-time workers, like their full-time equivalents, are entitled under the Working Time Regulations 1998 to be granted a minimum of four weeks' paid leave each year. This should, of course, be granted on a pro-rata basis, for example:

- A part-time employee who works two days a week (in an organisation where the standard working week is five days) will be entitled to eight paid days' holiday per annum.

- A part-time employee who works five days a week from 09.00 am to 1.00 pm will be entitled to 20 days' (ie part-days) paid holiday per year, payable at their normal part-time rate of pay.

Over and above annual leave, many organisations grant their staff paid leave on public holidays. Employers should take care firstly that this does not place any part-time employee at a disadvantage in comparison to an equivalent full-time worker. If, for example, the employer grants full-time employees eight paid public holidays per annum over and above their entitlement to annual leave, a part-time employee who was engaged on a 50 per cent contract would be entitled to four extra paid days' holiday each year.

Secondly, the employer should review whether there are any inequalities amongst their part-time workforce, taking into account the days of the week when part-timers normally work. For example, an employee who works Mondays and Tuesdays only, and whose employer grants paid leave to all staff on public holidays, would be likely to gain a significant benefit in comparison to an employee who works only on Wednesdays and Thursdays, simply because more public holidays fall on Mondays than on other weekdays. This inequitable treatment of some part-time staff as compared with others could give rise to discontent. There may also be a breach of the Part-Time Workers Regulations if part-timers lose out on paid public holidays in comparison to their full-time counterparts.

The employer could choose to solve this dilemma in one of three ways:

1. Grant additional paid days' holidays to any part-timers who do not work on Mondays, so as to bring their paid entitlement up to the same level as that of part-timers who do work on Mondays and are granted paid leave on public holidays.

2. Pay part-timers who do not work on Mondays an extra day's pay on each occasion when there is a Monday holiday for which equivalent part-time colleagues receive a paid day's holiday.

3. Have no prescribed public holidays, but grant full-time staff eight floating holiday days per year to be taken either on public holidays or (by agreement) on other days. Part-time staff would then be entitled to a pro-rata portion of the eight floating days consistent with the number of hours or days they work per week. This third approach would have the further advantage of benefiting those whose religion means that they do not celebrate Christmas or Easter and who would prefer time off at another time of the year, for example at a time that coincides with a date that is important to their faith (see Chapter 3, 'Time off for religious holidays', page 53).

The overall aim should be to ensure equality of treatment in the allocation of holiday entitlement and paid time off on public holidays for all staff, both full- and part-time.

The right to a written statement

Part-time workers are entitled under the Part-Time Workers Regulations to request a written statement giving the reason(s) for any treatment that they believe is in breach of their rights under the Regulations. If such a request is received, the employer must provide the employee with a written statement within 21 days, giving particulars of the reason(s) for the treatment.

Part-Time Workers Regs 2000

Model policy on part-time working

'It is the policy of this company that all part-time employees will be treated as valued and committed members of staff, irrespective of the number of hours they work per week or per month. Part-timers are entitled to equal (pro-rata) pay in relation to full-timers performing the same or similar work, and the company will make no distinction in pay rates on account of an employee's full-time or part-time status. The equality principle will also apply, wherever practicable, to contractual terms and non-contractual benefits, which will be offered to part-timers on an equivalent (pro-rata) basis, to that which is available to comparable full-time staff. The company will also ensure that opportunities for training and access to promotion are made available on an equal basis to full-time and part-time employees wherever possible.

Access to the company's pension scheme is open to all employees, irrespective of the number of hours they work, and benefits available under the scheme are equivalent (on a pro-rata basis) for both full-time and part-time employees. Entry to the company's pension scheme is, however, dependent upon the employee having gained a minimum of [x months'] length of service.

It is the policy of this company that no employee will be disadvantaged or afforded less favourable treatment of any kind on the grounds of the number of hours they work per week or per month.'

Moving to part-time work

There is no right contained in the Part-Time Workers Regulations for an employee to be permitted to work part-time. However, following implementation in April 2003 of the Flexible Working (Procedural Requirements) Regulations 2002 and the Flexible Working (Eligibility, Complaints and Remedies) Regulations 2002, employees (but not other workers) who have a minimum of six months' continuous service and who have a child under the age of 6 (or whose partner has a child under 6) may submit a formal request for flexible working to their employer. If an employee has a disabled child, a request may be submitted up until the child's 18th birthday. A request for flexible working in this context includes a request to switch from full-time to part-time hours. Both men and women are eligible.

An employer who is in receipt of a request for flexible working is not obliged to agree to it automatically but must (if the request is not agreed at the outset) follow through a defined procedure that includes:

- holding a meeting with the employee who has made the request within 28 days in order to explore how the request might be made to work (for example, by recruiting a job-share partner); the employee will be entitled to be accompanied at the meeting by a colleague if they wish

- providing a written reply to the request within 14 days of the meeting which must, if the request is rejected, explain the specific business grounds for the refusal and why this is relevant to the employee's case

- granting a right of appeal within 14 days if the request is refused, and hearing the appeal within another 14 days.

Further details of the right to request flexible working appear in Chapter 11 under 'Discrimination against parents', page 207.

A model response for employers in receipt of a request to switch to part-time working is provided below.

Model response to an employee's request to move from full-time to part-time working

I am in receipt of your application to move from full-time to part-time working, dated [date]. In order to deal with your request effectively, I would like to meet with you to discuss the request, review the practical implications of implementing it, and assess how it might be made to work in practice. We will need, for example, to review how the duties of your job might be managed differently or be divided up, and see whether there is a way forward that will fit in with your request.

We would also like to make sure that you are given a full opportunity to think through the implications of moving to part-time work, in particular in light of the associated reduction in pay.

May I suggest therefore that you come to a meeting with [name] on [date] at [time] in [place]. You may, if you wish, bring a fellow employee along with you to the meeting.

Following the meeting, a decision will be made on the practicability of your request to move to part-time working. Please be assured that the company will endeavour to grant your request for a move to part-time working if it is at all possible to do so. It is the company's policy to be flexible on the working hours' arrangements for all its employees.

If the above meeting arrangements are not suitable for you, please telephone or e-mail [name] on [telephone number and/or e-mail address] to make alternative arrangements.

Refusing a request to move to part-time work

If a request for flexible working is refused, there must be a specific business reason for the refusal. Valid reasons are contained within the legislation (incorporated into the Employment Rights Act 1996). Full details are provided in Chapter 11 under 'Discrimination against parents', page 207.

s80G ERA 1996

There are further implications of refusing to agree to permit an employee to move to part-time working as a result of a long line of cases decided under the Sex Discrimination Act (SDA) 1975. These are fully discussed below under 'Hours of work and when they risk being discriminatory against women' (this page).

Implementing a request for a move to part-time working

Any change to an employee's hours of work implemented as a result of a formal request for flexible working will be regarded as a permanent change to the terms of the employee's contract (unless expressly agreed otherwise). It follows that the employee will have no automatic right to revert to full-time working at a future date, and the employer, similarly, will not be able to insist that the employee reverts to full-time working when the child reaches the age of 6 (although there is nothing to prevent the employer and employee agreeing to a trial period – see also Chapter 11 under 'Discrimination against parents', page 207).

Under the Part-Time Workers Regulations 2000, where a switch from full-time to part-time working is agreed, the employee will have the right to terms and conditions under the new part-time contract that are no less favourable (on a pro-rata basis) that those that were applicable as part of the previous full-time contract. This means, for example, that it is not open to an employer to agree to an employee's request to move to part-time working on condition that the employee accepts a lower rate of pay.

Hours of work and when they risk being discriminatory against women

Where an employer operates arrangements (whether formal or informal) under which employees are required or expected to work long hours (or even full-time hours – see below) or to take part in shift working, these arrangements will have a disproportionately adverse impact on female staff. There has been a long line of court and tribunal decisions that have upheld the general principle that fewer women than men can comply with a requirement to work long hours or unsocial hours, owing to child-care responsibilities, and that women are therefore more likely than men to be disadvantaged by such arrangements. If faced with a tribunal claim for indirect sex discrimination from an employee on account of a requirement to work long or unsocial hours, the employer will have to show that the hours requirement was objectively justifiable in the particular case (see also

Chapter 10 under 'Indirect discrimination', page 181). In effect, the employer will have to prove, on the balance of probabilities, that the requirement for the particular employee to work the hours in question was appropriate and necessary for the effective performance of the job.

Examples of hours patterns that could be indirectly discriminatory against women include:

- a regular requirement for overtime

- compulsory weekend working

- an early start or a late finish

- occasional or regular night working

- shift working, especially if the shift pattern involves irregular hours or rotating shifts.

Case Examples

[1998] IRLR 364

In *London Underground Ltd v Edwards*, it was ruled that a change to the employer's shift roster was indirectly discriminatory against a female employee. The employer had implemented a new shift system for train operators, as a result of which employees could no longer take advantage of a previously available option to swap shifts with other operators. One employee, a single mother, was unable to comply with the new roster (in particular the early morning start-time on some days) because of her child-care responsibilities. She succeeded in a complaint of indirect sex discrimination despite the fact that she was the only employee who could not comply with the new pattern of working. The Court of Appeal held that the employer could not justify insisting that she should work the new shift pattern.

EAT [2001] (503/00)

In *Chief Constable of Avon & Somerset Constabulary v Chew EAT*, a female police officer succeeded in a claim for indirect sex discrimination when her employer insisted that she should work shift rosters in order to be entitled to work part-time. The employee, who had two pre-school-age children, had recently separated from her husband, and wished to work part-time on day shifts only.

The Employment Appeal Tribunal (EAT) reviewed the well-established principle that a requirement to work shifts or unsocial hours will have a disproportionately adverse impact on women as compared with men. The issue was not whether the police force could justify shift working in a general sense but rather whether it was justifiable for them to apply the

Continued

Continued

requirement to work shifts to the police officer in question under all the relevant circumstances. The evidence suggested that, at the relevant time, other posts involving regular day shift working were available. The EAT thus held that the police force's insistence that the police officer must work the shift patterns in order to be granted part-time working was not justifiable.

The above cases do not mean that an employer can never impose requirements for employees to work long hours or shift patterns. The important point to remember is that any requirement imposed on an employee must be justifiable based on the needs of the job. In reality this breaks down into two elements:

1. whether it is justifiable in a general sense for the employer to operate a policy or practice of requiring employees to work long hours or shift rotas

2. whether it is justifiable to apply such a policy or requirement to the individual employee in question under all the circumstances (which will depend in part on what, if any, other options are reasonably available).

It is advisable, therefore, in circumstances where the employer is considering introducing, or is reviewing, any hours or shift pattern, to:

- consider carefully the effect that such an arrangement might have on employees, both generally and individually

- adopt a positive approach towards any employee who has difficulty complying with hours requirements or a shift pattern

- endeavour either to adapt the policy or requirement to accommodate such an employee or exempt the employee from the requirement.

It is important to bear in mind that a failure to respond in this way without objective justification will be likely to amount to indirect sex discrimination.

Employers would be well advised in any event to review their practices concerning working hours, overtime requirements, shift patterns and weekend working etc to ensure that no female employee might potentially be placed at a disadvantage as a result of the employer's practices.

Avoiding sex discrimination when dealing with requests to switch from full-time to part-time working

In line with the above principles, the argument that fewer women than men can comply with a requirement to work full-time has been used successfully in a number of tribunal cases alleging indirect sex discrimination, in particular cases involving women returning to work following maternity leave.

The key issue is the same as explained above, ie whether the employer can show that the requirement for the individual employee to work full-time is justifiable on objective grounds related to the needs of the job. Again, this breaks down into two questions:

1. Can the employer justify the need for full-time hours to be worked in the particular job?

2 Can the employer justify the need for the full-time job to be done by one person, as opposed to two job-share partners?

[1998] IRLR 364

Whilst the first of these two requirements may be easy to justify on the basis of volume of work or the need for full-time cover, the second will be more difficult, as many jobs are in fact suitable for job-sharing, provided that management take an open-minded and positive approach towards this concept.

In order to ensure that the principles of equality are effectively applied, therefore, it would be advisable for employers to:

- carry out a review of the feasibility of part-time, job-share and other non-standard working practices within the organisation, so that an objective and positive approach can be taken to the issue of flexible working

- consider any request for part-time working or job-share arrangements with an open mind

EAT [2001] (503/00)

- take all reasonable steps to accommodate an employee's request for part-time working, whether this occurs on the occasion of a woman's return from maternity leave or in other circumstances.

Employers should pay heed also to the provisions of the Part-Time Workers (Prevention of Less Favourable Treatment) Regulations 2000 (see above under 'Equality of treatment for part-timers in employment', page 81) and the right for employees with a minimum of six months' service who have a child under 6 years of age to submit a request for flexible working (see above under 'Moving to part-time work', page 85).

Equivalent contractual terms for fixed-term employees

Hard on the heels of the Part-Time Workers Regulations, the Government implemented the Fixed-Term Employees (Prevention of Less Favourable Treatment) Regulations 2002 on 1 October 2002. In terms of the principle of non-discrimination, the Fixed-Term Employees Regulations largely mirror the Part-Time Workers Regulations, but with one key difference. As is clear from the titles of the two sets of Regulations, the Part-Time Workers Regulations protect all workers (and not only employees) against discriminatory treatment, whilst the Fixed-Term Employees Regulations apply only to employees, ie those engaged directly by the employer on a contract of employment. The Fixed-Term Employees Regulations do not, however, extend to cover temporary staff engaged via a contract with an employment agency.

A fixed-term contract is defined in the Regulations as a contract that is set up to:

- last for a specified period, ie the contract has a predetermined termination date, or

- continue until a particular task or project is complete, or

[1998] IRLR 364

- continue until the occurrence (or non-occurrence) of a specified event, for example the non-renewal of funding upon which the post is dependent.

Thus, a wide range of different employment 'arrangements' will fall within the definition of fixed-term work, including, for example, summer seasonal work, employment to cover absence on maternity, adoption, paternity or parental leave, extra cover for peak periods, and contracts to carry out a specific task such as setting up a new database or even running a series of training courses.

EAT [2001] (503/00)

Model contractual clauses stating that a contract is for a fixed term

1. *Contractual clause for an employee engaged for a fixed-term period specified by date*

   Your contract of employment will be for a fixed term commencing on [*state date*] and terminating on [*state date*], at which time the contract will automatically expire. In accepting this contract, you agree that your employment will terminate on the expiry date mentioned above unless we offer you an extension or renewal of the contract which you choose to accept.

Continued

Although this contract is for a fixed term, we reserve the right at our entire discretion to give you notice to terminate the contract at any time during the currency of the contract for any reason. In this case, we will give you a minimum of [state number of weeks] notice in writing.

Would you please sign below to indicate your acceptance of the terms of this fixed-term contract.

2. *Contractual clause for an employee engaged on a contract for the performance of a particular task or project*

Your contract of employment will be for a fixed term commencing on [*state date*] and continuing until the [*state name or description of task/project*] task/project is complete, at which time the contract will automatically expire. We cannot specify exactly how long the task will last/project will take, and cannot therefore guarantee you any minimum or maximum period of employment. In accepting this contract, you agree that when the task/project is complete, your contract of employment will terminate, unless we offer you an extension or renewal of the contract which you choose to accept.

Although this contract is for a fixed term, we reserve the right at our entire discretion to give you notice to terminate the contract at any time during the currency of the contract for any reason. In this case, we will give you a minimum of [*state number of weeks*] notice in writing.

Would you please sign below to indicate your acceptance of the terms of this fixed-term contract.

3. *Contractual clause for an employee engaged for a fixed term until the occurrence of a specific event*

Your contract will be for a fixed term commencing on [state date] and continuing until [*state event, eg a named employee returning to work after a period of leave*]. When this occurs, your contract will automatically expire. We cannot specify at this point in time exactly how long we will wish to retain your services, and cannot therefore guarantee you any minimum or maximum period of employment. In accepting this contract, you agree that when [the event occurs, eg the employee returns to work], your contract of employment will terminate unless we offer you an extension or renewal of the contract which you choose to accept. Although this contract is for a fixed term, we reserve the right at our entire discretion to give you notice to terminate your contract at any time during the currency of the contract for any reason. In this case, we will give you a minimum of [*state number of weeks*] notice in writing.

Would you please sign below to indicate your acceptance of the terms of this fixed-term contract.

The non-discrimination principle

Under the Fixed-Term Employees Regulations, employees engaged on fixed-term contracts must not be treated less favourably than comparable permanent employees, unless there is an objective reason for the different treatment fixed-term staff, or there is some other reason that provides objective justification for less favourable treatment of the individual. Protection against discrimination covers all terms and conditions of employment, including pay and pension benefits, and also general treatment at work. Thus, non-contractual benefits such as access to promotion, training and appraisal are in scope (see also Chapter 6 under 'Including part-time and fixed-term employees within the scope of training and development', page 102).

Drawing the correct comparison

In order to found a claim, a fixed-term employee has to compare their treatment with a permanent employee who is performing the same or similar work and is working or based at the same establishment. In the event that there is no equivalent permanent employee at the same establishment, then the fixed-term employee can draw a comparison with a permanent employee performing similar work at another of the employer's workplaces. Comparisons may not be made on a hypothetical basis, unlike comparisons for the purposes of sex, sexual orientation, race or religious discrimination legislation.

The comparison to be made is, however, not a term-by-term balancing act (as is required in a claim for equal pay under the Equal Pay Act 1970) but rather a 'whole package' comparison. Thus, an employer may justify treating a fixed-term employee less favourably in relation to one specific benefit, provided that the package as a whole is no less favourable than that of a permanent employee engaged to perform similar work. For example an employer may legitimately decide not to allocate a company car to an employee engaged for a three-month fixed term even though a permanent employee performing the same work is allocated a car, so long as the lack of a car is offset by, for example, a higher rate of pay.

Holidays and holiday pay for fixed-term employees

Fixed-term employees, like their permanent equivalents, are entitled under the Working Time Regulations 1998 to a minimum of four weeks' paid leave each year. If, however, a fixed-term employee works for less than a year, then the annual entitlement should be pro-rated accordingly. It is permissible, where an employee (permanent or fixed-term) leaves their employment part-way through a holiday year, for the employer to pay them for any holiday leave that they have accrued but not taken. Thus, where a fixed-term contract is set up to last, for example, six months (creating a statutory holiday entitlement of two weeks), the employee could be required to work through the six months without taking any holiday leave and then be paid for the two weeks upon termination of the contract (assuming the contract is not extended or renewed). A contractual clause for dealing with this matter is provided below.

Over and above annual leave, many organisations grant their staff paid leave on public holidays. Employers should take care that this does not place any fixed-term employee at a disadvantage in comparison with an equivalent permanent worker. If, for example, the employer grants permanent employees eight paid public holidays over and above their entitlement to annual leave, a fixed-term employee who was engaged for a period of six months would be entitled to four extra paid days' holiday. If fewer than four public holidays occurred during the employee's fixed-term contract, they would have to be paid for any outstanding entitlement on termination.

The overall aim should be to ensure equality of treatment in the allocation of holiday entitlement and paid time off on public holidays for all staff.

Contractual clause for fixed-term employees re holidays and holiday pay on termination

'The company's holiday year runs from [1 January to 31 December]. The annual holiday entitlement for all staff is [four weeks] per annum for each complete holiday year. Where you are engaged on a fixed-term contract that does not span a complete holiday year, your entitlement to holiday leave during that year will be calculated on a pro-rata basis according to the proportion of the year that you are employed.

Under the Working Time Regulations 1998, it is not permitted for an employee to carry over holiday leave from one holiday year to the next, and holiday must not be bought out except on termination of employment. You should therefore agree with your manager whether it is acceptable for you to take paid leave during the currency of your fixed-term contract. If your fixed-term contract is shorter than a year, and if you do not take paid holidays during the period of your employment, you will be entitled to be paid in lieu of holidays not taken when your employment ends.'

Access to permanent work

Fixed-Term Employees
Regs 2002

Under the Fixed-Term Employees Regulations, employers are obliged to inform fixed-term employees of any suitable permanent vacancies that arise within the organisation. Informing all staff of internal vacancies is good practice in any event, and is something that the employer should actively seek to achieve by using not only notice-boards on which to post vacancies but also (if one exists) the company intranet. Alternatively, fixed-term employees could be given the opportunity to learn of permanent vacancies by e-mail or even by post if some of them do not have ready access to e-mail.

The Regulations further stipulate that fixed-term employees must be given the same opportunity to apply for promotion, transfer and training as comparable permanent employees with the same length of service.

Restrictions on the use of fixed-term contracts

As well as implementing the non-discrimination principle in relation to employees engaged on fixed-term contracts, the Fixed-Term Employees Regulations introduced a restriction on the renewal of fixed-term contracts in the form of a cut-off date after four years' continuity of service.

This means that once a fixed-term employee has gained four or more years' continuous service and has had their contract renewed at least once, they are automatically entitled to have their contract converted to permanent status, unless the employer can justify continuing the employment on a fixed-term basis. Two examples demonstrate how this works in practice:

- Employee A is engaged on a fixed-term contract for three years. The contract is then extended for another two years (without a break). At the four-year point, employee A will be entitled to have the contract converted to a permanent contract, because there has already been a renewal.

- Employee B is engaged on a fixed-term contract for a period of five years. At the four-year point, nothing will happen because there has been no renewal of the contract. However, if the contract is renewed or extended upon completion of the five years, the new contract will have to be a permanent contract.

As can be seen from the second of the two examples above, the four-year provision does not affect the initial length of a fixed-term contract, which can be any length that is agreed between the employer and the employee.

An important point to note in relation to the four-year restriction is that it was not made retrospective. Specifically, any service on a fixed-term contract before 10 July 2002 (the date by which the Fixed-Term Employees Regulations should have been implemented) will not count towards the four-year cut-off. In effect therefore, this provision will not bite until 10 July 2006.

It is open to employers to modify the above provisions by way of a collective agreement with a trade union or a valid workforce agreement. Any modifications will, however, be dependent on agreement being reached between the employer and the trade union or the workforce, and are not capable of being imposed on the workforce unilaterally.

Waiver clauses

Prior to the implementation of the Fixed-Term Employees Regulations, it was permissible for an employer who engaged someone on a fixed-term contract for two years or more to include a waiver clause in the contract for the purpose of excluding the employee's entitlement to statutory redundancy pay on termination. This provision was abolished by the Regulations, but not retrospectively. Thus, any properly agreed waiver clause entered into prior to the date the Regulations were implemented (1 October 2002) will remain valid until the date the fixed-term contract expires. The waiver clause will not, however, be able to be included in any extension or renewal to the contract.

The right to a written statement

Fixed-term employees are entitled under the Fixed-Term Employees Regulations to request a written statement giving the reason(s) for any treatment that they believe is in breach of their rights under the Regulations. If such a request is received, the employer must provide the employee with a written statement within 21 days, giving particulars of the reason(s) for the treatment.

Model policy on fixed–term working

'This company operates a policy of employing staff on open-ended (permanent) contracts of employment in normal circumstances. Where, however, there are specific circumstances that justify employing someone on a temporary basis only, then the company will offer employment on a fixed-term contract. Fixed-term contracts will generally be offered where:

- it is clear from the outset that the need for the particular job to be done will end on a specific date

- the employment is for the purpose of completing a particular task or project

- a replacement is needed for an employee who is to be absent from work for a period of time (for example on maternity leave) and it is not known at the outset exactly when that employee will return to work

- the post is dependent on external funding or external approval and it is thought likely that the funding or approval (as the case may be) will be available only for a limited period.

It is the policy of this company that all fixed-term employees will be treated as valued and committed members of staff irrespective of the fact that their employment is temporary. Fixed-term employees are entitled to an equal (pro-rata) package of pay and benefits as compared with permanent employees performing the same or similar work, unless there is an objective reason for offering different terms.

The company will also ensure that opportunities for permanent work are communicated to fixed-term employees and that fixed-term employees are, where practicable, included in company training programmes.

Access to the company's pension scheme is open to all employees, irrespective of whether they are engaged on a permanent or fixed-term contract. Entry to the company's pension scheme is, however, dependent on the employee having gained a minimum of [*x months'*] length of service.

It is the policy of this company that no employee will be disadvantaged or afforded less favourable treatment of any kind on the grounds that they are employed on a fixed-term contract.'

Termination of a fixed-term contract

The expiry of a fixed-term contract without renewal is, rather curiously, regarded as a dismissal in UK law. This is despite the fact that the employer and employee will have agreed at the outset that the contract will terminate on a particular date or on a particular occasion. The dismissal will be by reason of redundancy, or possibly on grounds of 'some other substantial reason' (SOSR).

It is important to remember that where an individual is employed on a series of separate, but continuous, fixed-term contracts, they will gain the same service-related employment rights as someone engaged on a normal open-ended contract. Such rights will include the right to claim unfair dismissal after one year's continuous service and the right to be paid statutory redundancy pay after two years' continuous service.

Normally, the dismissal because of the expiry of a fixed-term contract will be fair in law, but in certain circumstances an employment tribunal may take the opposite view, for example if:

- the employer recruits a replacement for the fixed-term employee shortly after the expiry of the contract (suggesting that the reason for the fixed-term employee's dismissal was not in fact the expiry of the contract, but in reality some other reason) – and matters could be even worse if the replacement employee was of the opposite sex or a different race

- there was another job into which the fixed-term employee could have been transferred on the expiry of their contract, but the employer did not discuss this opportunity with the fixed-term employee to establish whether such a transfer would have been of interest to them

- the employer in some other way acted unreasonably in terminating the fixed-term employee's contract.

To ensure fairness in termination, therefore, the employer should first review (in consultation with the fixed-term employee) whether the employee can be offered alternative work (whether permanent or fixed-term). If no alternative work is available, the employer should still be certain that the real reason for the proposed dismissal of the fixed-term employee is (for example) that the term has expired, the work is complete or the person whom the fixed-term employee replaced has returned to work.

Points to note

- Part-time employees have the same statutory employment rights as full-time employees, irrespective of the number of hours they work.

- The Part-Time Workers (Prevention of Less Favourable Treatment) Regulations 2000 provide that employers must not treat their part-time workers less favourably than comparable full-timers just because they work part-time, unless there is an objective reason justifying different treatment in the particular case.

- Employees who have a minimum of six months' continuous service and who have a child under the age of 6 (or whose partner has a child under 6) may submit a formal request to their employer for part-time working in order to care for the child.

- Arrangements (whether formal or informal) under which employees are required or expected to work long hours or to take part in shift working will have a disproportionately adverse impact on female staff and will therefore constitute unlawful indirect sex discrimination unless they can be objectively justified.

- Under the Fixed-Term Employees (Prevention of Less Favourable Treatment) Regulations 2002, employees engaged on fixed-term contracts must not be treated less favourably than comparable permanent employees, unless there is an objective reason for the different treatment.

- Once a fixed-term employee has gained four or more years' continuous service and has had their contract renewed at least once, they are automatically entitled to have their contract converted to permanent status, unless the employer can justify continuing the employment on a fixed-term basis.

Action points

- Conduct a review of the work done by part-time staff and check whether part-timers are receiving pay and benefits on a par with full-timers performing similar work.

- Ensure that no part-timer is excluded from training, appraisal or from opportunities for promotion or transfer on account of their part-time status.

- Check that part-time employees are granted equivalent paid time off on public holidays (on a pro-rata basis) in comparison with equivalent full-timers, and also that there are no inequalities as between different part-timers.

- Make sure that proper procedures are followed when in receipt of a statutory request for flexible working, including holding a meeting with the employee to explore how the request might be made to work.

- Review objectively whether any requirement for an employee to work long or unsocial hours is appropriate and necessary for the effective performance of the job.

- Adopt a positive approach towards any employee who has difficulty complying with hours requirements or shift patterns, and endeavour either to adapt the requirement to accommodate the employee or exempt the employee from the requirement.

- Carry out a review of the feasibility of part-time, job-share and other non-standard working practices within the organisation so that an objective and positive approach can be taken to the issue of flexible working.

- Take all reasonable steps to accommodate an employee's request for part-time working, whether this occurs on the occasion of an employee's return from maternity leave or in other circumstances.

- Take care that fixed-term employees are not placed at a disadvantage in respect of holidays (including public holidays) on account of being engaged for only a temporary period.

- Take steps to make sure all fixed-term employees are properly informed of any suitable permanent vacancies that arise within the organisation.

- Take care to ensure procedural fairness when terminating an employee's fixed-term contract, as the expiry of a fixed-term contract without renewal constitutes a dismissal in UK law.

CHAPTER 6

DISCRIMINATION IN EMPLOYEE DEVELOPMENT

This chapter takes a look at equality and diversity in the areas of training, appraisal, transfer and promotion. Access to opportunities for promotion, transfer and training are expressly covered in the anti-discrimination legislation. Employers should aim not only to avoid any potentially unlawful discrimination, but should also strive to ensure fairness and equality of treatment for all staff in relation to opportunities for development. Well-designed, objective procedures should be used to deal with employee training and promotion, and employers should take care in particular to ensure that women and members of ethnic groups are not overlooked for promotion or training, especially if they are in the minority to begin with.

Offering access to training and development opportunities without discriminating

It is very important, when making decisions about employees' training and development, that managers should refrain from making assumptions about individuals based on generalisations or on their own past experiences of people with whom they have worked. For example, it would be sexually discriminatory to deny training to a female employee based on an assumption that the employee might leave in the near future to start a family, or to accompany her husband, should he be relocated to another area by his employer. Such assumptions about the likely behaviour patterns of women would be discriminatory if they placed a female employee at a disadvantage (ie led to her being denied or refused an opportunity for training). In contrast, if there was evidence that a particular woman did in fact plan to leave in the foreseeable future (whatever her reason), then that fact would constitute a valid, non-discriminatory reason for the employer to decline to invest in that employee's training. The outcome would obviously be the same in the event of a male employee whose plans to leave the organisation in the near future were known to management.

Similarly, it would be discriminatory on racial grounds to refuse training to an employee of foreign nationality based on an assumption that the employee might decide to return to their own country soon after completion of the training. Such generalised assumptions may well be quite untrue in relation to a particular individual and may cause them a detriment on racial grounds. Instead of making generalised assumptions, the employer should consider the individual employee when deciding whether to offer training. For example, it would not be discriminatory to decline to nominate an employee for a training course on account of the employee's limited abilities or unwillingness to attend.

Scheduling of training

When organising internal training events, employers should pay heed to the likely diverse circumstances of their workforce in relation to the days of the week and times of day that individuals are likely to be available to attend the training.

Scheduling a training programme over a weekend, for example, may place female employees who work normal office hours at a disadvantage (as compared with male employees) on account of the greater likelihood of women having the predominant responsibility in the family for child-care. A female employee may be unable to attend a training event held at a weekend, in particular if she is a single parent. Training courses that extend into the evening may have the same detrimental effect on women more than on men (unless of course the employees in question normally work evening shifts). Such scheduling could therefore amount to indirect sex discrimination if a female employee was placed at a disadvantage by the scheduling of the training, for example if she was unable to attend, or if she was to incur the overt disapproval of management for not attending.

An employer who insists on running internal training courses at weekends may also run the risk of claims for indirect religious discrimination from those whose religious beliefs mean that they cannot work on a Saturday or on a Sunday (as the case may be).

In order to avoid such problems and to ensure that valued employees are not thoroughly demotivated, the employer should seek to organise training programmes within the normal working hours of the employees who form the target audience of the training. If, however, there are strong business reasons for running training at times that are outside employees' normal working hours, the employer should make sure that employees are informed of the dates and times of the training well in advance so that they at least have an opportunity to make personal and domestic arrangements enabling them to attend. If, despite such advance notice, a particular employee cannot attend, that employee should not be penalised in any way.

Another consideration, where training spans whole days, will be to make sure opportunities are available within the timetable for employees to take a break for the purposes of religious observance.

It will be a step towards diversity if employers regularly review any policies and practices on both internal and external training provision that affect employee development, in order to ensure that there are no potentially discriminatory criteria or conditions attached to them.

Including part-time and fixed-term employees within the scope of training and development

Both the Part-Time Workers (Prevention of Less Favourable Treatment) Regulations 2000 and the Fixed-Term Employees (Prevention of Less Favourable Treatment) Regulations 2002 provide that employers should not exclude part-timers or fixed-term employees respectively from opportunities for training on account of their part-time or fixed-term status. The Guidance Notes issued by the Department of Trade and Industry (DTI) to accompany the Part-Time Workers Regulations state also that training should be scheduled so far as possible so that staff, including part-timers, can attend. Neither set of Regulations places a positive duty on employers to offer training to part-time or fixed-term employees, but employers are instead under a duty not to exclude these categories of staff from training.

With respect to fixed-term employees, the Fixed-Term Employees Regulations impose an obligation on employers to treat a fixed-term employee who has the same length of service as a comparable permanent employee no less favourably than that permanent employee as regards access to training opportunities. In other words, it would be a breach of the Regulations to exclude from training a fixed-term employee with (for example) one year's service if a permanent employee with one year's service performing a comparable job would be offered the training, unless there is objective justification for the less favourable treatment of the employee engaged on the fixed-term contract.

Further information about the rights of part-time and fixed-term employees is contained in Chapter 5.

Making adjustments for a disabled employee in training

DDA 1995

Under the Disability Discrimination Act (DDA) 1995, an employee who is disabled has the right not to be treated unfavourably in relation to opportunities for training and development. Employers should therefore ensure that:

- disabled staff are given the same training and development opportunities as others

- negative assumptions about the abilities of disabled staff are not made

- arrangements for training do not place any disabled employee at a disadvantage

- training methods and scheduling are flexible enough to accommodate any disabled employee who is eligible to attend.

In order to comply with the duty to make reasonable adjustments in respect of a disabled employee whose disability would otherwise place them at a substantial disadvantage, employers may wish to consider making some of the following adjustments in respect of training:

- Move the training venue to a location with easier access for an employee who has limited mobility or who uses a wheelchair.

- Reschedule a training course to accommodate a disabled employee whose condition means that they need to attend a medical appointment or undergo medical treatment at a particular time.

- Ensure that tables, desks, chairs etc are suitable for an individual with a physical disability.

- Consider anyone who has a visual impairment when designing training, for example by producing written training material in Braille or in extra-large print.

- Provide an induction loop for an employee who has a hearing impairment so that they can use this in conjunction with their hearing aid at the training venue.

- Obtain a copy of the script of any video that is to be used during the training course for an employee with a hearing impairment (if this is possible).

- Redesign training, for example by allowing a longer period overall and a slower pace for an employee with a mental impairment that affects their ability to concentrate, learn or understand.

- Design training with more frequent breaks, so that individual sessions are shorter for employees whose disability affects their span of concentration or who cannot sit for lengthy periods.

- Permit a disabled employee to be accompanied on the training programme by someone who can provide them with support or assistance.

- Provide special coaching or mentoring either before or after the main training event for an employee with learning difficulties.

When considering an employee with a mental impairment for training, managers should beware of making negative assumptions about an individual's potential to learn or develop. An employee with learning difficulties, for example, may be quite capable of learning if they are afforded extra time to assimilate the necessary information, or extra coaching or support.

Induction training

One of the most important forms of training for any organisation (and one that is often afforded only lip-service) is induction training for newly employed staff. If a new employee is not made to feel comfortable and confident during the first few days or weeks of their employment, there will be a higher-than-average chance that they will leave. This will result in a considerable waste of time, energy and money for the employer, who will inevitably have to repeat the recruitment exercise.

Starting a new job is stressful for most people. They may initially feel out of place, uncomfortable and under pressure to make a positive impression to a maze of people whom they do not know. A new employee who belongs to a minority group (for example, a woman in a predominantly male environment or an employee from a minority ethnic group) may feel particularly 'out of place' when thrown into a completely new environment, as they may, over and above these ordinary stresses, have to cope with the worry of being perceived as 'different'.

It is therefore very important that all new employees, but especially those from minority groups, are made to feel welcome and valued, and are made aware of what is expected of them during the first few weeks of their employment. Every individual is different, and whilst some new recruits may settle down quickly, others will take longer to start to feel that they are fitting in, or they may experience difficulties in becoming integrated.

One positive approach towards induction would be to nominate a mentor for each new employee for the first few weeks of their employment. This would give the new recruit access to an experienced person (preferably someone from a different part of the organisation) who would be able to provide advice and guidance on a range of general issues. This approach would, of course, require the mentors to be properly trained in the processes of mentoring.

To improve the process of induction generally, employers may wish to:

- design induction so that new employees are offered a range of different introductory sessions with different people in different departments

- avoid cramming induction into the first day or two of the new employment

- endeavour to give the new employee something useful and productive to do as early as possible in their employment

- make it clear to all new employees during induction what people need to do in order to make progress within the organisation

- make sure induction includes information about the informal processes that exist within the organisation, as well as the official policies and procedures

- nominate an individual in respect of each new start (for example a mentor) from whom the employee can seek specific guidance or advice or to whom they can take any problems they experience in becoming integrated into the organisation

- ensure that managers who carry responsibility for induction training are properly trained themselves.

Positive action that is permitted to encourage minority groups to access training

Whilst positive discrimination in employment is not permitted by UK law, certain forms of positive action are allowed provided the action taken is in the form of encouragement to members of an under-represented or disadvantaged group to take up opportunities for employment or training. In effect, positive action will widen the pool for development, promotion or selection.

The circumstances in which positive action may be taken are, however, limited. Specifically, positive action in relation to gender and race may be undertaken only when either men or women, or people from a particular racial group are under-represented in the organisation as a whole or in a particular type of employment. The equivalent provisions related to religion and sexual orientation permit employers to take steps to encourage people of a particular religion (or sexual orientation) to take advantage of training opportunities, provided such action is carried out to prevent or compensate for disadvantages linked to religion (or sexual orientation) suffered by those of that religion (or sexual orientation).

Positive action in training is therefore a lawful means of attempting to redress an existing imbalance, and is specifically aimed at helping to fit employees from an under-represented or disadvantaged group for particular work. Further information about positive action appears in Chapter 1 (pages 12–15).

It is important to note, however, that offering training to an employee just because they belong to a minority group is not permitted in UK law. What is permitted is training set up specifically and exclusively for people from an under-represented or disadvantaged group. Furthermore, although single-sex training or training restricted to members of a particular racial or religious group is permitted under the positive action provisions, where training is made generally available by an employer the employer may not then give priority to members of a minority group. In other words, the positive action provisions affecting training dictate an 'all or nothing' approach. For example, in an organisation where women are under-represented in management positions, it would be lawful for the employer to offer management training exclusively to female employees in order to encourage more women to progress into management. Where, however, the employer elected to offer management training to all employees (ie both men and women), it would not be open to them to give priority to a female employee in the process of deciding who was to be nominated for a particular training course.

Forms of positive action relevant to employee development

Positive action can include (for example):

SDA 1975 s47(3)

- offering training to people who have been out of full-time employment because of domestic or family responsibilities, to enable them to get back into work (this is expressly permitted in the Sex Discrimination Act 1975)

- designing focused training for people from groups that are under-represented in a particular type of work, for example to increase the chances for promotion into supervisory or management posts for women or people from minority racial groups

s36 RRA 1976

- offering training to overseas nationals who are not ordinarily resident in Britain and who are not expected to remain in Britain, for example if the training will be needed when they return to their home country (this is expressly provided for in the Race Relations Act 1976)

- encouraging ethnic minority employees to apply for promotion or transfer opportunities

- promoting flexible working practices (which are likely to benefit all staff) and training managers in how to manage flexible working and work-life balance.

Managing positive action effectively

In order to manage positive action effectively, managers should pay heed to the following matters:

- Make positive action part of the employer's overall equal opportunities policy.

- Consult employees before deciding what measures to take in order to avoid the risk that positive action might be perceived as preferential (and by implication unfair) treatment.

- Communicate any planned positive action clearly to all staff to inform them what measures are planned, why they are planned and the fact that the proposed measures will not place anyone who is not from the particular minority group at a disadvantage.

- Brief those who will be conducting the training properly to ensure they understand the key objectives of the training.

- Evaluate any training based on positive action after the event to ascertain whether it has been effective in achieving its aims. This can be done by comparing the numbers of the under-represented group in particular types of employment before the training and at a predetermined interval after the training.

Conducting performance appraisals without discrimination

As with other aspects of the employment relationship, performance appraisal should be conducted without any direct or indirect discrimination against individuals on grounds of gender, marital status, race, religion or belief, sexual orientation, age or disability.

The starting point for ensuring a fair and non-discriminatory appraisal scheme is to review the scope of the scheme and make sure that no one is excluded from appraisal on any of the prohibited grounds. If appraisal is offered to some groups of employees and not others (for example to 'white-collar' staff and not 'blue-collar' workers), this could lead to indirect discrimination if the gender or racial composition of each of the two groups is different. If fixed-term employees are excluded from appraisal, this would in most cases be unlawful under the Fixed-Term Employees (Prevention of Less Favourable Treatment Regulations) 2002, unless their exclusion could be objectively justified. The same principle applies to part-time employees under the Part-Time Workers (Prevention of Less Favourable Treatment) Regulations 2000. Excluding part-timers, and even possibly casual workers, from appraisal could also amount to indirect sex discrimination if the majority of part-timers or casuals in the organisation are women.

One particular pitfall to avoid is the inadvertent exclusion from appraisal of a woman who is absent from work on maternity leave. Once the employee has returned to work, her manager should ensure she is given a full opportunity to undergo an appraisal that is as equal as is possible to the standard appraisal offered to other staff (taking into account that she has been absent from work for a period of time).

Case Example

In the French case of *Caisse Nationale d'Assurance Vieillesse des Travailleurs Salariés v Thibault ECJ Case*, a female employee successfully claimed before the European Court of Justice (ECJ) that she had been the victim of sex discrimination when she was denied an annual performance assessment, and along with it the chance of promotion, because she had taken maternity leave. The reasoning of the ECJ was that, had the employee not been pregnant and taken maternity leave, she would have been given a performance appraisal, and could have therefore qualified for promotion. Since pregnancy and maternity leave are exclusive to women, the employee's exclusion from the annual performance assessment for reasons related to maternity leave amounted to direct sex discrimination.

Criteria for appraisals

Having ensured that no employees are unreasonably excluded from the appraisal process, the next step for management should be to examine the assessment criteria of any existing scheme to ensure these do not discriminate indirectly against any group of employees. For example, if employees' performance is measured in terms of flexibility (ie flexibility in terms of availability to work additional hours at short notice), this would discriminate indirectly against female employees, who are less likely than male employees to be able to comply with any request to work overtime at short notice.

Criteria used for assessing job performance should be job-oriented and measurable, and not person-oriented (which would allow the appraiser's opinion of the appraisee as a person to be the determining factor). Criteria could, for example, be based on tasks completed, standards achieved and targets met, rather than factors such as 'attitude', 'reliability' or 'flexibility', which would allow the appraiser's subjective view of the individual's personal qualities to take precedence. If an assessment of the employee's communication skills forms part of the appraisal, care should be taken not to discriminate against employees of foreign nationality whose first language is not English.

Appraisal interviewing

Appraisal interviews are notoriously difficult to conduct effectively. One barrier may be the appraiser's personal opinions about the appraisee, their work or future potential. It is important that those conducting appraisals have been properly trained in the art of appraisal interviewing. Such training should include awareness training on prejudice and stereotyping based on such factors as sex, marital status, sexual orientation, race, cultural background, religion, appearance, age and other factors.

Checklist for ensuring equality of treatment in appraisal

- Aim to make appraisal available to all staff at all levels within the organisation rather than restricting it to only some groups of staff. If, however, appraisal is offered to employees in some jobs but not others, make sure that the excluded group(s) are not predominantly of one sex or race.

- Ensure the appraisal scheme is designed to measure employees' job performance objectively, for example against agreed targets.

- Design appraisal criteria so that they cannot in any way be based on the personal qualities of the appraisee as perceived by the appraiser.

- Identify training needs based on the objective needs of the job and specific training needs of the individual.

- Examine the criteria to be used in appraisal to ensure there is no indirect discrimination in any of the factors used to evaluate individuals' job performance or future potential.

- Make sure that any female employees who are absent from work on maternity leave during the period over which appraisals are being conducted receive an appraisal on their return to work.

- Provide full training to all those who are to conduct appraisal interviews.

- Evaluate and monitor appraisal results, in particular to ensure that the potential of women or employees from minority racial groups to progress within the organisation is not rated lower than that of others.

Ensuring promotion opportunities are available equally to all

The duty to ensure equality of treatment in promotion is similar in principle to the duty not to discriminate during the process of recruitment and selection (see generally Chapter 1 for full details). The GOQs (genuine occupational qualifications) and GORs (genuine occupational requirements) that are permissible in recruitment to new posts are also permissible in respect of selection for promotion or transfer. (Chapter 1 contains detailed information about GOQs and GORs.)

Specifically, the anti-discrimination legislation provides that employers must not discriminate in the access afforded to opportunities for promotion. This wording clearly covers a wide range of situations involving the availability of opportunities for promotion as well as the employer's decisions as to whom to promote. For example, an employee who was allocated only menial or unchallenging tasks could argue that this practice restricted or prevented them from gaining access to opportunities for promotion. If the allocation of menial tasks could be shown to be linked to discrimination on grounds of sex, race etc, then a case for unlawful discrimination in opportunities for promotion could be made out.

Ensuring any criteria or conditions for promotion are not indirectly discriminatory

As in the process of recruitment, it is important, when operating procedures for selection for promotion, to ensure that any criteria applied to the promoted post are not indirectly discriminatory (see 'Ensuring any criteria or conditions attached to the job are not indirectly discriminatory' in Chapter 1, page 15).

[1997] IRLR 560

Case Example

In *Falkirk Council v Whyte and ors*, for example, an employee at a prison who had been unsuccessful in an application for promotion to a management post claimed indirect sex discrimination on account of the employer's policy of applying 'management training and supervisory experience' as 'desirable' criteria for the post. She argued that female prison officers were less likely than male officers to have the requisite management training and experience, and that she had suffered a disadvantage when she was rejected because of the application of these criteria.

The employer argued at tribunal that because the management training and supervisory experience criteria were not applied to the selection process as essential factors, the employee's rejection for the post could not have been discriminatory. However, the evidence was that the employer had in fact applied these criteria as decisive factors. The employee who had been rejected for the promoted post had therefore suffered a disadvantage as a result of the imposition of the requirement to have management training and supervisory experience. The Employment Appeal Tribunal (EAT) took the view that the imposition of this requirement was not objectively justified in the particular case.

Employers should therefore think twice before specifying requirements based on length of service, length of experience, flexibility, mobility (see below) and full-time working as either necessary or desirable criteria for promotion to a particular post. Such provisions can discriminate indirectly against women, who are more likely than men to be disadvantaged by them as a result of family and child-care responsibilities (see Chapter 10, 'Indirect discrimination', page 181). It is important, if a particular criterion is to be applied in the selection decision, that it can be objectively justified as relevant or necessary for the effective performance of the job in question.

Indirect discrimination on grounds of marriage

Discrimination on grounds of marriage is unlawful under the SDA 1975 (see also Chapter 11, 'Marital status', pages 196, 204), as the following case demonstrates.

SDA 1975

Case Example

In *Chief Constable of Bedfordshire Constabulary v Graham*, a female police officer succeeded in a case of unlawful discrimination based on marital status following the rescinding of an offer of appointment to the post of Area Inspector in the division that her husband commanded. The Chief Constable took the view that the officer's appointment would have been inappropriate, principally because of concerns that the officer might not be a competent witness against her husband in the event of criminal proceedings. Other reasons for the rescinding of the appointment were concerns that the police officer's colleagues might have difficulties in circumstances where they wished to bring a grievance against her, and that it might be difficult for the Force to take action in the event that she underperformed in the new job.

The EAT held that the rescinding of the appointment constituted both direct and indirect marriage discrimination (and also indirect sex discrimination). The decision not to allow her to take up the appointment was, firstly, directly discriminatory simply because it was related to the fact that she was married. The EAT rejected the contention of the employer that there could be no marital discrimination where the action complained of was taken not on grounds of marriage *per se*, but on the grounds that the individual was married to a particular person. Secondly, the Chief Constable's decision was indirectly discriminatory. This was because the application of a 'requirement' to Mrs Graham that, in order to be allowed to take up the post, she should not be in a cohabiting relationship with another police officer, was one with which fewer married police officers (as compared to unmarried officers) could comply. The EAT held that the action taken by the Chief Constable could not be objectively justified.

[2002] IRLR 239

Procedure for determining who is to be promoted

It often happens that an individual is selected for a promotion without any formal procedure having been undertaken by the employer. Whilst this practice may be convenient for the employer who may have earmarked a particular employee for a particular post, it does run the dual risk of:

- alienating other employees who would have valued the opportunity to apply for the promoted post

- being an arbitrary practice capable of being challenged as indirectly discriminatory against, for example, women or ethnic minority employees who may be vulnerable to being overlooked for promotion. If, say, a woman on maternity leave could show that she had more suitable experience or qualifications in relation to the promoted post than the person selected, the employer would have great difficulty at tribunal in defending a claim for sex discrimination.

Even if the employee who is appointed to the promoted post is the most suitable candidate, making an appointment without first affording the opportunity to apply for the job to other employees who may consider themselves capable of performing it will breach the inherent principle of equal opportunities and send out the wrong signals. Conversely, adopting a policy of making opportunities available to all employees to apply for all promoted posts will act to promote equality and diversity throughout the organisation, and will minimise the likelihood of appointments being perceived as unfair or discriminatory.

It follows that, to promote equality and diversity, all available vacancies should be widely advertised internally, using all available methods, for example notice-boards, internal magazines, e-mail and any company intranet. Managers should take steps to make sure that employees at different branches or locations are also informed of vacancies. Arguably, it is only where people from all sectors of the organisation are given full opportunity to be considered for promoted posts that the aims of diversity can fully be achieved.

Affording opportunities for promotion to fixed-term and part-time employees

Reg 3(6-7) Fixed-Term
Employees Regs 2002

The Fixed-Term Employees (Prevention of Less Favourable Treatment) Regulations 2002, contain a specific provision that entitles employees engaged on fixed-term contracts to receive information from their employer about any suitable available vacancies that arise in the establishment. Furthermore, fixed-term employees have the right to be treated equally in comparison to permanent employees with the same length of service with regard to the opportunity to obtain permanent employment. These provisions would entitle fixed-term employees to be considered on an equal footing to comparable permanent employees in relation to any available promoted posts.

DISCRIMINATION IN EMPLOYEE DEVELOPMENT

The Part-Time Workers (Prevention of Less Favourable Treatment) Regulations 2000 provide that employers must not subject part-time workers to any detriment on account of their part-time status. This principle would be breached if a part-time employee was refused a promotion just because they worked part-time, unless the employer was able to justify the refusal on objective grounds unrelated to the individual's existing part-time status. Managers should not assume that part-timers do not want promotion or are unsuitable for promotion, whether the promoted post is part-time or full-time. Instead, all staff should be given an equal opportunity to apply for the promoted post in question.

Fuller information about the rights of part-time and fixed-term employees is given in Chapter 5.

Checklist for good practice in dealing with promotions

- Review, and if necessary revamp, promotion procedures to ensure that each stage of the procedure, including vacancy notification, interviewing, assessment and final selection, is being carried out objectively and without discrimination on any ground.

- Ensure that procedures for promotion are communicated to all staff (including fixed-term and part-time workers) so that everyone understands the process used to identify and assess internal candidates for promotion.

- Scrutinise any traditional routes to promotion into supervisory and management posts to make sure the employer's practices do not indirectly discriminate against female employees or those from minority racial or religious groups.

- Review and if necessary change any rules that restrict or preclude transfers between certain jobs.

- Think carefully before specifying the criteria for selection into a promoted post to ensure that they can be objectively justified.

- Ensure all job vacancies are advertised internally at all the employer's branches and locations so that all employees are consistently informed about promotion opportunities.

- Ensure that fixed-term and part-time staff are given fair and appropriate consideration for promoted posts.

- Introduce a process whereby unsuccessful internal candidates are given feedback explaining why their application for a promoted post was unsuccessful, and giving positive guidance on how they might improve their chances of promotion in the future.

- Monitor promotions to provide a record of the numbers of men/women and members of different racial groups who are promoted. If any imbalances are identified relative to the total numbers of people employed, explore the causes and take appropriate steps to eliminate them.

When mobility clauses can be discriminatory

It is common for employers to include mobility clauses in the contracts of employment of certain staff, typically senior management and project employees in large national organisations. However, a blanket policy to incorporate a clause into employees' contracts requiring them to agree to relocate to a different UK (or overseas) location at the employer's request is not advisable, as it would discriminate indirectly against women. This principle was established in the case of *Meade-Hill & anor v British Council*.

[1995] IRLR 478

Case Example

In *Meade-Hill*, the employee, who had been promoted, was issued with a new contract which included a wide-ranging mobility clause requiring her to agree to work anywhere in the UK at the employer's discretion. Even though this clause did not immediately affect the employee (who was not being required to relocate at the time in question), she applied to a court seeking a declaration that it was unenforceable on the grounds that it amounted to indirect sex discrimination. Her argument was founded on the principle that a larger proportion of women than men are secondary wage earners, and consequently fewer women than men can in practice comply with an employer's instruction to relocate.

On appeal, the Court of Appeal upheld the employee's complaint, ruling that the mobility clause had been 'applied' immediately the contract had been entered into and that its application was not objectively justified in all the circumstances of the case.

It is not, in any event, clever psychology for an employer to try to force an employee (whether male or female) to move to a different location against their will. A much better policy would be to seek to agree mobility requirements individually with employees as and when the need to fill a vacancy arises, without any pressure being placed on a particular employee to move, whether permanently or temporarily. Even though mobility may be a justifiable requirement in some jobs, it is important to consider the employee's personal circumstances at the time a transfer is being mooted and not penalise an employee who, for family or other personal reasons, cannot, or does not wish to, move to a different location.

In contrast, a limited mobility clause requiring employees to agree to move to a different location within reasonable distance of their home would be helpful to an employer in the event that they decide to move premises or transfer employees between different workplaces in the same city or district.

Model mobility clause

Where an employer does agree with an employee that a mobility clause is an appropriate and fair element to include in an employment contract, the clause should be carefully worded. A clause along the following lines would allow reasonable flexibility:

'It is a condition of your contract that you may be asked, whether permanently or temporarily, to transfer to another place of work anywhere in the UK, or to travel both inside and outside the UK on company business. You will be expected to agree to any such request upon reasonable prior notice. If, however, there is a valid reason why you are unable to relocate or work in a different location at the time you are asked to do so, the company will consider your circumstances and will not unreasonably penalise you for refusing.'

Points to note

- Scheduling training programmes over a weekend or during evenings may place female employees who work standard office hours at a disadvantage as compared with men, and should therefore be avoided in these circumstances.

- Both the Part-Time Workers Regulations 2000 and the Fixed-Term Employees Regulations 2002 provide that employers should not exclude part-timers or fixed-term employees respectively from opportunities for training on account of employees' part-time or fixed-term status.

- Positive action in training is a lawful means of attempting to redress an existing imbalance (for example in the proportions of men and women in a particular type of work), and is specifically aimed at helping to fit employees from an under-represented or disadvantaged group for particular work.

- The starting point for ensuring a fair and non-discriminatory appraisal scheme is to review the scope of the scheme and make sure that no one is excluded from appraisal on any of the prohibited grounds.

- It will be unlawful to exclude part-time or fixed-term employees from appraisal purely on grounds of their part-time/fixed-term status, although the exclusion of a particular individual may be objectively justified.

- Criteria used for assessing job performance should be job-oriented and measurable (for example against agreed targets) and not person-oriented (which would allow the appraiser's subjective view of the individual's personal qualities to be the determining factor).

- Anti-discrimination legislation provides that employers must not discriminate in the access afforded to opportunities for promotion, which means a wide range of situations involving the availability of opportunities for promotion as well as the employer's decisions as to whom is to be promoted are covered.

- Adopting a policy of making opportunities available to all employees to apply for all promoted posts will promote equality and diversity throughout the organisation and minimise the likelihood of appointments being perceived as unfair or discriminatory.

- A blanket policy to incorporate a clause into employees' contracts requiring them to agree to relocate to a different UK location at the employer's request is not advisable, as it would discriminate indirectly against women.

Action points

- Review regularly any policies and practices on both internal and external training provision that affect employee development in order to ensure that there are no potentially discriminatory criteria or conditions attached to them.

- Ensure that disabled staff are given the same training and development opportunities as others, and that arrangements for training and training methods do not place any disabled employee at a disadvantage.

- Consider nominating a mentor for each new employee for the first few weeks of their employment to help them become integrated into the organisation.

- Consider designing focused training for people from groups that are under-represented in a particular type of work, for example to increase the chances for promotion into supervisory or management posts for women or people from minority racial groups.

- Communicate any planned positive action clearly, including the fact that the proposed measures will not place anyone who is not from a minority group at a disadvantage.

- Make sure employees on maternity leave are not excluded from the employer's appraisal process.

- Examine the assessment criteria of any existing appraisal scheme to ensure these do not discriminate indirectly against any group of employees.

- Ensure that the criteria applied to promoted posts are not indirectly discriminatory, for example against women, married people or people from minority racial groups.

- Take care, if requirements based on length of service, length of experience, flexibility, mobility or full-time working are to be applied as criteria for promotion to a particular post, that the criteria in question can be objectively justified as relevant or necessary for the effective performance of the job.

- Ensure that all job vacancies are advertised internally at all the employer's branches and locations, so that all employees are consistently informed about promotion opportunities.

- Ensure that fixed-term and part-time staff are given fair and appropriate consideration for promoted posts.

- Seek to agree mobility requirements individually with employees as and when the need to fill a vacancy arises, without any pressure being placed on a particular employee to relocate, whether permanently or temporarily.

CHAPTER 7

HARASSMENT AS DISCRIMINATION

Harassment of any kind in the workplace can have devastating effects, both on the well-being of its victim and on the morale (and consequent effectiveness) of the workforce generally. Harassment can undermine an employee's confidence, make them feel demeaned and degraded, create enormous stress (leading potentially to mental illness), and ultimately have a seriously detrimental impact on the productivity not only of the victim, but also on other employees who find themselves working in a culture of fear and resentment.

The law governing harassment has developed substantially in recent years, both as a result of court and tribunal decisions that have interpreted harassment as a detriment under discrimination law, and as a result of new legislation which has, for the first time, provided a statutory definition of harassment.

Chapter 10 provides further explanation and interpretation of the law on harassment, page 187.

Recognising when behaviour may amount to unlawful harassment

Anti-discrimination legislation is not yet entirely consistent as regards its approach towards the interpretation of harassment. Most of the differences will disappear in time as a new statutory definition of harassment is introduced to the various strands of discrimination law. The Race Relations Act (RRA) 1976 was amended in July 2003 to include a statutory definition of harassment (see below), although this definition applies only to harassment on grounds of race, ethnic origins and national origins, and not to harassment on grounds of colour or nationality. Both the Disability Discrimination Act 1995 and the Sex Discrimination Act 1975 are expected to be amended (in 2004 and 2005 respectively) to include a similar statutory definition of harassment. The newer

RRA 1976

DDA 1995, SDA 1975

legislation, namely the Employment Equality (Religion or Belief) Regulations 2003 and the Employment Equality (Sexual Orientation) Regulations 2003, both contain a parallel statutory definition.

Racial harassment – statutory definition

The RRA 1976 was amended in July 2003 to make specific provision to render harassment on grounds of race or ethnic or national origins unlawful, and to introduce a statutory definition of racial harassment.

The definition in the RRA 1976 is:

s3(A) RRA 1976

A person subjects another to harassment where, on the grounds of that other's race or ethnic or national origins, he engages in unwanted conduct which has the purpose or effect of –

(a)   violating that other's dignity, or

(b)   creating an intimidating, hostile, degrading, humiliating or offensive environment for that other.

The amended Act also states that:

Conduct shall be regarded as having the effect specified in paragraphs (a) and (b) if, and only if, having regard to all the circumstances, including, in particular, the perception of that other, it should reasonably be considered as having that effect.

Thus, the principle that an employee is entitled to decide for themselves what conduct they perceive as unwanted and offensive has been introduced to statutory law as a free-standing ground of unlawful discrimination, with the proviso that treatment that has an alleged discriminatory effect must also be capable of being interpreted as harassment by a reasonable person. This provides an objective dimension and a yardstick of reasonableness for judging whether or not conduct that has had an alleged detrimental effect on the person experiencing it amounts to unlawful harassment. The person's subjective perception of the alleged harassment stands to be balanced against an objective, reasonable viewpoint, taking into account all the circumstances of the particular case.

For example, if an over-sensitive Afro-Caribbean employee unreasonably took offence at a one-off innocent remark about black people, but most reasonable people would not have perceived the remark as offensive in the circumstances in which it was made, then a complaint to a tribunal alleging unlawful racial harassment would be unlikely to succeed. On the other hand, if, for example, a Pakistani employee was genuinely offended on account of racist banter in the workplace in circumstances where their British colleagues found the same remarks amusing, then the Pakistani employee would nevertheless be able potentially to succeed in a claim for racial harassment. It has been established for some time as a result of court and tribunal decisions that it is for each individual to determine individually what they find offensive.

An interesting element of the definition of harassment is the concept that a complaint of harassment can be brought on the grounds that an employee's working environment was intimidating, hostile, degrading, humiliating or offensive to them. One consequence of this approach is that it will be possible for an individual to succeed in a claim for unlawful harassment even where the conduct complained of was not directed at them personally. For example, if management condone an atmosphere at work in which it is commonplace for employees to engage in homophobic banter, then this might be said to have created an offensive working environment for an employee who is gay, irrespective of whether any of the banter was directed at that particular employee.

One inconsistency in the legislation, however, is that the provisions in the RRA 1976 governing harassment apply only to harassment on grounds of race, ethnic origins or national origins. This means that harassment on grounds of colour or nationality will stand to be dealt with under the 'detriment' provisions of the Act as interpreted by the courts and tribunals over the years (see below under 'Sexual harassment', page 121).

Religious harassment

Since the implementation of the Employment Equality (Religion or Belief) Regulations 2003, which contain a statutory definition of harassment as a distinct form of discrimination (parallel wording to that contained in the RRA 1976 – see above), employees are expressly protected against any harassment on grounds of their religion or belief. For example, if a Muslim employee was incessantly teased about their beliefs or religious practices, this could amount to harassment. The law prohibiting religious harassment is also likely to impinge on behaviour in workplaces where employees have allegiances to football clubs linked to sectarian rivalry, such as the rivalry between Rangers and Celtic supporters in Glasgow. It is possible that the wearing of clothing displaying football slogans with a sectarian significance could create an offensive working environment for some employees.

Harassment on grounds of sexual orientation

The implementation of the Employment Equality (Sexual Orientation) Regulations 2003 made it unlawful to harass someone at work on the grounds that they are, or are thought to be, gay, lesbian or bisexual (or heterosexual). One difficulty with this strand of the discrimination legislation is that an employer will be less likely to possess the knowledge as to whether a particular individual is gay or lesbian. Such lack of knowledge will not, however, allow an employer to escape liability for any unlawful harassment that takes place in the course of the individual's employment.

Sexual harassment

UK sex discrimination legislation does not (as yet) contain a definition of sexual harassment. As early as 1986, however, the courts and tribunals recognised that sexual harassment at work could amount to a detriment and hence be a form of direct discrimination. The case that set the precedent was *Strathclyde Regional Council v Porcelli*.

[1986] IRLR 134

Case Example

In *Strathclyde Regional Council v Porcelli [1986] IRLR 134*, a woman had been subjected to a campaign of inappropriate touching and suggestive remarks by two male colleagues who resented her and wanted to force her out of her job. The Scottish Court of Session ruled that the behaviour meted out to the woman would not have occurred if she had been a man, and that it therefore amounted to less favourable treatment under the SDA 1975. They further stated that harassment need not be based on a sex-related motive for it to constitute unlawful sex discrimination, and that provided the unfavourable treatment to which the woman was subjected included a significant sexual element to which a man would not be vulnerable, then it would be regarded as direct sex discrimination.

Although there is as yet no definition of sexual harassment in UK law, the EC Code of Practice on the protection of the dignity of women and men at work provides a framework for defining it, by stating that:

- sexual harassment is 'unwanted conduct of a sexual nature, or other conduct based on sex affecting the dignity of women and men at work'

- sexual harassment can consist of 'physical, verbal or non-verbal conduct'

- conduct of a sexual nature will amount to sexual harassment where it is 'unwanted, unreasonable and offensive to the recipient'

- it is for each individual to determine what behaviour is acceptable to them and what they regard as offensive.

It can be seen from the EU's approach to harassment (which has been observed and upheld for many years by UK courts and tribunals) that the decision as to whether particular conduct amounts to sexual harassment lies with the victim. It follows that managers responsible for staff should take care not to view behaviour purely subjectively, as this may lead them to view an allegation of sexual harassment as insignificant in circumstances where the recipient of the behaviour has been genuinely offended. The important criterion is whether the recipient of the conduct finds it offensive, and not whether the manager regards the same conduct as trivial or a joke. More recently, the Employment Appeal Tribunal (EAT) confirmed in *Reed & anor v Stedman* that it is up to the recipient of the conduct in question to decide what type of conduct is acceptable and what is offensive.

[1999] IRLR 299

The other key factor in determining whether harassment constitutes unlawful sex discrimination is whether it can be shown that the victim was treated unfavourably on grounds of their sex (as opposed to some other reason unconnected with gender). Bullying at work that has no sexual motive or that is not sex-based or sexual in nature cannot give rise to a complaint under the SDA 1975 (although the victim may – if the bullying is sufficiently serious – be able to resign and claim constructive dismissal, provided they have a minimum of one year's continuous service with their employer).

Whether the conduct complained of constitutes a detriment

In the *Reed* case (above), the EAT expressed the view that some conduct will be of such a nature that it will be obvious it was unwanted from the victim's perspective, whilst in other cases behaviour may be borderline. In the former case, the employee will not have to provide evidence to a tribunal that they were disadvantaged by the treatment meted out to them, as this will be accepted at face value. In the latter case, however, the employee would have to show (in order to prove detriment) that the conduct continued after they had made it clear to the perpetrator that it was unwelcome. The EAT stated that, provided any reasonable person would understand the victim to be rejecting the conduct in question, its continuation should be regarded as harassment. This approach is in line with the EC Code of Practice, which states 'Sexual attention becomes sexual harassment if it is persisted in once it has been made clear that it is regarded by the recipient as offensive.'

[2003] UKHL 11

An interesting development occurred in the case of *Shamoon v Chief Constable of Royal Ulster Constabulary*, in which the House of Lords approved the principle that an employee may be subjected to a detriment even though the action or behaviour complained of caused no physical or economic consequence.

Disability harassment

Courts and tribunals have tended over the years to adopt a broadly similar approach to complaints of disability harassment, ie harassment is capable of amounting to a detriment that can give rise to a successful claim for unlawful direct discrimination. Harassment that is related in some way to an employee's disability will therefore constitute unlawful disability discrimination where it causes the employee a disadvantage and it can be shown that, but for the fact that the employee was disabled, the harassment would not have occurred.

Single incident or series of incidents

A complaint of discrimination can be taken to tribunal as a result of either a single serious incident of harassment or a series of relatively minor incidents, which, when viewed collectively, can be classed as a campaign of conduct amounting to unlawful harassment or causing detriment to the victim. The EAT held (in *Driskel v Peninsula Business Services Ltd & ors* that a series of verbal incidents may become a discriminatory detriment if persisted in, irrespective of whether the employee expressed an objection at the time the individual remarks were made. In the same case the EAT held that an employer will not be able to defend a claim for sexual harassment on the basis that vulgar comments and sexual remarks were made equally both to men and women. They took the view that, even though both sexes were subjected to the same remarks, women were likely to find the remarks more intimidating than men, and hence the effect of the remarks was to place women at a disadvantage as compared with men.

[2000] IRLR 151

Company statement defining and outlawing harassment

The following model statement could be used as part of an organisation's equal opportunities policy.

'As part of our commitment to equal opportunities, the Company aims to develop and encourage a working environment and culture in which harassment and bullying are neither tolerated nor acceptable, and in which employees feel confident in coming forward to report any incidence of harassment.

It is the responsibility of management to ensure that this policy is upheld at all times. It is the responsibility of all members of staff to treat their colleagues with respect and dignity and to ensure that their behaviour does not cause offence or upset to others.

Disciplinary action up to and including summary dismissal will be taken against any employee who is found to have harassed or bullied another person during the course of their employment.

Any employee who feels uncomfortable or distressed by the conduct of another person at work may raise the issue informally in the first instance with [nominated person] or invoke the Company's [grievance procedure/ complaints procedure]. No employee will be penalised in any way for raising a genuine complaint about harassment, and all complaints will be taken seriously.'

Harassment as a crime

In addition to the employment laws that protect workers from harassment, the implementation of the Criminal Justice and Public Order Act 1994 in England and Wales made it a criminal offence for an individual to commit an act of deliberate harassment against another person. This Act does not apply in Scotland. To be covered by the Act, however, the harassment must be shown to have been intentional. This contrasts with the discrimination laws, under which a claim can be made out irrespective of whether there was a deliberate intention to harass the victim.

More specifically, it is an offence under the Criminal Justice and Public Order Act intentionally to commit an act that causes another person harassment, alarm or distress either:

- by using threatening, abusive or insulting language or behaviour, or disorderly behaviour, or

- by displaying any writing, sign or other visible representation which is threatening, abusive or insulting.

The Act covers all forms of harassment, irrespective of the motive behind it, and so harassment on grounds of sex, race, religion, sexual orientation etc are prohibited, as well as harassment on other grounds not covered by employment law, such as harassment motivated by personal dislike or difference in political opinion. Thus an employee who is being intentionally harassed by a colleague at work may have recourse to justice by complaining directly to the police over and above the potential right to bring a complaint against their employer to tribunal alleging discrimination on one of the prohibited grounds.

Another criminal law governing harassment which applies throughout the UK is the Protection from Harassment Act 1997. This Act makes it a criminal offence to pursue a course of conduct that amounts to harassment, or which causes a person to fear that violence will be used against them, on at least two occasions. The principal objective of this Act was to provide protection to individuals who were the victims of stalking. There is no requirement under this Act for the behaviour in question to be intentional for it to be an offence.

Furthermore, the Anti-terrorism, Crime and Security Act 2001 created an offence of religiously aggravated harassment. The Act amended the Crime and Disorder Act to include a new category of 'religiously aggravated criminal offences'. Thus, harassment or hostility at work based on a person's membership of a religious group could be a criminal offence, as well as affording the victim the opportunity to bring a claim against their employer for unlawful harassment under the Employment Equality (Religion or Belief) Regulations 2003. A 'religious group' is widely defined in the Act as 'a group of persons defined by reference to religious belief or lack of religious belief'.

Different forms of harassment

Harassment can take many forms, some blatant and others more subtle. In general, harassment may be physical, verbal or non-verbal. Many types of conduct will be capable of being interpreted as unlawful harassment if the conduct is 'on grounds of' sex, marital status, sexual orientation, gender re-assignment, race, religion or belief, or disability (and – after October 2006 – age), and if it has had the effect of making the victim feel distressed in some way or has created a working environment in which the employee was made to feel uncomfortable.

Physical harassment

Where an employee is physically abused by a colleague, there is unlikely to be any doubt that the abuse constitutes a detriment, or that it amounts to harassment under the anti-discrimination legislation, provided only that the physical abuse can be shown to have been on grounds of gender, race, disability etc.

Forms of physical harassment could include:

- unwelcome fondling, patting or touching

- threatened or actual sexual assault

- physical assault motivated by race

- pranks played against (for example) a disabled employee.

Verbal harassment

According to the 2002 Report by the Wainwright Trust (an educational and research charity), verbal harassment, including sexist and racist 'banter', is the most common form of harassment. Verbal harassment could include a wide range of behaviour, such as:

- language that is of a sexual nature or racially offensive, whether oral or in writing – for example, derogatory remarks made about a colleague in an e-mail

- office gossip or detrimental speculation about an employee's private sexual activities or religious practices

- sexist or racist remarks made to or about an employee, or jokes or banter based on sex, race, religion, sexual orientation or disability

- calling someone by a name based on sex or race – for example, calling a female colleague 'blondie' or an Asian employee 'Paki', both of which might be regarded as demeaning or insulting

- offensive terminology such as the word 'wog' when referring to a black employee, 'cripple' when describing a disabled person or 'lezzie' said to a lesbian

- deliberate isolation of someone at work or non-co-operation on grounds of gender, race, religion, sexual orientation or disability

- teasing directed at an employee on account of the fact they have a same-sex partner or a son or daughter who is gay or lesbian

- teasing on the subject of religious convictions or religious practices

- persistent sexual advances or pestering for sexual favours.

When considering terminology related to an individual's race or disability, it is worth bearing in mind that language evolves, and words that were once acceptable may now be regarded as derogatory.

Non-verbal harassment

Some examples are:

- sexually suggestive gestures

- leering at someone in a manner that is overtly sexual

- the display of pin-up calendars or pictures of naked women (or men)

- the display of racist publications

- sexually explicit or racist material displayed on computer screens

- the conspicuous display of a tattoo or the wearing of a badge that contains a slogan that is racist or offensive to people of a particular religion

- gestures that are derogatory or demeaning towards gay or lesbian people

- the blatant and conspicuous wearing of jewellery with an obvious religious message

- the wearing of clothing displaying football slogans that have a sectarian significance.

The above lists of examples are, of course, not exhaustive but demonstrate the scope of behaviour that could, depending on the context, be viewed as unlawful harassment.

Banter in the workplace

The new definition of harassment as a distinct form of unlawful discrimination has implications for employers who condone banter in their workplaces. Legislation on race, religion and sexual orientation clearly states that where unwanted conduct has the effect of 'creating an intimidating, hostile, degrading, humiliating or offensive environment' for an employee, it will be regarded as unlawful harassment. Sex and disability discrimination legislation will be amended in the future to contain similar wording. If the working environment is one in which sexual or sexist remarks, coarse or vulgar humour, racial, racist or homophobic banter or jokes about religious practices are commonplace, and if any individual employee genuinely finds this type of environment degrading, humiliating or offensive, the employer may find themselves facing claims at an employment tribunal for unlawful harassment. The fact that other employees are being subjected to the same banter or jokes will be irrelevant, provided only that the remarks and banter are capable of causing offence in the mind of a reasonable person. In addition, it will not be necessary for an individual to show that the remarks that caused offence were directed at them personally, as the legislation requires only that the conduct in question created an uncomfortable environment for them.

An example could be where one or more employees regularly engages in racist banter at work and a black employee (for example) who works within earshot of the banter feels demeaned by the jokes or finds the terminology used offensive. If the conduct occurs regularly, the employee who is upset by it could be said to have been subjected to a working environment that is degrading or humiliating, simply by being required to work in the presence of such banter. It may be that those engaging in the banter had no malicious motive, did not intend to cause offence and were unaware that they were causing offence. Nevertheless, provided the employee in question genuinely finds the conduct unwanted, and assuming it is sufficient to reasonably be considered to have a detrimental effect, it will be capable of giving rise to a claim of unlawful race discrimination.

It may be helpful to bear in mind that an employee who is feeling upset by banter in the workplace may not feel comfortable about the prospect of telling their colleagues that they find the banter unacceptable, or about complaining to management about it. They may feel that working relationships may be damaged, that they will be seen as a trouble-maker, ostracised by their colleagues or not taken seriously. These fears are understandable, and management should not assume in the absence of any complaints that no problems of this nature exist. The key is to put in place policies, procedures and practices designed to prevent discriminatory harassment, including offensive banter, rather than waiting to deal with a problem after it has arisen (see Chapter 9).

It is strongly advisable, therefore, for employers to review the culture in which their employees work and take steps to actively discourage any banter that could be viewed as discriminatory in order to avoid the risk of claims for unlawful harassment from an employee offended by it. This may involve introducing guidelines for all employees explaining the parameters of the laws on harassment and providing examples of what is, and is not, acceptable conduct.

The potential consequences of harassment for the organisation

Employers are liable in law for any act of discriminatory harassment carried out by one employee against another in the course of their employment. Liability cannot be avoided by pleading ignorance of the fact that the harassment was taking place, or by asserting that there was no deliberate intention to offend the victim. Even where the employer has taken steps to prevent discrimination, for example by introducing an anti-harassment policy, a tribunal will examine whether there were any further preventative steps at all that the employer could have taken that were reasonably practicable (a principle emanating from the case of *Canniffe v East Riding of Yorkshire Council*). Chapter 10 explains more fully how an employer is liable for discrimination in the workplace, page 176.

Claims to tribunal for unlawful harassment

In the event of a serious incident of harassment, or a series of events that might collectively be viewed as a course of conduct that creates an uncomfortable working environment, the employee could succeed in a claim for unlawful discrimination at an employment tribunal. A complaint would be particularly likely to succeed where the employee had already made management aware that the behaviour of a colleague was causing them offence or distress, and the complaint had been ignored, dismissed as trivial or inadequately dealt with.

There is no minimum length-of-service requirement to bring a case of discrimination to a tribunal, and no age limit. In most cases, the employer will be ordered to pay the complainant compensation for injury to feelings and for financial loss (if any). Information about tribunal claims and the compensation that can be awarded following a successful claim for unlawful discrimination or harassment can be found in Chapter 10, pages 190–192.

The possibility of a claim for constructive dismissal

An employee who is being seriously harassed at work may also be able to succeed in a complaint of unfair constructive dismissal based on the assertion that the way in which they were treated was so intolerable that it amounted to a fundamental breach of contract and left them with no alternative but to resign. Serious harassment, or a failure on the part of management to deal adequately with a genuine complaint of harassment, would in most cases be regarded by the courts as a breach of trust and confidence, a duty that exists within every contract of employment. In *Morrow v Safeway Stores plc*, the EAT held that a breach of the implied term of trust and confidence would always amount to a fundamental or repudiatory breach of the employee's contract.

Employees do, however, require a minimum of one year's service to bring a complaint of unfair constructive dismissal to tribunal.

Non-financial consequences of harassment in the workplace

Over and above the impact on the employer of any financial award they are ordered to pay to an employee following a campaign of harassment, there may be serious consequences for morale. Harassment of any kind can have devastating effects on the person subjected to it, and will also create a working atmosphere of fear in which employees will not be enabled to give of their best. An individual who is the victim of harassment may lose their confidence and feel anxious and unhappy; the stress caused by the harassment may even cause them to become seriously ill.

Dealing effectively with a complaint of harassment

It is very important for employers to take any complaint of harassment seriously in the first instance, and deal with it promptly, effectively and fairly. It is, however, understandably difficult to tackle such a complaint, for a host of reasons. The personal nature of the behaviour complained of, the fear of emotional reactions or unpleasant confrontation, the worry that working relationships might be damaged and even a fear that if the matter is looked into, more problems might crawl out of the woodwork are all likely to create anxiety for the manager responsible for dealing with a complaint. Nevertheless, these difficulties must be tackled if the problem is to be solved, as it is the unarguable responsibility of management to make sure that all complaints are dealt with without either procrastination or excuses.

Investigating the complaint

The first step in dealing with a complaint of harassment in the workplace will always be to conduct an investigation into the alleged incident(s). The investigation should of course be as thorough as possible, and must be unbiased. For this reason, the person dealing with the investigation should have no connection with the allegations or with the alleged harasser.

Confidential meetings will be needed, firstly with the complainant, and subsequently with the alleged harasser. At these meetings, the person being interviewed should be allowed to bring a colleague or trade union representative along with them if they wish. It may also be appropriate to hold meetings with any witnesses to the incident(s) of alleged harassment in order to gather relevant information.

The aim at this stage is to gather as much evidence as possible about what happened so as to be able to give the person accused of harassment an opportunity to respond fully to the complaint against them. It should of course be borne in mind that, however serious or credible an employee's complaint may seem, there are always two sides to every story. The employee accused of harassment must also be treated fairly, and in an unbiased and non-accusatory manner.

Checklist for investigating a complaint of harassment

The following represents a checklist of how a manager should proceed to investigate an employee's complaint of harassment.

- Hold a confidential meeting with the employee who has raised the complaint of harassment to discuss the details of their complaint. Specific examples of what was said or done (and the manner and tone in which things were said or done) should be sought, with times and dates of relevant incidents, if possible.

- Give the employee the opportunity to be accompanied by a colleague or trade union representative at the meeting if they wish.

- Write to the alleged harasser (ensuring confidentiality) explaining that there has been a complaint of harassment made against them, and inviting them to attend a meeting to establish the facts. It should be made clear that this meeting will be an investigatory meeting and that the employee is not being accused of any wrong-doing.

- Hold the meeting with the alleged harasser at which they should be given the opportunity to be accompanied by a colleague or trade union representative of their choice (if they wish).

- Give the alleged harasser full details of all the allegations that have been made against them, in other words the specifics regarding the behaviour that has allegedly caused offence. It is important that they are given all the facts and allegations so that they have a fair opportunity to defend themselves.

- Listen to the alleged harasser's side of events and allow them to provide a full explanation of their conduct and the reasons (if any) behind it. Ask probing questions if necessary to get at the truth.

- Try to establish whether the person accepts, partly accepts or completely refutes the allegations made against them.

Continued

Continued

- Be prepared to adjourn the meeting for further investigation if the alleged harasser provides new information that needs to be checked out.

- Once discussions are concluded, inform the employee what will happen next and within what timescale.

- Keep a confidential record of the key points discussed at each meeting.

If, following investigations, there are reasonable grounds to believe that the allegations of harassment are well-founded, the employer will in most instances decide to take disciplinary action against the employee who perpetrated the harassment. The disciplinary process should, however, be dealt with as a separate set of proceedings and, if possible, should be carried out by someone other than the person who conducted the investigations (see below).

Support for the employee who has been harassed

Any employee who has been the victim of harassment at work will inevitably have suffered distress and anxiety as a result of the way they have been treated. In particular, if the harassment has been going on for a period of time, the adverse effect on the employee may be substantial. It may also have taken a considerable amount of courage for the employee to come forward with the complaint.

It follows that it will be very important, once it has been established that the employee has indeed been the victim of harassment, for the employer to offer the employee their full support. This will include reassurance that the problem will be fairly and thoroughly dealt with, and a firm commitment to put a stop to the harassment, but may also involve the need to provide moral support to help the employee come to terms with what has happened.

One excellent way of providing moral and practical support is to appoint an appropriate person to fulfil the role of employee counsellor. This may be done either by appointing a member of staff who has received professional training in counselling techniques or by providing employees with access to an external confidential advice service through an independent counselling organisation.

If a counsellor is appointed, their role could include:

- providing a sounding-board to employees who believe they are being harassed to help them view the problem objectively and decide what to do

- offering information and guidance to employees on the courses of action open to them and the likely outcomes

- helping the employee to plan how they might go about making an informal direct approach to the harasser to explain that certain behaviour is unacceptable and asking for it to stop

- accompanying an employee to an informal meeting with the alleged harasser to help the employee explain their case (if that is the course of action decided upon)

- talking to the alleged harasser (in confidence) if the victim of the harassment feels unable to make a personal approach to explain that a particular aspect of their behaviour is causing offence or upset, and why the victim finds it unacceptable

- supporting an employee who wishes to raise a formal complaint if this is the course of action the employee would prefer (especially in the event of serious allegations)

- counselling both parties as to future behaviour once the complaint has been discussed and resolved.

Dealing fairly with the perpetrator of harassment

Harassment of any kind in the workplace is a serious issue, and one that should always be treated seriously by management. In some cases, instances of harassment will provide solid grounds for the perpetrator of the harassment to be dismissed, whilst in other cases a formal written warning may be appropriate. Any warning issued should make it clear that any further type of harassment or victimisation of the employee, or any other employee, is likely to lead to the employee's dismissal. By contrast, in cases where the individual was genuinely unaware that their conduct was causing offence, an informal warning may suffice so long as the person clearly understands and accepts that the conduct causing offence or embarrassment must not recur.

It is important for the person dealing with the alleged perpetrator of harassment to refrain from making accusations, showing emotion or jumping to premature conclusions. The person accused of harassment has as much right to be treated fairly as the person complaining of the harassment. As with any form of alleged misconduct in the workplace, it is important that the manager responsible for handling it should act fairly and reasonably in dealing with the problem.

Transfer to another job

Once a problem of harassment has been uncovered, it may be difficult, if not impossible, for the alleged harasser and the victim to continue to work together. Furthermore, if the allegations of harassment are established as being well-founded, it may be inappropriate to allow the harasser to continue to work anywhere near their erstwhile victim.

If there has been a complete breakdown in trust or where, despite reassurances that the problem has been resolved, the employee flatly refuses to continue to work alongside the harasser, the employer may have to consider transferring one or other of the employees involved to another job or even another department.

Caution should be exercised, however, if consideration is being given to transferring the employee who has been the victim of harassment, as a transfer may be viewed as a further detriment (and thus discriminatory). If, however, the employee genuinely wishes to move, and provided the transfer in question is on terms and conditions at least as favourable as the employee's current terms, this may provide a satisfactory solution. The employer should discuss the option of a transfer with the employee with a view to exploring whether it is a viable option, rather than imposing a transfer unilaterally.

A more appropriate course of action may be to transfer the harasser to another post (but only after it has been established that the allegations of harassment were well-founded). Once again, however, the matter would have to be discussed and agreed with the employee, otherwise a transfer to a different job could amount to a breach of the employee's contract (irrespective of the motive behind the transfer).

In contrast, in circumstances where the harassment has been of a relatively minor nature, and provided the employer has taken appropriate steps to deal with the matter, the employee should be encouraged to continue in the same job, with the reassurance that there will be no further instance of the behaviour complained of. An unconditional apology from the erstwhile harasser would be a welcome step towards a viable future working relationship. In a case of this nature, counselling will be helpful.

Following up

If, following the conclusion of proceedings to deal with a complaint of harassment, the harasser and the person whom they harassed continue to work in the same part of the organisation, an appropriate manager should follow up by monitoring the situation to ensure that:

- the working relationships between the various people are now harmonious and no further instances of harassment have taken place

- neither party is engaging in recriminatory behaviour against the other

- the complainant is not being victimised (whether by the harasser or by colleagues) on account of the fact that they complained.

Checklist for dealing with an employee accused of harassment

The following checklist is intended to assist managers to plan and conduct a disciplinary interview with an employee accused of harassment.

- Write to the employee to set up a disciplinary interview, giving reasonable notice and providing full information as to the conduct that will be the subject of the disciplinary proceedings.

- Inform the employee that they have the right (if they wish) to bring a fellow worker or trade union official to the interview.

- Approach the interview with an open mind, and refrain from making any premature decisions as to what the outcome will or should be.

- Explain clearly to the employee what the interview is about, what specific conduct has been reported and what the evidence is against them (including the content of any witness statements).

- Give the employee a proper chance to put forward any mitigating factors or other form of defence.

- Listen actively to what the employee has to say and consider any mitigating factors fully.

- Remain calm and neutral throughout the interview.

- Be patient and do not rush the interview.

- Act objectively and reasonably towards the employee.

- Following the interview, adjourn to decide on the course of action.

- Communicate the outcome of the disciplinary proceedings to the employee in writing.

- Follow any in-house disciplinary procedure fully, whatever the nature of the employee's misconduct.

Following any disciplinary action taken, whether in the form of a warning or dismissal, the employee must be allowed the right of appeal. The appeal should, if the size of the organisation allows it, be dealt with by someone who has not been involved in either the investigation or the disciplinary proceedings.

Finally, the employer should keep confidential records of all meetings held in connection with the allegations of harassment and the process used to address and resolve the complaint and the outcome. In so doing, it will be important to adhere to the relevant provisions of the Data Protection Act 1988.

Points to note

- The Race Relations Act 1976 was amended in July 2003 to make specific provision to render harassment on grounds of race or ethnic or national origins unlawful and to introduce a free-standing statutory definition of racial harassment.

- Conduct at work may be regarded as unlawful harassment if it violates another person's dignity, or creates an intimidating, hostile, degrading, humiliating or offensive environment.

- Employees are expressly protected by statute against any harassment in the course of their employment on grounds of their religion or belief, and on grounds of sexual orientation.

- Although UK sex discrimination law does not (as yet) contain a definition of sexual harassment, courts and tribunals have consistently held that sexual harassment at work can amount to a detriment and hence be a form of direct discrimination.

- The EC Code of Practice on the protection of the dignity of women and men at work defines sexual harassment as 'unwanted conduct of a sexual nature, or other conduct based on sex affecting the dignity of women and men at work' and further states that conduct of a sexual nature will amount to sexual harassment where it is 'unwanted, unreasonable and offensive to the recipient'.

- A complaint of sex discrimination can be taken to tribunal as a result of either a single serious incident or a series of relatively minor incidents, which, when viewed collectively, can be classed as a campaign of conduct causing detriment to the victim.

- An employee who is being seriously harassed at work may bring a claim for unlawful harassment to tribunal and may also be able to succeed in a complaint of constructive dismissal if they have resigned because of the harassment, and provided they have a minimum of one year's service.

- In most cases, instances of harassment will provide solid grounds for the employer to take disciplinary action (including dismissal in serious cases) against the perpetrator of the harassment.

Action points

- Take care not to view a complaint of harassment purely subjectively, as the key criterion that determines whether conduct amounts to unlawful harassment is whether the recipient of the behaviour found it unwelcome or offensive.

- Recognise that if sexual or sexist remarks, racial, racist or homophobic banter or jokes about religious practices are condoned in the workplace, this could be viewed as unlawful harassment, irrespective of whether the banter or jokes were directed at a particular employee.

- Do not assume that there is no harassment problem in the workplace just because there have been no complaints.

- Review the culture in which employees work and take steps to actively discourage any banter that could be viewed as discriminatory.

- Consider the potentially serious consequences of harassment in the workplace in terms of employee morale and damage to productivity.

- Take all complaints of harassment seriously in the first instance, and deal with them promptly, effectively and fairly.

- Conduct a thorough and unbiased investigation into any alleged incident of harassment in order to be able to give the person accused of the harassment an opportunity to respond fully to the complaint against them.

- Hold confidential meetings firstly with the employee who has raised the complaint of harassment and subsequently with the alleged harasser, giving both parties the opportunity to be accompanied at the meetings if they wish.

- Give the alleged harasser full details of all the allegations that have been made against them so that they have a fair opportunity to defend themselves.

- Offer any employee who is found to have been the victim of harassment full support, including counselling if possible.

- Consider transferring one or other of the employees involved to another job or even another department in cases where there has been a complete breakdown in working relationships following harassment.

- Discuss the option of a transfer with the employee concerned (normally the harasser rather than the person who was their victim), but take care not to impose a transfer unilaterally.

- Monitor the situation following the resolution of a complaint of harassment to ensure that no further instances of harassment have taken place and that the complainant is not being victimised.

- Keep confidential records of all meetings held in connection with the allegations of harassment, the process used to address and resolve the complaint and the outcome.

CHAPTER 8

DISCRIMINATION AT TERMINATION OF EMPLOYMENT

Discrimination at the time of the termination of a person's employment could be linked to the reason for dismissal, the motive behind it, the process for redundancy selection or the manner in which the dismissal or redundancy was carried out. A discriminatory dismissal will always be unlawful, entitling the employee to bring a complaint to an employment tribunal irrespective of their age or length of service.

Employers should therefore ensure that the reason for an employee's dismissal is not related in any way to gender, trans-gender status, marital status, race, religion, sexual orientation or (unless it can be justified) disability. They should also take care to ensure that all procedures and processes that lead, or might lead, to termination of employment are carried out objectively and are free from discrimination. This chapter aims to help employers to achieve these objectives.

Discipline and dismissal – ensuring procedures are not discriminatory

Whenever an employer has grounds to invoke their disciplinary procedure (whether or not this is thought likely to lead to the employee's dismissal), it is essential that the processes must be free from all forms of discrimination.

Whether to proceed with disciplinary action where the employee is absent from work with a stress-related illness

One particularly difficult area is dealing with an employee whose conduct or performance is unsatisfactory and where, additionally, the employee has a stress-related illness that is causing absence from work. A stress-related illness may, depending on how it affects the employee, amount to a disability in law (see Chapter 11 for a discussion on conditions that may amount to disabilities, pages 224–225).

[2002] ICR 516

Case Example

In *Rowden v Dutton Gregory* the employee, who was a secretary in a firm of solicitors, had been absent from work with a stress-related illness. A disciplinary hearing had been convened, but when the employee was unable to attend, her employer went ahead without her and subsequently took the decision to dismiss her on grounds of various types of misconduct, poor timekeeping and excessive sickness absence. The employee brought claims for unfair dismissal and disability discrimination to an employment tribunal. The employer conceded the unfair dismissal claim before the tribunal, but the disability discrimination claim went on to appeal.

The Employment Appeal Tribunal (EAT) held ultimately that the actions of the employer in holding a disciplinary hearing whilst the employee was absent from work with an illness that amounted to a disability had caused the employee a detriment and thus constituted disability discrimination. The employer had also failed in their duty to make reasonable adjustments by not making alternative arrangements in relation to the disciplinary hearing in order to prevent the process from placing the employee at a substantial disadvantage.

The EAT also held that, since two of the reasons for the employee's dismissal, namely poor timekeeping and excessive sickness absence, were related to the employee's disability, and since these two reasons had a significant impact on the employer's decision to dismiss, the dismissal itself was discriminatory. The employee therefore succeeded in showing that both the disciplinary process and the decision to dismiss amounted to disability discrimination.

It may be advisable, therefore (depending on the circumstances), not to proceed with disciplinary action against an employee who is signed off work with a stress-related illness, but instead to wait until the employee returns to work before dealing with the matter. Alternatively, the employer could ask an occupational doctor to advise on whether the employee is fit to attend a meeting (even though they may not be well enough to work).

Where the stress-related illness has arisen following the instigation of disciplinary proceedings and the employer suspects that the employee's absence is an avoidance tactic, caution must still be exercised. The employer should:

- refrain from making automatic assumptions that the employee is deliberately trying to evade disciplinary action

- inform the employee in writing that the disciplinary action will be postponed for a reasonable period in order to allow them to recover sufficiently to take part in the proceedings

- seek the employee's consent to contact their GP or seek advice from an occupational doctor as to whether the employee is well enough to attend an investigatory or disciplinary meeting

- make it clear to the employee in a firm but non-threatening way that the disciplinary investigation or action (as the case may be) must be dealt with, and that it is in everyone's interests to deal with it as soon as possible

- give the employee the option (if it is considered appropriate) to appoint a representative (for example a colleague or trade union official) to attend a meeting on their behalf.

Disciplining or dismissing staff because of lack of flexibility or unwillingness to work long or unsocial hours

Another difficult area is dealing with an employee who is unable, or unwilling, to be flexible as regards hours of work, for example when it comes to shift working or a requirement for overtime. This may be because of family commitments, in particular child-care responsibilities. Another example could be an employee who refuses to work on a particular day of the week, or date during the year, possibly for reasons related to their religion or belief.

Unwillingness to work long or unsocial hours owing to child-care responsibilities

There may be a tendency for some managers to view an apparent unwillingness to work long or unsocial hours, or different shifts, as a negative factor, possibly justifying disciplinary action in the event of an outright refusal to work at the required times. This could, however, create a problem for the employer if the employee in question is a woman with caring responsibilities, because any unfavourable treatment of the woman in such circumstances would be likely to constitute indirect sex discrimination. This is because courts and tribunals have, over many years, accepted the general principle that fewer women than men can work long hours or unsocial hours owing to their child-care responsibilities. The Sex Discrimination Act 1975 states that any provision, criterion or practice that is likely to be to the detriment of a larger proportion of women than men, and which places a particular woman at a disadvantage will be indirect sex discrimination and unlawful unless the employer can justify it.

[1995] IRLR 355

Case Example

In *London Underground Ltd v Edwards*, the employer changed their rostering system in such a way that Ms Edwards, a train driver, could not comply with a requirement to start work at 04.45 am on some mornings. This was because she was a single parent. Ms Edwards succeeded in her claim that the new arrangements were indirectly discriminatory against her as a woman, and the Court of Appeal held that it was not justifiable for the employer to have insisted that she comply with the early morning start-time. Whilst there was nothing inherently unlawful about the new rostering system, the employer, as a large undertaking, could have exempted Ms Edwards from the requirement to do the early shift, or made alternative arrangements to accommodate her needs without causing any difficulty in terms of the efficiency of the business.

Similarly, any disciplinary action, or dismissal, of a woman on the grounds of a refusal to work longer hours or unsocial hours (or even full-time hours as opposed to part-time hours) will be indirect sex discrimination unless the requirement to work the hours or shift pattern in question can be shown to be objectively justifiable based on the needs of the business, and it can also be shown that the employer was justified in applying the requirement to the woman as an individual.

Checklist of when the dismissal of a woman may constitute sex discrimination

If a female employee is dismissed in any of the following circumstances, it is likely that her dismissal would be judged to be sex discrimination by an employment tribunal:

- dismissal for any reason linked to the fact the employee is pregnant

- dismissal on account of the inconvenience the employee's impending absence on maternity leave was thought likely to cause

- enforced retirement at an earlier age than that at which a man in similar circumstances would have been compelled to retire

- termination on the grounds that the woman has raised a genuine complaint of sexual harassment

- dismissal because the employee cannot work shifts, work extensive overtime or work full-time, criteria that place women at a disadvantage as compared with men

- selection for redundancy based on lack of flexibility as regards hours of work or shift working

- dismissal for any reason where a man would not have been dismissed in similar circumstances.

Unwillingness to work on certain days or dates based on religion or belief

An employee's religious belief may involve practices associated with not working on a particular day of the week or on specified dates during the year. It follows that (for example) requiring a practising Christian employee to work on a Sunday where that employee held strong religious views that Sunday working was unacceptable would constitute indirect religious discrimination (see Chapter 10, 'Indirect discrimination', page 181). Even though the employer might well apply the Sunday working requirement equally to all employees, it would nevertheless place people who shared the particular employee's religious beliefs at a disadvantage, thus constituting indirect religious discrimination. In order to be lawful therefore, the employer would have to show that the requirement to work on Sundays was proportionate to the achievement of a legitimate aim, taking into account all the relevant circumstances.

Employers may also face requests from Jewish employees or Seventh Day Adventists (for example) to be exempted from working on Saturdays (or on Fridays after dusk). If not working on a particular day is genuinely a key facet of an employee's religious beliefs, then a refusal without justification to accommodate the individual's request will be discriminatory. Similarly the dismissal of an employee for refusing to work on Saturdays, where the refusal was on grounds of the person's religious beliefs, could constitute unlawful religious discrimination. Once again, the key question is whether a refusal to grant an employee's request was proportionate to the achievement of a legitimate aim (see also Chapter 10 under 'Indirect discrimination', page 181).

Time off on special religious days

As discussed in Chapter 3 ('Time off for religious holidays and when a refusal may be discriminatory or in breach of the individual's human rights', page 52), some employees may not wish to work on certain days of the week, or may require time off for certain special religious days during the year. It is advisable for all employers to be as flexible as possible in the application of their policies and requirements for working time so that individual needs can be accommodated whenever possible.

If an employer chose to take an inflexible stance, and disciplined or dismissed an employee who, for example, refused to work on a Sunday because of strongly held Christian views about Sunday's being a day of rest, this would constitute indirect religious discrimination. Such action would thus be unlawful unless it could be justified. The test for justification is that the 'provision, criterion or practice' must be proportionate to the 'achievement of a legitimate aim'. The employer may well be pursuing a legitimate aim, for example the aim of meeting business deadlines during peak periods of work, but it would in most instances be difficult to demonstrate that it was proportionate to the achievement of that aim to discipline an employee who wished to be exempted from Sunday working for religious reasons. This would be especially so if the employee had, for example, offered to work overtime on another day of the week.

Thus, if it can be shown that an exception could have been made for the employee in question (ie the employee could have been exempted from the requirement to work on Sundays) without damaging the employer's interests, any disciplinary action or dismissal of the employee would be unlawful.

A better way forward is for the employer to discuss the issue of working hours and flexibility with individual employees where appropriate in order to seek agreement on alternative arrangements that will meet the employee's needs without prejudicing the needs of the business.

Dismissing a disabled employee on grounds of lack of capability

The Employment Rights Act 1996 does permit employers to dismiss employees who are not capable of performing their jobs, for example on account of ill-health or injury. Such dismissals are thus capable of being fair under that Act provided fair procedures have been followed prior to the employee's dismissal.

The question of whether such a dismissal would be in breach of the Disability Discrimination Act 1995 is, however, quite a separate matter. The burden of justifying the dismissal of an employee on grounds related to disability is a high one. The dismissal of a disabled employee should only be contemplated after the employer has:

- made all possible reasonable adjustments to facilitate the ongoing employment of the disabled employee (see below)

- established that there is no alternative work within the organisation that the employee could reasonably do (after training)

- reasonably concluded that there are no other adjustments that can reasonably be made to support the employee

- obtained appropriate medical advice confirming the effects of the employee's condition on their ability to perform their job and indicating that there is little or no likelihood of a material improvement in their condition in the foreseeable future

- concluded that despite any adjustments that have been made, the employee's disability, or its effects (for example excessive absence from work), is causing the employer a substantial problem

s98(1) ERA 1996
- satisfied themselves that lack of capability is a substantial reason for dismissal under the Employment Rights Act 1996

- acted reasonably throughout the process of considering termination of the employee's employment.

Case examples in which dismissal for a reason related to an employee's disability was justified

In *A v London Borough of Hounslow* the employee had recently begun work as a physics/IT technician at a secondary school. Soon after he began work, the results of a medical examination (upon which his offer of employment was dependent) disclosed that he had schizophrenia and that, although his condition was stable, there was no guarantee that he would never suffer a relapse. Although the chances of a relapse were small, the advice from the school's occupational health specialist was that if it were to occur, the employee could pose a serious risk to himself, the other staff and the pupils. As a result of this advice, the school dismissed the employee, who subsequently asserted that this course of action amounted to disability discrimination. [2001] EAT 1155/98

It was clear from the facts of the case that the employee's condition amounted to a disability, and that his dismissal was for a reason related to disability. The question was whether the dismissal could nevertheless be justified on grounds that were material and substantial. The EAT held that, even though the employee's condition had been under control for a number of years, the prospect of a relapse and the danger it might create for pupils and teachers amounted to 'an incalculable risk'. They thus found that the employer's actions were justifiable.

In *Allen v H Hargarve & Co* the employee was a butcher who, owing to tenosynovitis (inflammation of the tendons owing to repetitive action), had been on long-term sick leave and could no longer perform his job. The work in the employer's slaughterhouse was physically heavy and involved working at speed and under pressure. The only possible alternative position was tray-washing, but in order for the employee to be able to perform this work, the employer would have had to make alterations to the machine that would have prevented other employees from using it. In any event, the company had no vacancies at the time in question either in tray-washing or cleaning. Taking into account all these circumstances, the EAT judged that the dismissal of the employee was justified. The reasons for the dismissal were material and substantial – because they related to the employee's physical condition, his inability to perform his job, the machinery and the non-availability of other jobs. EAT 150/99

It can be seen from the above cases that dismissal for a reason related to an employee's disability is not automatically unlawful. Such a dismissal must, however, be justified by factors that are material and substantial if a claim for unlawful disability discrimination is to be avoided or defended successfully. The main criterion is that the employer must first have exhausted all possible avenues as regards their duty to make reasonable adjustments to support the disabled employee prior to considering termination of employment. If there are further adjustments that the employer could have made, but failed to make, then the dismissal will not be justified (see Chapter 11 for a general discussion on disabled employees and the duty on the employer to make reasonable adjustments, page 226).

It is important to note also that the responsibility to make adjustments lies with the employer, and it is not up to the disabled employee to offer suggestions (although they should of course be encouraged to do so). In *Fu v London Borough of Camden*, for example, the EAT judged that the employer should have considered the adjustments suggested by the employee (who had had long absences from work) and the extent to which they could have helped to overcome her medical symptoms and helped her return to work.

[2001] IRLR 186

Nevertheless, if the employer is in a position where there is no action, or further action, that they can reasonably take to enable the disabled employee to cope adequately with their job (or another suitable job), or to return to work, then dismissal may be a lawful option. The point may come where, even though management have adopted a supportive approach towards the employee to date, the employee's absence(s) from work may have become excessive or job performance may have dropped well below the standard that is acceptable. In such circumstances, dismissal may eventually be the only course of action that realistically remains open to the employer. In this case the employer should proceed according to the checklist below.

Checklist of actions prior to dismissing a disabled employee on grounds of lack of capability

- Review the employee's job performance and/or sickness and absence record to assess whether it is sufficiently unsatisfactory to justify dismissal, taking care not to assume automatically that recent poor performance or a recent high level of absence will continue indefinitely.

- Review the feasibility of altering the employee's job duties, or offering the employee alternative work, including part-time work.

- Consider what reasonable adjustments, or further adjustments, could be made to the employee's working arrangements or conditions to facilitate better performance or a return to work, and discuss these with the employee.

Continued

Continued

- Keep in regular touch with an employee who is absent from work to discuss how they are, and the likely length of time they expect to be absent.

- Discuss with the employee how they feel about their employment and (if the employee is on sick leave) the likelihood of a return to work, and what type of work they think they may be capable of doing on their return.

- Seek expert medical advice from an occupational doctor, a specialist in the employee's condition or (with the employee's written consent) their GP (better still, seek medical advice from more than one source).

- Inform the employee of any time limits that have been set for appraising the situation.

- Review whether the employee is receiving statutory or occupational sick pay, and for how much longer payment is set to continue (so as to avoid any breach of contract claim).

- Tell the employee, as soon as it is thought to be the case, that their continued employment may be at risk, and the reasons for taking that view.

- Adopt a supportive approach towards the employee at all times.

Examples of reasonable adjustments to facilitate the retention in employment of a disabled employee

The following represents a list of suggested examples of adjustments that could be made for a disabled employee who is no longer capable of performing their job (whether completely or partially):

(For an employee who is on long-term sickness absence from work)

- offering the employee a phased return to work, for example the possibility of part-time working, whether temporarily or permanently

- agreeing to permit the employee to do some or all of their work from home as a step towards returning to office-based employment

- discussing the possibility of redeployment into a different job, for example a less demanding role

- providing training or coaching on the employee's return to work, for example a mini-induction to help the employee to become re-integrated into the workplace (especially if the employee's absence has been a long one)

- providing a mentor for the employee who can be assigned to provide general support and keep an eye on how the employee is coping with being back at work.

(For an employee who is still at work but who is no longer capable of full or satisfactory job performance)

- agreeing (within reason) to a higher than usual tolerance of job performance, conduct or attendance that is falling short of the organisation's normal standards

- suggesting a transfer to alternative work, if a suitable post is available, for example where the employee, although incapable of handling the job they are employed to do, could adequately perform a different job (obviously any transfer should only be with the employee's consent)

- altering the employee's job duties, for example by transferring some of the duties that the disabled employee can no longer manage to other employees (again, only after full consultation with all those affected)

- reducing the employee's working hours (with consent), or exempting the employee from shift working or overtime working

- agreeing to permit regular time off work for hospital appointments, rehabilitation or medical treatment

- providing training, coaching or supervision

- providing special equipment to help the employee perform their duties.

It is essential for the employer to consult the disabled employee fully about the prospect of adjustments to working conditions, job duties and any other arrangements before coming to any final decision. Such discussions should have, as their main objective, the aim of establishing a way of facilitating the continued employment of the employee if at all possible.

Dismissal on account of a genuine occupational requirement

There are limited exceptions to the general principle that it is never lawful to dismiss an employee for reasons that relate to race, religion or sexual orientation (but not gender). In certain limited circumstances, an employer may dismiss an employee on racial or religious grounds or on grounds of sexual orientation based on the argument that being of a particular race, religion or sexual orientation is a genuine occupational requirement (GOR) for the specific post. For the GOR to apply, however, it must be genuinely necessary in order to ensure effective performance of the job in question for the job-holder to be a person from a defined racial group, someone who belongs to a specific religion, or someone of a particular sexual orientation. In these circumstances, it is lawful for the employer to decline to offer employment or promotion, or dismiss the employee, provided also that the race/religion/sexual orientation requirement is proportionate in the particular case.

It is important to note that the GOR exception applies (at present) only to dismissals that are on grounds of the individual's race, ethnic origins, national origins, religion or sexual orientation (and not yet to gender). Dismissal could be lawful (ie not discriminatory), for example, where an employee changed their religion to one that made them unsuitable in relation to the performance of the job in which they were employed Another example could be where being of a particular sexual orientation was a GOR for a particular post and it was discovered that the post-holder was not of that particular sexual orientation. The exceptions are narrowly drawn, however, and would apply only in very limited circumstances. Employers should note also, that even if a GOR can legitimately be applied, this does not mean that the employee's dismissal will be fair under the Employment Rights Act 1996. The fairness of any dismissal will depend on a wide range of factors, for example whether there was a reasonable alternative to dismissal, such as transfer to another job.

Further and more detailed information about GORs and how they apply in practice can be found in Chapter 1 under 'Genuine occupational requirements and qualifications' (page 5).

Designing redundancy criteria to be discrimination-free

In order to comply with the various anti-discrimination laws, an employer undertaking a programme of redundancy must ensure that all employees are treated consistently irrespective of their sex, trans-gender status, marital status, racial group, sexual orientation, religion or disability. This would apply at all stages of the redundancy programme, impinging for example on:

- the process of consultation

- the treatment of employees who volunteer for redundancy

- the criteria used to select individuals for redundancy

- consideration for any alternative employment

- any redundancy payments granted over and above the statutory minimum.

Deciding on criteria for selection for redundancy

When an employer is deciding on the criteria to use to select employees for redundancy, they should keep in mind the principles of equality and diversity and:

- use a range of criteria, rather than just one

- ensure that the criteria are objective, ie based on factors that are capable of being evidenced

- aim to identify criteria that are fair and reasonable in all the circumstances, but which allow the employer to retain those employees whose skills, experience and talents will best meet its future needs

- use only criteria that are capable of being applied objectively and fairly

- (if attendance is to be used as a criterion in the selection process) exclude from the calculation any instances of sickness absence related to pregnancy and all forms of family leave (eg maternity leave, paternity leave, adoption leave, parental leave and time off work to care for dependants)

- avoid using flexibility of working hours as a criterion in the selection process, as this could in some circumstances discriminate indirectly on grounds of gender or religion

- establish a procedure under which no single manager can take redundancy selection decisions alone

- treat part-time and fixed-term employees in the same way as full-time and permanent staff. In *Whiffen v Governing Body of Milham Ford Girls' School & anor* the Court of Appeal held that an employer's policy of selecting teachers engaged on fixed-term contracts for redundancy first (before any permanent staff were considered) was indirectly discriminatory against women. Such a policy would, in any event, be in breach of the Fixed-Term Employees (Prevention of Less Favourable Treatment) Regulations 2002.

[2001] IRLR 468

Warning – Checklist of redundancy selection criteria that might be discriminatory

- Using absence records might be discriminatory against a disabled employee who, as a result of their disability, has needed time off work for rehabilitation or ongoing medical support.

- Taking other forms of absence into account could discriminate against women, for example sickness absence during pregnancy or absence on account of child-care problems.

- Using mobility as a criterion could discriminate indirectly against women, who in general are less likely than men to be able or willing to move to a different location with their job.

- Insisting on using qualifications as a factor in the selection process could be racially discriminatory where the qualifications specified were not strictly necessary for the jobs in question and where it could be shown that employees of foreign nationality were less likely than British employees to possess them.

- Using LIFO (last in, first out) as a determining factor can discriminate indirectly against women (or employees from ethnic minority groups), who, statistically, tend to have shorter service than men.

Continued

Continued

- Applying a requirement for flexibility in terms of hours and shift working would discriminate indirectly against women, who are less likely than men to be able to work long or unsocial hours owing to child-care responsibilities.

- Applying flexibility as a criterion could also discriminate indirectly against people from certain religious groups who, as a result of their religious beliefs, may not be able to work on certain days or dates.

- Placing strong emphasis on skills that tend to be possessed more often by men than women (or vice versa), for example giving marks for physical strength, would place women at a disadvantage.

- Using communication skills, levels of assertiveness or perceived ability to 'fit in' as criteria, as these may indirectly disadvantage employees from certain racial or religious groups, for example people who have been brought up in a culture where assertiveness or outgoing behaviour are not valued or encouraged.

- Using age as a criterion in the redundancy process, eg selecting those who are near to retirement age for compulsory redundancy first, before applying other criteria to the workforce at large. Depending on the gender make-up of the workforce, this could be indirectly discriminatory against men (or women).

- Selecting part-time or fixed-term employees for redundancy first, which would be in breach of the Part-Time Workers Regulations 2000 and the Fixed-Term Employees Regulations 2002 respectively, and would also potentially be indirectly discriminatory against women.

Redundancy selection in relation to an employee on maternity leave

When considering how to execute a redundancy programme, employers should make sure that any employee on maternity leave is treated no less favourably than employees at work, and, if alternative work is available or becomes available whilst the employee is absent, that she is offered the work as an alternative to dismissal.

When reviewing whom to select for redundancy from amongst a group of employees doing the same or similar work, employers should take particular care not to overlook the requirement to consult an employee who is absent from work on maternity leave. A failure to consult an employee over prospective selection for redundancy because she is absent on maternity leave is likely to be regarded as direct sex discrimination. This is what happened in the case of *McGuigan v T G Baynes & Sons*.

[1998] EAT 111/97

Case Example

In *McGuigan v T G Baynes & Sons,* Ms McGuigan was on maternity leave when her employer decided there was a need to make one employee out of three in her department redundant. Ms McGuigan's two colleagues were both male. A points-scoring exercise was carried out, as a result of which Ms McGuigan was selected. None of the three employees was consulted about the selection process, nor were they informed how the redundancy decision had been arrived at. Ms McGuigan subsequently complained to an employment tribunal of unfair dismissal and sex discrimination. Both complaints were ultimately upheld.

The employer attempted to defend their actions by asserting that they had not consulted any of the employees in the department, and that Ms McGuigan's treatment had therefore been no less favourable than that of her male colleagues. The EAT, however, held that the employee's absence on maternity leave had been an 'effective and predominant' cause of the employer's failure to consult her. This was despite the fact that the other employees had not been consulted either. Case law had clearly established that less favourable treatment on grounds of pregnancy or maternity leave will entitle a woman to succeed in a case of direct sex discrimination without comparing her treatment to that of a male colleague.

Avoiding disability discrimination during the redundancy selection process

Employers undertaking a redundancy exercise must ensure that the methods used to select staff for redundancy do not place any disabled employee at a disadvantage. Managers should take care when reviewing staff's abilities not to view an employee's disability in a negative light, or allow the fact that an employee is disabled to count against them in any points-scoring exercise. Equally, it will be important to exclude from consideration the effects of an employee's disability. Specifically, employers should avoid applying the following criteria to disabled employees:

- sickness absence, where much of it has been on account of the employee's disability

- breadth of skills, as this could cause a detriment to an employee whose disability meant they were incapable of performing certain tasks

- flexibility, as this criterion could work to the disadvantage of an employee who could not work at certain times on account of their disability

- productivity, where a disabled employee's impairment had the effect of slowing down their work performance to a rate below the average

- physical fitness or level of energy, which would discriminate against any employee with a physical disability.

The duty to offer disabled employees suitable alternative employment

In relation to the duty to offer redundant employees suitable alternative employment, the EAT held (in *Kent County Council v Mingo*) that an employer is not permitted to give preferential treatment to redundant employees over disabled employees who are also seeking redeployment on account of being unable to continue in their current job.

[1999] EAT 1097/98

The implications of compulsory retirement ages

Most employers are aware that it is unlawful to operate different retirement ages for men and women. A retirement age specified by the employer for a job or group of jobs can (as the law stands at the moment) be any age, so long as there is no differentiation between male and female employees (and no discriminatory impact on other grounds, such as race).

It is, however, permissible to operate different retirement ages for different groups of employees provided no discrimination results from the application of the policy. Where an employer has decided to do this, it is important to:

- ensure there is a valid, objective reason for the difference in retirement ages

- check to make sure the groups of workers to whom different retirement ages apply do not have a substantially different gender (or racial) profile.

If, for example, a group of employees in one part of the organisation consisted predominantly of women, and if that group had a retirement age that was higher or lower than a group of employees elsewhere that comprised mainly men, a claim for unlawful sex discrimination could potentially be brought to tribunal. In these circumstances, the burden of proof would be on the employer to prove to the tribunal's satisfaction that the difference in retirement ages could be objectively justified on grounds unrelated to sex.

An employee who is aged 65 or over, or who is over their employer's normal retirement age, is, as the legislation stands at present, precluded from taking claims for unfair dismissal or redundancy pay to an employment tribunal. These provisions are conditional on the existence of a retirement age that is the same for men and women. An interesting development, however, is that the cut-off age of 65 has been challenged at tribunal on the grounds that it is indirectly discriminatory against men. Further information on this, including outline details of future age discrimination legislation, is available in Chapter 11 under 'Age', page 229.

Avoiding post-employment discrimination

Discrimination after an individual's employment has ended is now unlawful under all the anti-discrimination laws as a result of two entirely separate developments. The first was the implementation of legislation – specifically, amendments to the RRA 1976 and the SDA 1975 to that effect were implemented in July 2003. Equally, the Employment Equality (Religion or Belief) Regulations 2003 and the Employment Equality (Sexual Orientation) Regulations 2003 both expressly provide that discrimination and harassment after an employment relationship has ended will be unlawful whenever 'the discrimination or harassment arises out of and is closely connected to that relationship'.

The legislation does not specify any time-based limitation on the right not to suffer post-employment discrimination. It would seem, therefore, that the right applies indefinitely after an individual's employment has ended, so long as the ex-employee can show a connection between their treatment and their employment.

Examples of post-employment discrimination could include:

• a refusal to give a reference (see below)

• the provision of an adverse reference (see below)

• a post-dismissal appeal hearing in which (for example) sexist or racist remarks were made

• refusal to grant the ex-employee benefits such as admission to sports and social facilities where other ex-employees have been granted these benefits

provided these actions were on grounds related in some way to the ex-employee's gender, race, religion or sexual orientation.

[2003] UKHL 33

In a separate development, the House of Lords ruled (in six conjoined cases, the lead case being *D'Souza v London Borough of Lambeth*) that an employment relationship can outlast the existence of the contract of employment, and the right for ex-employees to bring claims of unlawful discrimination against their ex-employer must be applied to all forms of less favourable treatment, including direct and indirect discrimination, victimisation and harassment. Thus, discrimination perpetrated against an ex-employee is covered by the relevant legislation, provided the employee's treatment arose out of their employment relationship and provided it caused them a detriment on grounds of gender, race or disability.

This decision took place prior to the implementation of the Employment Equality (Religion or Belief) Regulations 2003 and the Employment Equality (Sexual Orientation) Regulations 2003, but since both sets of Regulations expressly outlaw post-employment discrimination and harassment, this is largely irrelevant. The point is that any form of post-employment discrimination on any of the prohibited grounds will be capable of challenge at an employment tribunal provided there is some connection between the ex-employee's treatment and their previous employment.

Giving references

As discussed in the previous section, discrimination on any of the prohibited grounds after an individual's employment has ended will be unlawful if the treatment of the person is in any way connected to their previous employment. Employers should therefore take great care in the compilation of references requested in respect of a previous employee to ensure that nothing is stated that could put the person at a disadvantage on grounds of gender, race, religion etc. Three particular areas where risks may occur are in respect of:

- a disabled ex-employee whose performance was below standard for reasons related to disability

- a female employee who, owing to child-care responsibilities, was unable to be flexible in terms of working time

- an employee who was unable to work on certain days or dates owing to their religion or belief.

Employers should take care not to make any negative statements in a reference about any ex-employee in any of these areas. For example, if a Jewish employee had, whilst employed, been unwilling to work on Saturdays (the Jewish Sabbath) owing to their religious beliefs, the employer should avoid presenting this information as a negative element in a reference. It could be discriminatory under the Employment Equality (Religion or Belief) Regulations 2003, for example, to describe such a person as 'inflexible', or as 'unwilling to work at weekends', as this type of reference would put the person at a disadvantage compared with others for whom references may be given. Similarly, it would be sex discrimination to describe a previous female employee as inflexible if, owing to child-care responsibilities, she was unable to work variable hours.

Employment Equality (Religion or Belief) Regs 2003

Termination of a fixed-term contract

The expiry of a fixed-term contract without renewal is regarded as a dismissal in UK law. This is despite the fact that the employer and employee will have agreed at the outset that the contract will terminate on a particular date or on a particular occasion. The dismissal will be by reason of redundancy, or possibly on the grounds of 'some other substantial reason' (SOSR).

Normally, the dismissal because of the expiry of a fixed-term contract will be fair in law, but in certain circumstances an employment tribunal may take the opposite view, for example if:

- the employer recruits a replacement for the fixed-term employee shortly after the expiry of the contract (suggesting that the reason for the fixed-term employee's dismissal was not in fact the expiry of the contract, but in reality some other reason – and matters could be even worse if the replacement employee was of the opposite sex or a different race)

- there was another job into which the fixed-term employee could have been transferred on the expiry of their contract, but the employer did not discuss this opportunity with the fixed-term employee to establish whether such a transfer would have been of interest to them

- the employer in some other way acted unreasonably in terminating the fixed-term employee's contract.

To ensure fairness in termination therefore, the employer should first review (in consultation with the fixed-term employee) whether the employee can be offered alternative work (whether permanent or fixed term). If no alternative work is available, the employer should still be certain that the real reason for the proposed dismissal of the fixed-term employee is (for example) that the term has expired, the work is complete or the person whom the fixed-term employee replaced has returned to work.

Further and more detailed information about employees engaged on fixed-term contracts is available in Chapter 5.

Points to note

- Disciplining or dismissing a female employee because she is unable or unwilling to be flexible as regards hours of work may be indirectly discriminatory on grounds of gender unless objectively justified.

- Disciplining or dismissing an employee because they refuse to work on a day where it would contravene their religious beliefs to do so would constitute indirect religious discrimination and would be unlawful unless the employer could justify the requirement for the employee in question to work on the particular day.

- The dismissal of an employee on grounds of incapability is potentially fair under the Employment Rights Act 1996 (provided fair procedures have been followed) but the question of whether such a dismissal would be in breach of the Disability Discrimination Act 1995 is an entirely separate matter.

- A dismissal on grounds related to disability must, if it is to be lawful, be justified by factors that are material and substantial.

- If there are any adjustments, or further adjustments, that an employer could reasonably have made for a disabled employee, but failed to make, the dismissal of that employee will not be capable of justification.

- The responsibility to make adjustments for a disabled employee lies with the employer, and it is not up to the disabled employee to offer suggestions (although they should of course be encouraged to do so).

- In certain limited circumstances, an employer may dismiss an employee on racial or religious grounds or on grounds of sexual orientation, based on the argument that being of a particular race, religion or sexual orientation is a genuine occupational requirement (GOR) for the specific post and the race/religion/sexual orientation requirement is proportionate in the particular case.

- Employers undertaking a redundancy exercise must ensure that the methods used to select staff for redundancy do not place any disabled employee at a disadvantage, for example by allowing the disability to count against the employee in a points-scoring exercise.

- A retirement age specified by the employer for a job or group of jobs can (as the law stands at the moment) be any age, so long as there is no differentiation as between male and female employees and no discriminatory impact on other grounds such as race.

- Discrimination after an individual's employment has ended is unlawful under all the anti-discrimination laws whenever the discrimination or harassment arises out of and is closely connected to the employment relationship.

- The expiry of a fixed-term contract without renewal is regarded as a dismissal in UK law by reason of redundancy or on grounds of 'some other substantial reason'.

Action points

- Exercise caution with regard to taking disciplinary action against an employee who is signed off work with a stress-related illness.

- Review whether an employee who has difficulty complying with a shift roster can be exempted from the requirement to work shifts, in order to accommodate their needs and avoid claims of indirect sex discrimination or indirect religious discrimination.

- Discuss the issue of working hours, shift patterns and flexibility with individual employees where appropriate to seek agreement on arrangements that will meet the employee's needs without prejudicing the needs of the business.

- Explore all possible avenues as regards reasonable adjustments to support a disabled employee prior to considering termination of their employment.

- Consider what reasonable adjustments, or further adjustments, could be made to facilitate the return to work of a disabled employee who has been absent on account of a disability-related condition.

- Tell an employee who is absent from work, as soon as it is thought to be the case, that their continued employment may be at risk, and the reasons for taking that view.

- Consider offering a disabled employee who has been absent from work owing to illness or injury a phased return, for example the possibility of part-time working or home-working for a temporary period, or redeployment into a less demanding job.

- Take steps to ensure that all employees are treated consistently at all stages of a redundancy programme irrespective of their sex, trans-gender status, marital status, racial group, sexual orientation, religion, age or disability.

- Use a range of criteria to select employees for redundancy, and ensure that they are objective, ie based on factors capable of being evidenced.

- Refrain from using flexibility in terms of working time as a redundancy selection criterion, because this would discriminate indirectly against women, who are less likely than men to be able to work long or unsocial hours owing to child-care responsibilities, and possibly against people from certain religious groups who, as a result of their beliefs, may not be able to work on certain days or dates.

- Make sure that employees on maternity leave are treated no less favourably than employees at work during any redundancy exercise, and take particular care not to overlook the requirement to consult an employee absent on maternity leave.

- Take care in the compilation of references requested in respect of a previous employee to ensure that nothing is stated that could put the person at a disadvantage on grounds of gender, marital status, race, religion, sexual orientation or disability.

- Review whether an employee whose fixed-term contract is about to expire can be offered alternative work, and, if none is available, be certain that the real reason for the proposed dismissal of the fixed-term employee is (for example) that the term has expired or the work is complete.

CHAPTER 9

PREVENTING DISCRIMINATION AND PROMOTING EQUALITY AND DIVERSITY

Taking positive steps to prevent discrimination and promote equality and diversity in the workplace is much better than leaving things to chance and risking tribunal claims for unlawful discrimination. In order to start the journey down this road, employers should:

- devise and implement an equal opportunities policy and an anti-harassment policy (or dignity at work policy)

- thoroughly brief all employees about the policies and any accompanying procedures

- train all managers and supervisors in equal opportunities matters and in the avoidance of discrimination, including harassment

- monitor the implementation of the policies to ensure that they are being put into practice consistently.

Avoiding liability for claims of discrimination

s41(3) SDA 1975; s31(3) RRA 1976; s58(5) DDA 1995; s11(3) Part-Time Workers Regs 2000; s12(3) Fixed-Term Employees Regs 2002; s22(3) Employment Equality (Sexual Orientation) Regs 2003; s22(3) Employment Equality (Religion or Belief) Regs 2003

Where proper preventative measures are introduced, they will place the employer in a relatively strong position to defend any claims of unlawful discrimination or harassment taken against them. This is because all the anti-discrimination laws include the statement that an employer facing a claim for unlawful discrimination will have a defence if they can show that they 'took such steps as were reasonably practicable to prevent' the discrimination in question (see the Sex Discrimination Act 1975, Race Relations Act 1976, Disability Discrimination Act 1995, Part-Time Workers (Prevention of Less Favourable Treatment) Regulations 2000, Fixed-Term Employees (Prevention of Less Favourable Treatment) Regulations 2002, Employment Equality (Sexual Orientation) Regulations 2003, and the Employment Equality (Religion or Belief) Regulations 2003). This means that if an employer can provide evidence to a tribunal that they did everything they reasonably could to prevent discrimination in the workplace, they may be held not liable for any discriminatory conduct that does occur despite the measures taken. The burden of proving this defence is, however, a high one, and tribunals will not only scrutinise the employer's policies and procedures, but will examine the extent to which they were actually put into practice.

Thus, the adoption of appropriate policies and procedures represents a very important first step in the journey towards protecting the employer from liability for claims of unlawful discrimination. Articulately written policies will not, however, be enough on their own to provide the employer with protection against liability. In the event of a claim to tribunal for unlawful discrimination, the tribunal will also wish to examine closely whether:

- the policies and procedures genuinely have full management commitment and support

- the policies and procedures have been communicated properly to all staff in ways that ensure clear understanding

- management and (where relevant) staff have received adequate training in equal opportunities

- disciplinary procedures have been amended so as to include acts of discrimination and harassment as serious misconduct.

It is important to understand that adopting and practising preventative measures is the only way that an employer will be able to escape liability for any discriminatory conduct perpetrated by one of their workers.

However, it is also very important for an employer to take prompt and decisive steps to deal with any instance of discrimination or harassment as soon as they become aware of it. Taking appropriate measures to deal promptly and effectively with discriminatory conduct will not remove the employer's liability for the discriminatory act in an overall sense, but it will play an important part in convincing a tribunal that, because the discrimination was promptly remedied, the employer had taken such steps as were reasonably practicable and necessary.

Devising and implementing effective policies and procedures

Although there is no legal requirement for employers to put an equal opportunities policy in place, there will be many benefits in doing so. The objectives of an equal opportunities policy could include:

- to ensure that no employee or job applicant is treated unfavourably on grounds of sex, race, religion etc

- to increase general awareness of the importance of equal opportunities in t
  workplace, and make it clear why discrimination or harassment of any ki
  is unacceptable

- to set out minimum standards of behaviour expected of workers and wh
  workers can expect from the organisation

- to help towards the creation of an environment in which workers feel
  comfortable and confident that they will be treated with respect and dignity

- to enable all workers to perform at their best

- to make it clear that the employer takes equality and the prevention of
  discrimination seriously and that anyone who acts in breach of the policy will
  be liable to disciplinary action up to and including summary dismissal.

Over and above an effective equal opportunities policy and anti-harassment
policy, it will be important to have an accompanying complaints procedure,
designed specifically to provide a route for workers who are the victims of
discrimination or harassment to report the problem and receive support from the
employer. The employer's normal grievance procedure will not normally be
adequate for this purpose, simply because it often happens that the perpetrator of
discrimination and harassment is the worker's supervisor, who will also be the
person to whom grievances must be taken under the grievance procedure. It is
best to have a separate complaints procedure that is designed specifically to deal
with instances of alleged discrimination and harassment.

Providing training in equality, diversity and the avoidance of discrimination

In order to ensure that the employer's equal opportunities policy and anti-
harassment policy are put into practice, and to minimise the likelihood of
instances of discrimination or harassment, full training in equality, diversity and
the avoidance of discrimination should be provided to all staff. Training is
especially important for managers, supervisors and anyone who is responsible for
recruitment and promotion decisions, as it is clearly vital that people in positions
of authority understand how the various laws impact upon their actions.
Employers may wish also to make awareness training in equal opportunities
matters available to all staff on a voluntary basis.

Equal opportunities training should aim to achieve the following objectives:

- to provide information about the fundamental principles of UK discrimination
  legislation, and the concepts of direct and indirect discrimination,
  victimisation and harassment

- to identify the different grounds on which discrimination can occur, eg grounds of gender, sexual orientation, part-time status, colour, religion etc

- to identify the types of behaviour that can constitute unlawful discrimination, eg failure to promote, pay differences, discriminatory questions at interview etc

- to clarify the many forms that harassment can take, eg physical, verbal and non-verbal

- to provide examples of the types of joke, banter and casual remark that may cause offence and therefore constitute unlawful harassment

- to explore the meaning of equality and diversity, and identify the barriers to achieving them

- to encourage all employees to adopt a positive attitude towards equality and diversity

- to encourage employees to recognise, understand and reject stereotyped assumptions, prejudice and negative attitudes towards certain people or groups

- to raise awareness of the employer's policies and procedures relating to equality and the prevention of discrimination, and their underlying values

- to identify actions and behaviours that promote equality and diversity in the workplace.

Model policies and procedures

This section provides a range of model policies and procedures that employers may wish to adopt or adapt to suit their needs.

Model equal opportunities policy

This equal opportunities policy represents a statement of the company's general approach towards equal opportunities. It is not intended to form a contractually binding statement.

Policy statement

The Company is committed to ensuring equal opportunities, fairness of treatment, dignity, work–life balance and the elimination of all forms of discrimination in the workplace. One of the key objectives of the policy is for the Company to provide a working environment in which workers feel comfortable and confident that they will be treated with respect and dignity.

It is the Company's stated policy to treat all workers equally and fairly, irrespective of their sex, marital status, trans-gender status, sexual orientation, race, colour, nationality, ethnic origin, national origin, culture, religion, age or disability. A similar policy is adopted towards job applicants. The Company is also committed to ensuring that no policy, procedure, provision, rule, requirement, condition or criterion will be imposed on any worker without justification if it would put that worker at a disadvantage on any of the above grounds. Furthermore, harassment in any form is unacceptable and staff should also familiarise themselves with the Company's anti-harassment policy.

Scope of the policy

This equal opportunities policy applies to the Company's recruitment and selection practices, employees' terms and conditions of employment (including pay), opportunities for promotion, transfer and training, general treatment at work, disciplinary and grievance procedures, and termination of employment.

Communication of the policy

Implementation of this policy will be supported by a full programme of communication to ensure that all workers are aware of their responsibilities and rights, and of the Company's commitment to equality.

Training in equal opportunities

All staff who have responsibility for recruitment, selection, promotion and/or appraisal, or who supervise other staff, will receive equal opportunities training. Other staff will have the opportunity to attend awareness training in equality and diversity.

Review of the policy

The Company will review this policy on a regular basis in order to ensure that individuals are selected, promoted and otherwise treated on the basis of their relevant abilities and merits.

Monitoring

The effectiveness of the policy will be judged by monitoring the numbers and composition (in terms of gender, racial group, age and disability) of:

- successful and unsuccessful job applicants

- staff who receive training

- staff who are promoted

- staff who benefit or suffer detriment as a result of performance assessment

- staff who raise grievances

- staff who are the subject of disciplinary action

- staff who leave the Company.

An annual report containing the result of the monitoring will be prepared and published by the Board.

Responsibility for implementation of the policy

The overall responsibility for the policy lies with [*state name of senior manager*]. All workers are, however, expected to act within the spirit and intention of the policy and the law relating to equal opportunities and discrimination at all times. The employer will view any breach of the policy, or any type of discriminatory action against another worker, very seriously. Any worker who breaches the principles of equal opportunity enshrined in this policy will be liable to disciplinary action up to and including summary dismissal.

Reporting breaches of the policy

Any worker who believes they have been the victim of a breach of this policy, or who has witnessed a breach of this policy affecting another worker, should report the matter immediately either to their line manager or to [*state name of appropriate contact, for example an HR manager*]. Alternatively, a worker who wishes to make a complaint may use the Company's formal complaints procedure.

Model clause covering employees' rights in pregnancy and maternity for insertion into an equal opportunities policy

The Company respects employees' rights not to be subjected to any unfavourable treatment for any reason connected with pregnancy, childbirth or maternity leave. It is therefore the Company's policy to ensure that employees who become pregnant do not suffer any form of detrimental treatment because of pregnancy, an intention to take maternity leave or because they have taken maternity leave. It follows that all employees who become pregnant will be treated fairly and equally in relation to pay, promotion, transfer, training, appraisal, time off work, occupational sick pay etc.

Model policy on flexible working

The Company believes that the promotion of flexible working can increase staff motivation, promote work-life balance and improve performance. It is the Company's policy to endeavour to be flexible on working patterns for all its workers. Flexibility extends to the number of hours that an employee works, the days and start/finish times of those hours, overtime working, shift working and the place of work.

The Company must, however, recognise that the law grants employees who have a minimum of 26 weeks' continuous service and who have parental responsibility for a child under the age of 6 (or under the age of 18 where the child is disabled) the statutory right to request a change to their working pattern. If necessary, therefore, the Company will give priority to requests for flexible working from employees who have the statutory right to request flexible working.

Whenever an employee submits a request for flexible working, full and fair consideration will be given to the request, taking into account the likely effects that the employee's desired working pattern might have on the Company, the work of the employee's department and the employee's colleagues. Agreeing to one employee's request will not therefore set a precedent or create any right for another employee to be granted a similar change to their hours of work or place of work.

Model policy relating to the recruitment, training and retention of disabled workers

It is the Company's policy to support the employment and retention of people with disabilities. This is the case irrespective of whether the individual's impairment is physical or mental. The Company is committed to taking all reasonable steps towards accommodating the needs of disabled workers and job applicants to enable them to be employed, and to continue in employment so long as they are able to do so and wish to do so.

The Company will refrain from making assumptions about the type of work that people with disabilities can or cannot do. Applicants for employment, promotion or transfer will be given full and fair consideration and support. Furthermore, all disabled job applicants who meet the minimum requirements for the job as set out in the job description and employee specification will be guaranteed an interview.

All workers, including those who have a disability, will have equal access to training and opportunities for promotion based solely on their individual merits, taking into account any adjustments that could reasonably be made in the circumstances.

When a worker becomes disabled, or where an existing disability worsens, the Company will do everything it reasonably can to retain the disabled person in employment. If redeployment becomes necessary, the disabled worker will be viewed as a priority within any general redeployment exercise.

In general, the Company will take all reasonably practicable steps to make adjustments to working arrangements, working practices and, where appropriate and feasible, to premises, in order to facilitate the employment or continued employment of a disabled person. The worker will be fully consulted over any proposed adjustments, and where appropriate, expert medical advice will be sought in order that the Company can do its best to support the disabled worker.

Model anti-harassment policy

The Company is committed to ensuring fairness of treatment, dignity, and the elimination of all forms of discrimination, including harassment and bullying, for all its workers. This policy aims to ensure that no worker is subjected to any form of harassment or bullying, and that the Company provides a working environment in which workers feel comfortable and confident that they will be treated with respect and dignity at all times.

Harassment and bullying at work are contrary to the interests of the Company because such behaviour is likely to make the victim feel upset, embarrassed, humiliated or intimidated. Such effects will lead to lower levels of motivation and job performance, and may also lead to ill-health.

The Company adopts a zero-tolerance approach towards harassment and bullying. Although managers and supervisors have a particular duty to ensure this policy is adhered to, all workers have an individual responsibility for their own conduct and must comply with both the spirit and the wording of the policy at all times. This will include time spent on the Company's premises and also time spent working for the Company at other locations. This policy applies also to conduct at Company-organised social events.

All workers should be aware that harassment on grounds of sex, trans-gender status, sexual orientation, race, religion and disability are unlawful, and that, additionally, intentional harassment on any grounds constitutes a criminal offence. The Company will be held liable for unlawful harassment, but the individual perpetrator of the harassment may also be convicted of a criminal offence, or may be ordered by an employment tribunal to pay compensation to their victim for unlawful discrimination. There is no limit on the level of such compensation.

The Company will view any type of harassment or bullying perpetrated against another worker very seriously. Any member of staff who acts in breach of this policy will be liable to disciplinary action up to and including summary dismissal.

What is harassment/bullying?

There is no single definition of what constitutes harassment or bullying. Harassment may take many forms and may be based on sex, trans-gender status, sexual orientation, race, nationality, colour, ethnic origins, national origins, culture, religion, age or disability. Harassment, broadly, is unwanted conduct that violates a person's dignity or creates an uncomfortable working environment for that person. It may be physical, verbal or non-verbal. Harassment may consist of a single serious incident, or may involve persistent behaviour of a particular type or different types.

It is important to understand that the question of whether or not particular behaviour constitutes harassment depends on whether the victim genuinely finds it offensive or otherwise unacceptable, and not how anyone else perceives the same behaviour.

Bullying is behaviour that is threatening, intimidating, malicious, abusive or insulting. Often bullying is an abuse of power, position or knowledge and is designed to undermine, humiliate, denigrate or harm the victim. Bullying will have the effect of eroding an individual's confidence and self-esteem, and will cause anger, stress and/or anxiety. Both bullying and harassment can seriously damage working relationships, productivity and morale.

Examples of unacceptable behaviour include (but are not limited to):

- banter, jokes or comments that may be construed as sexually explicit, sexist, racist, homophobic or derogatory on grounds of religion or disability

- calling someone by a name based on sex, race etc (for example, calling an Asian employee 'Paki')

- spreading malicious rumours or insulting someone (particularly on grounds of gender, sexual orientation, race, religion or disability)

- ridiculing or demeaning someone

- picking on someone or setting them up to fail

- the display of pin-up calendars or pictures of naked women (or men)

- the display of racist publications

- sexually explicit or racist material displayed on computer screens

- exclusion or victimisation

- overbearing supervision or other misuse of power or position

- unwelcome sexual advances – for instance, touching, standing too close

- displaying offensive pictures

- making threats or comments about job security without foundation

- deliberately undermining a worker by overloading them and then constantly criticising them

- preventing individuals progressing by intentionally blocking promotion or training opportunities.

The above behaviours may take place face to face, on the phone or in writing, including e-mail.

(*Acknowledgement*: ACAS, *Bullying and Harassment at Work: A guide for managers and employers*, from which some of the above points are taken.)

The overall responsibility for this policy lies with [*state name of appropriate senior manager*].

Model complaints procedure (discrimination and harassment)

The Company is opposed to all forms of unlawful discrimination and harassment and seeks to create and maintain a working environment where all workers are treated with dignity and respect. In order to achieve this aim, the Company has devised this complaints procedure to give employees a means of challenging any unlawful discrimination or harassment that they experience or witness.

All complaints of discrimination or harassment will be treated seriously by the Company and will be dealt with promptly, efficiently and, so far as is possible, in confidence. The main aim of this procedure is to resolve complaints of discrimination or harassment so that the discriminatory treatment is remedied or the harassment stopped.

Any worker may use this procedure if they believe they have:

- been treated unfavourably in contravention of the Company's equal opportunities policy on grounds of sex, trans-gender status, sexual orientation, marital status, race, religion, age or disability

- been subjected to any form of harassment or bullying at work

- witnessed the harassment of a colleague.

Employees who, in good faith, raise a genuine complaint under this procedure will not be subjected to any unfavourable treatment or victimisation as a result of making a complaint.

The procedure

Any worker who believes that they have been the victim of discriminatory treatment or harassment, or who has witnessed discrimination or harassment, may choose to take either informal or formal action.

Informal action

Where possible, the worker should talk directly and informally to the person who they believe has discriminated against them or harassed them, and explain clearly their objection to the other employee's actions or conduct. In the case of harassment, the worker should explain clearly what aspect of their colleague's behaviour is unacceptable, or is causing offence, and request that it should stop. It may be that the person whose conduct is causing offence is genuinely unaware that their behaviour is unwelcome or objectionable.

If the worker feels unable to approach the person whose actions or conduct is causing offence, or if they have already done so but to no avail, or if the complaint is one of very serious harassment, they may elect to raise a formal complaint (see below).

Alternatively, the complaint can be raised informally with [*state name or job title of appropriate contact, eg an HR officer or senior manager*], in which case the nominated person will try to assist the employee to find an informal solution to the problem.

Formal action

The worker may raise the complaint (preferably in writing) with [*state name or job title of appropriate person*].

The complaint must identify the person who is alleged to have perpetrated discriminatory treatment or harassment, and give specific examples of the actions or conduct that the worker believes constitute discrimination or harassment. Specific incidents should be highlighted, with times and dates, and the names of any witnesses if possible.

The person responsible for dealing with the complaint should act immediately to:

- inform the HR department of the complaint

- investigate the complaint (see below)

- take steps to conciliate if, after discussion, both parties agree this is an acceptable course of action, or

- take formal action if this is appropriate.

In the event of serious allegations of harassment, the manager should consider whether to suspend the alleged perpetrator of the harassment in order to prevent any further contact between the parties until the matter can be fully dealt with (suspension should, however, be done in a way that does not penalise the employee accused of discrimination or harassment, nor prejudge the allegations).

Investigation

The Company undertakes to investigate all complaints of discrimination and harassment objectively and confidentially. The responsible manager's investigation into the complaint will be handled with due respect for the rights of both the complainant and the alleged perpetrator. Both parties will be separately interviewed as soon as possible and granted the right, if they wish, to be accompanied by a colleague or trade union representative at their interview.

In advance of the interview with the alleged perpetrator of the discrimination/harassment, the person must be informed in writing of the exact nature of the complaint against them. At the interview itself, the alleged perpetrator must be given a full and fair opportunity to state their side of events, and explain any conduct that forms the basis of the worker's complaint against them.

Following the investigation into the complaint, the responsible manager will produce a written report setting out the findings on the specific complaints made by the worker. This will be done within two weeks of the completion of the interviews. A copy of the report will be given both to the worker and the alleged perpetrator of the discrimination, and a copy placed on the appropriate personnel file(s), but will otherwise be kept confidential. If there are parts of the report that contain statements from third parties (eg other workers) that would identify the third party in spite of their reasonable expectation to the contrary, these parts will not be included in the copies of the report supplied to the worker and the alleged perpetrator.

The outcome of the investigation

If, following investigation, it is apparent that the complaint is well-founded, prompt action will be taken to remedy the discrimination or stop the harassment and prevent its recurrence.

The outcome of the investigation into the worker's allegations of discrimination or harassment may be (depending on what is established during the investigation and the interviews) that:

- the complaint is well-founded and the alleged perpetrator of the discrimination or harassment is disciplined or dismissed (in line with the Company's disciplinary procedure)

- the allegations made by the worker are not viewed as discrimination or harassment and no further action is taken

- the worker's complaint is found to be false or malicious, in which case disciplinary action may be taken against them

- standards for future conduct are set, which could involve training.

The Company regards all forms of harassment and bullying as gross misconduct, and any worker found guilty of such behaviour will be liable to disciplinary action up to and including summary dismissal. Disciplinary action will also be taken against any worker found to have made a deliberately false or malicious complaint of discrimination, harassment or bullying.

Appeals

If the worker who has made the complaint is not satisfied with the outcome, they may appeal in writing to [*state name or job title of a more senior manager*], setting out the reasons for their dissatisfaction. The appeal must be submitted within two weeks of receipt of the written report from the manager who handled the complaint.

The senior manager responsible for the appeal will convene a hearing with the worker to establish the grounds for their dissatisfaction and explore possible resolutions, having notified them of their right to be accompanied by a colleague or trade union representative at the hearing. The hearing will normally be held within two weeks of receipt of the worker's written appeal.

Following the appeal hearing, the senior manager will reply to the worker within a further two weeks describing any action that they propose to take and the timescale, or informing the worker that the appeal has not been upheld and that no further action will be taken.

If it is not possible to respond within the time periods stated above, the worker will be given an explanation as to the reasons, and asked to agree to a reasonable extension of the timescale.

This will be the final stage of the procedure.

Records

Records will be kept detailing the nature of the allegation of discrimination or harassment, the Company's response, any actions taken, the reasons for them and the outcome. Details of these will be retained on file by the HR manager, who will ensure the records are held in accordance with the Data Protection Act 1998. The HR manager will also be responsible for making arrangements for statistical data to be released about the procedure and its usage for the purposes of monitoring.

Points to note

- Where proper measures are introduced to prevent discrimination and harassment, they will place the employer in a much stronger position to defend any claims of discrimination taken against them to tribunal.

- Taking measures to deal promptly and effectively with discriminatory conduct when it happens will not remove the employer's liability for the discriminatory act in a general sense, but will help to convince a tribunal that the employer did what was reasonably practicable and necessary to remedy the problem.

- Although there is no legal requirement for employers to put an equal opportunities policy in place, there will be many benefits in doing so.

- Over and above an effective equal opportunities policy and anti-harassment policy, it will be important to have an accompanying complaints procedure, so that workers who are the victims of discrimination or harassment can report any problem and receive support from the employer.

- Training in equal opportunities matters is especially important for managers, supervisors and anyone else responsible for recruitment and promotion decisions, but ideally should be provided to all staff.

Action points

- Devise and implement an equal opportunities policy and an anti-harassment policy.

- Ensure that the equal opportunities policy and anti-harassment policy are communicated properly to all staff in ways that ensure clear understanding.

- Amend disciplinary procedures so as to include acts of discrimination and harassment as serious misconduct.

- Take prompt and decisive steps to deal with any instance of discrimination or harassment as soon as they come to light.

- Ensure that there is a complaints procedure that is separate from the normal grievance procedure and designed specifically to deal with instances of alleged discrimination and harassment.

- Provide full training in equality, diversity and the avoidance of discrimination to all staff.

CHAPTER 10

THE SCOPE AND STRUCTURE OF DISCRIMINATION LEGISLATION IN BRITAIN

This chapter aims to explain how the various laws governing discrimination in employment are framed and structured, the range of people who are protected against discrimination in employment, the different forms of discrimination that can take place and some steps employers can take to protect themselves against complaints of discrimination.

In achieving these aims, this chapter will hopefully provide the reader with an understanding of how anti-discrimination law works in an employment context and a framework within which various HR and management activities can be implemented. It can be very important for both HR and line management to develop an understanding of the key legal principles and the scope of discrimination legislation in order to ensure that equality and diversity can be managed effectively and discrimination avoided.

The scope of discrimination legislation

Currently there are eight pieces of anti-discrimination legislation in Great Britain (England, Wales and Scotland). These are:

- the Sex Discrimination Act 1975 – covers unfavourable treatment on grounds of gender, gender re-assignment and marital status

- the Equal Pay Act 1970 – covers equality of treatment as between men and women in pay and contractual terms

- the Race Relations Act 1976 – covers unfavourable treatment on grounds of colour, race, nationality, ethnic origins and national origins; was amended in July 2003 in line with the EC Race Directive (Council Directive 2000/43)

- the Disability Discrimination Act 1995 – covers discrimination that is in any way related to an individual's disability

- the Employment Equality (Sexual Orientation) Regulations 2003 – protects people against discriminatory treatment on grounds of sexual orientation, whether gay, lesbian, bisexual or heterosexual (implemented in December 2003)

- the Employment Equality (Religion or Belief) Regulations 2003 – prohibits discrimination on grounds of religion or belief (implemented in December 2003)

- the Part-Time Workers (Prevention of Less Favourable Treatment) Regulations 2000 – confers the right to equality of treatment to part-time workers as compared with equivalent full-time workers engaged on the same type of contract

- the Fixed-Term Employees (Prevention of Less Favourable Treatment) Regulations 2002 – confers the right to equality of treatment to fixed-term employees as compared with equivalent permanent employees.

The different grounds for discrimination covered by each of these laws is explored fully in Chapter 11, pages 196–197.

The impact of European law on UK discrimination legislation

Apart from the DDA 1995, all the anti-discrimination legislation in Britain is governed by European law (and the DDA will be subject to EU law in the future). Because EU law has supremacy over national law, it will take precedence in the event of a conflict or inconsistency between the two. Furthermore, the principle of supremacy applies irrespective of the timing of the implementation of national law, ie it makes no difference whether the relevant UK legislation was implemented before or after the EU measure that regulates it.

Eligibility to complain of discrimination

In general, the anti-discrimination laws in Britain offer protection not only to an organisation's direct employees, but to a much broader range of people who work for the organisation (known as 'workers'). The one exception is the Fixed-Term Employees (Prevention of Less Favourable Treatment) Regulations 2002, which apply only to employees (ie those engaged directly by the organisation on a contract of employment).

Job applicants are also covered by the SDA 1975, the RRA 1976, the DDA 1995, the Employment Equality (Sexual Orientation) Regulations 2003 and the Employment Equality (Religion or Belief) Regulations 2003.

Workers and job applicants are protected against discrimination irrespective of their age, the number of hours they work or their length of service.

The application of the DDA 1995 is at present restricted to employers who have 15 or more staff – see Chapter 11, 'Disability', for more details, page 221.

Definition of 'employment'

The definition of 'employment' for the purposes of defining who is protected is 'employment under a contract of service or of apprenticeship or a contract personally to do any work'. Protection therefore extends to cover:

- part-time workers

- temporary staff and those engaged on fixed-term contracts

- workers engaged via a contract with an employment agency, including those whose contract with the agency is set up through their own personal services company

- employees of other organisations who may visit the employer's premises, for example to repair equipment or deliver goods

- self-employed people who perform work personally

- apprentices.

Essentially any worker who is engaged to perform work for an employer on a personal basis (ie the individual performs the work personally rather than organising others to do the work or delegating the work) is protected against discriminatory treatment on grounds of sex, race, disability, sexual orientation and religion or belief (and, in the future, age).

Matters covered by the non-discrimination principle

Protection against discrimination on the prohibited grounds is afforded to job applicants at every stage of the recruitment process, including during any interview and in the arrangements made for selection (see Chapters 1 and 2). For existing workers, protection is available in relation to:

- the terms and conditions of the job (see Chapter 3)

- any other benefits, facilities and services that a worker can access in connection with their employment (see Chapter 3)

- opportunities for promotion, transfer and training (see Chapter 6)

- arrangements made for termination of employment, including dismissal (see Chapter 8)

- (in some cases) post-employment discrimination, provided the treatment meted out to the individual has a connection with their employment (see Chapter 8)

- discrimination in the form of 'any other detriment', which has been interpreted simply as meaning any treatment that puts an individual at a disadvantage. In *Shamoon v Chief Constable of Royal Ulster Constabulary*, the House of Lords ruled that a complainant does not have to show that they have suffered economic or physical loss in order to establish that they have suffered a detriment. The Lords held further that, so long as the complainant's view that their treatment was to their detriment is reasonable, this will be sufficient to give rise to a detriment.

[2003] UKHL 11

Exclusion of overseas workers

Workers are usually excluded from the scope of discrimination legislation if they work wholly outside Great Britain (but see also below under 'Work done for the purposes of a business run at an establishment in Great Britain', page 176). 'Great Britain' excludes Northern Ireland (the latter is included within the term 'United Kingdom'), although similar anti-discrimination legislation is in force there. The Channel Islands and the Isle of Man are also excluded. People who work offshore in the oil and gas industry within British waters are, however, covered, as are employees who work on board ships, hovercraft or aircraft registered in Great Britain (unless they work on a ship that operates wholly outside British waters).

The general principle is that, so long as a worker does some of their work in Britain, they will be eligible to complain in a British tribunal of any treatment that amounts to unlawful discrimination. Thus, protection would cover (for example):

- British workers who are based in Britain but spend a great deal of their time working overseas

- British employees temporarily assigned overseas but who make regular or occasional trips back to Britain for work-related purposes

- overseas employees temporarily posted to Britain

- those working in Britain for foreign-registered corporations under contracts that are governed by law other than English or Scots law

- those based overseas who make regular or occasional business trips to Britain.

A worker's eligibility to bring a complaint of discrimination to a British employment tribunal will be unaffected by the fact that the worker is engaged on a foreign contract. Equally, the worker's nationality is irrelevant to the question of eligibility to bring a claim.

Work done for the purposes of a business run at an establishment in Great Britain

Under the Employment Equality (Religion or Belief) Regulations 2003, the Employment Equality (Sexual Orientation) Regulations 2003 and the RRA 1976 (for the purposes of discrimination on grounds of race or ethnic or national origins only), an employee who works wholly outside Great Britain is protected against discrimination if their work is done for the purposes of a business run at an establishment in Great Britain and if the employee is, or was, ordinarily resident in Great Britain either when they were recruited or at some time during their employment. British employees who are assigned to other countries and who do not, in the course of their work, return to the UK, will therefore be protected by these statutes.

Employers' and employees' liability for discrimination in the workplace

s41(1) SDA 1975

Discrimination legislation very clearly places responsibility on employers for any discriminatory actions on the part of their workers. For example, the SDA 1975 states:

> Anything done by a person in the course of his employment shall be treated for the purposes of this Act as done by his employer as well as by him, whether or not it was done with the employer's knowledge or approval.

Similar provisions occur in the RRA 1976, the DDA 1996, the Employment Equality (Religion or Belief) Regulations 2003 and the Employment Equality (Sexual Orientation) Regulations 2003.

This means that whenever an individual says or does something discriminatory 'in the course of employment', the employer may be held liable in law for any detrimental effect that such conduct has on any other worker. Ignorance of the fact that discrimination was taking place will not provide the employer with a defence, nor will it be a defence for the employer to argue that there was no intention to discriminate.

The meaning of 'in the course of employment'

The interpretation of the phrase 'in the course of employment' has evolved considerably over the years. Obviously, the employer will be liable for the words and actions of an employee that take place whilst the individual is engaged in the normal duties or activities of their job. Conversely, the employer will not generally be liable for employees' discriminatory conduct that takes place outside of work and in the employee's own time. The distinction may not, however, always be absolutely clear. For example, in *Chief Constable of the Lincolnshire Police v Stubbs*, the Employment Appeal Tribunal (EAT) held that the employer was liable for incidents of sexual harassment perpetrated by one police officer against another which occurred at organised social gatherings that took place in a pub after work. The social occasions were sufficiently linked to the officers' employment for the employer to be liable. [1998] EAT 145 & 1231/97

Employers should be aware therefore that they could be held liable for any acts of discrimination (for example, harassment) perpetrated by one employee against another at any work-related event, whether the event takes place on work premises or at an external venue. Examples could include office parties, workplace social functions and residential training programmes.

In the case of *Jones v Tower Boot Co Ltd*, the Court of Appeal held that the phrase 'in the course of employment' should be given a broad interpretation in accordance with a lay person's normal understanding of the words. The decision in this case marked a departure from the previous application of the common-law principles of vicarious liability in cases of discriminatory harassment. [1997] IRLR 168

It may be useful to incorporate a clause along the following lines into employees' contracts, an equal opportunities policy document or anti-harassment policy:

Model contractual clause governing employees' conduct at work and work-related events

The Company is committed to ensuring equal opportunities and fair treatment in the workplace for all its workers. All workers are expected to comply with the policy at all times and to act in accordance with its objectives.

These principles apply during all working time, irrespective of whether the employee is working at the employer's premises or elsewhere, and also at all work-related events, including work-related social functions.

Claims against co-workers

Although the principal claim for discrimination in the course of employment must be taken against the employer, it is also open to the complainant to name one or more individuals who were personally responsible for the discriminatory treatment. This type of claim occurs most often in cases of harassment, which is of course a very personal, and potentially offensive, form of discrimination. It is not possible, however, for an employee to bring a case to an employment tribunal against a co-worker alone, as the principal case must be brought against the employer.

It is advisable for employers to ensure that all their workers are made aware that they may be held personally accountable at an employment tribunal for any discriminatory conduct, and that they may have to pay compensation to their victim out of their own pockets if the case against them succeeds. For example, in the high-profile case of *Yeboah v Crofton*, the Court of Appeal ordered an individual personally to pay £45,000 compensation to an ex-fellow-employee on account of various incidents of very serious race discrimination. The Court endorsed the employment tribunal's decision that the individual was personally liable because he had knowingly 'aided' unlawful discrimination against a colleague, and that this would be the case even in circumstances where the employer could escape liability for the conduct in question. This award was in addition to the compensation paid by the employer.

[2002] IRLR 634

When an employer may be liable for discrimination perpetrated by a third party

As a result of case law, it was established some years ago that an employer maybe held liable for an act of discrimination inflicted on one of their workers by a third party. Third parties in this context could include any outside person such as a customer, a supplier or a member of the public. The precedent was set in the case of *Burton and Rhule v De Vere Hotels*.

[1996] IRLR 596

Case Example

In *Burton and Rhule v De Vere Hotels*, two black Afro-Caribbean waitresses succeeded in their claims for racial discrimination against their employer (a hotel) on account of offensive racist remarks directed towards them by the entertainer at a function held in the hotel (at which they were waiting at tables).

The EAT ruled that an employer would be liable for discriminatory treatment perpetrated by an outsider if they were in a position to prevent the discrimination from happening or at least reduce the extent of it, and in these circumstances take no action to prevent or control the discriminatory treatment.

At the time of writing, it is not entirely clear whether this principle is likely to continue to be upheld, following a recent House of Lords statement (in another case) that the *Burton and Rhule* case was wrongly decided. It remains to be seen how courts and tribunals treat this issue in the future. In any event, employers would always be advised to take appropriate measures to prevent, or put a stop to, any harassment suffered by any of their workers at the hands of an outsider.

Direct discrimination

Discriminatory treatment on grounds of sex, race, sexual orientation and religion can be direct or indirect. Direct discrimination occurs where a particular individual is treated less favourably than another worker on one of the prohibited grounds. The comparator must be someone whose circumstances in employment are the same or not materially different. The construction of the law also allows a comparison to be made with a hypothetical comparator in similar circumstances (where there is no actual comparator). For a claim to be made, therefore, the worker need only show that they were treated less favourably than another worker of the opposite sex, different race or religion, or different sexual orientation was or would have been treated in the same or similar circumstances, and that sex, race, religion or sexual orientation (as the case may be) was the reason, or one of the reasons, for the treatment.

Readers should note, however, that in claims under the Equal Pay Act 1970, there has to be an actual comparator of the opposite sex for someone to found a claim, ie hypothetical comparisons are not permitted. Similarly, under the Part-Time Workers (Prevention of Less Favourable Treatment) Regulations 2000 and the Fixed-Term Employees (Prevention of Less Favourable Treatment) Regulations 2002, the complainant must compare their treatment with a real person (respectively, a full-time employee engaged on the same type of contract or a permanent employee).

An example of a hypothetical comparison made in a claim for race discrimination could be where a black employee had evidence to show that a white employee in similar circumstances would have been treated more favourably than they were in fact treated, and that this treatment was on racial grounds. In other words, if the evidence suggests that, but for the employee's race, they would have been treated more favourably, then a claim for unlawful race discrimination could succeed. It would not be necessary for race to be the only reason for the employee's unfavourable treatment, so long as it was a substantial or important factor.

Everyone is protected equally under the legislation, for example men and women are equally protected under the SDA 1975, and everyone, whatever their sexual orientation, is covered under the provisions of the Employment Equality (Sexual Orientation) Regulations 2003.

The position is somewhat different, however, under the DDA 1995, where the worker merely has to show that they were treated unfavourably for a reason that relates to their disability. In *Clark v TDG Ltd (trading as Novacold)*, the Court of Appeal held that, in cases of disability discrimination, the test of whether a disabled employee has suffered less favourable treatment should be based on the reason for their treatment and not on the fact of their disability. This means that

[1999] IRLR 318

there is no need to draw a direct comparison with an employee who is not disabled, as the only relevant issue is whether the disabled employee suffered unfavourable treatment for a reason related to their disability.

Examples of direct discrimination

- Declining to appoint a job applicant because they have revealed during the interview that they are gay.

- Refusing to promote a woman who is qualified for the job because the department head takes the view that a man would cope better with certain aspects of the work.

- Refusing to transfer a black employee to a customer-facing role based on the view (whether accurate or not) that the employer's customers would prefer to deal with a white person.

- Refusing to recruit a qualified job applicant because they have revealed that they would wish time off on particular days on account of their religion.

- Refusing to renew a fixed-term contract on the grounds that the employee has become pregnant (in circumstances where the contract would otherwise have been renewed).

- Dismissing an Asian employee on the grounds that they do not fit in following tensions between employees that are linked to racial differences.

- Refusing to take a request from a male employee to switch to part-time working seriously, where a female colleague in similar circumstances has been allowed to work part-time.

- Refusing to appoint a disabled job applicant who is suitably qualified for the particular job on the basis of an assumption that the applicant would be unable to perform the job and without reviewing what adjustments the employer could reasonably make.

Further, more detailed, information on direct discrimination on the various grounds is provided in Chapter 11.

Indirect discrimination

The concept of indirect discrimination is somewhat complex. The SDA 1975, the Employment Equality (Sexual Orientation) Regulations 2003 and the Employment Equality (Religion or Belief) Regulations 2003 all contain varying definitions of indirect discrimination, whilst the RRA 1976 provides two different definitions, depending on whether discriminatory treatment is on grounds of colour or nationality on the one hand, or on grounds of race, ethnic origins or national origins on the other.

The other laws do not include indirect discrimination within their scope. In all cases, the legislation allows an employer potentially to defend indirectly discriminatory treatment by showing either that it is justified in all the circumstances or that it is proportionate to the achievement of a legitimate aim. The definitions and distinctions between the various provisions are explained below.

Different definitions of indirect discrimination under different statutes

Colour and nationality

In respect of discrimination under the RRA 1976 on grounds of colour or nationality, the principles are that indirect discrimination will occur where:

- the employer applies a requirement or condition to everyone

- the requirement or condition is such that the proportion of persons of a particular racial group who can comply with it is considerably smaller than the proportion of persons not belonging to that racial group who can comply

- the application of the requirement or condition has caused an individual a detriment because they cannot comply with it. If, however, the condition is one with which the person can comply, then there will be no discrimination.

An employer will be able to justify an indirectly discriminatory requirement or condition if there is an objective, job-based reason for its application even though it may have had a detrimental impact on an individual (or group of individuals). In other words, if there is an objective, job-based reason for the requirement or condition, it will not be unlawful.

Gender

Under the SDA 1975, the criteria for indirect discrimination are based on the following:

- The employer applies a provision, criterion or practice to men and women equally. The phrase 'provision, criterion or practice' has a broader meaning than 'requirement or condition' and could, for example, cover any policy, procedure, rule or practice that the employer adopted, whether formally or informally.

- The provision, criterion or practice has a disproportionately adverse impact on women (or men) generally.

- An individual is put at a disadvantage by the provision, criterion or practice.

Once again, the outcome of any claim for indirect sex discrimination will depend on whether the employer can justify the requirement. The criteria for justification are similar to those in place for indirect discrimination on grounds of colour and nationality (above), ie the employer must show that there is an objective, job-based reason for the provision, criterion or practice that has nothing to do with gender. If the provision is necessary or relevant to the effective performance of the employee's job, it will be justifiable.

Race, and ethnic or national origins

Following implementation of the Race Relations Act 1976 (Amendment) Regulations 2003, the principles for race, ethnic origins and national origins are that indirect discrimination will occur where:

- the employer applies a provision, criterion or practice to everyone

- the provision, criterion or practice puts, or would put, people of a particular race or ethnic or national origins at a disadvantage when compared with others. This wording suggests that the person alleging indirect discrimination would have to show only that the provision, criterion or practice was likely to have an adverse impact on the racial group to which they belong, rather than providing detailed statistical evidence to back up their claim

- the provision, criterion or practice must actually have disadvantaged the person alleging discrimination. There is no requirement, however, for the individual to show that they could not actually comply with the particular provision in practice.

It is open to the employer to put up a defence against any claim for indirect discrimination on grounds of race, ethnic or national origins, but the test is not one of justification, as is applicable to claims based on discrimination on grounds of gender, colour or nationality. Instead, the onus on the employer is to show that the application of the particular provision, criterion or practice was a proportionate means of achieving a legitimate aim. Breaking this down, there must first be a 'legitimate aim', ie a proper objective that the organisation wishes to achieve. Secondly, the means devised to achieve the aim (ie the provision, criterion or practice) must be relevant to its achievement, and proportionate, ie not excessive. So if, for example, an employer imposes rules that are not relevant to the achievement of a legitimate aim, or introduces provisions that are excessively rigorous or restrictive in relation to the achievement of an aim, and if the rules or provisions also place people from a particular racial group at a disadvantage, the employer would be unlikely to be able to justify their actions in the event of a claim for indirect race discrimination.

Religion or belief and sexual orientation

The wording in the newer areas of anti-discrimination legislation (religion or belief and sexual orientation) is similar to that used for indirect discrimination on grounds of race or ethnic or national origins as described above. Thus indirect discrimination will occur where:

- the employer applies a provision, criterion or practice to everyone

- the provision, criterion or practice puts, or would put, people of a particular religion or belief (or sexual orientation) at a disadvantage when compared with others

- the provision, criterion or practice has disadvantaged the person alleging discrimination.

An employer may defend themselves against a complaint of indirectly discriminatory treatment on the basis that the application of the particular provision, criterion or practice was a proportionate means of achieving a legitimate aim.

Examples of factors that may be indirectly discriminatory

- A decision that employees must be available to work during evenings or at weekends. This type of requirement could discriminate indirectly against women, since women are less likely than men to be able to comply with the hours' requirement owing to child-care commitments. This would be especially so if employees were asked to work overtime at short notice.

- Insisting that a particular female employee must be included within a shift roster and take her turn at night shift working. A woman who is a single parent might not be able to work at nights because of child-care responsibilities. Because more women than men are single parents (about 90 per cent of single parents are women), the imposition of the shift pattern could amount to indirect sex discrimination unless the employer could show that it was justified on job-based grounds (see, for example, the case of *Chief Constable of Avon & Somerset Constabulary v Chew [2001]* in Chapter 5 under 'Hours of work and when they risk being discriminatory against women', page 88. EAT 503/00

- A demand that candidates for a particular post must be of a minimum height. Such a requirement would clearly place women at a disadvantage when compared with men and, unless the height requirement could be justified objectively on job-based grounds, would be unlawful.

- A condition that applicants for a particular post must be willing to travel away from home on the employer's business for long spells. Because fewer women than men would be able to comply with this, owing to family commitments that might prevent them from being away for long periods of time, the condition would discriminate indirectly against women. It would be up to the employer to demonstrate that such travelling was necessary for the effective performance of the particular job.

Continued

Continued

- A criterion included as part of the recruitment process that applicants for a particular post must be able to speak, read or write fluent English. This criterion would discriminate indirectly against job applicants of foreign nationality whose first language was not English and would be unlawful unless fluency in English was a genuine requirement of the job in question. Unless the job in question involved special demands, it could be difficult for an employer to demonstrate that the application of the criterion of fluency was proportionate. Requiring the post-holder to speak English at a standard that could be readily understood would be more likely to be upheld as lawful.

- A rule that employees must not have beards. This would be indirectly discriminatory against (for example) Sikh men, whose religious beliefs mean that they do not shave. The rule would be unlawful unless it could be justified. For example, if the rule was imposed as part of the employer's health and hygiene policy in relation to jobs that involved food-handling, it would be capable of justification.

- A rigid policy that employees must wear a prescribed uniform if, for example, the uniform included a requirement to wear short-sleeved shirts. This would discriminate indirectly against, for example, some Muslim women who are required by their religion to have their arms covered at all times.

Victimisation

As well as affording protection to employees and job applicants against direct and indirect discrimination, the laws prohibiting discrimination on grounds of sex, race, disability, sexual orientation and religion or belief all preclude an employer from victimising an employee on the grounds that the employee has:

- made a complaint to a court or tribunal alleging discriminatory treatment (including the initial act of lodging the complaint)

- given information or evidence in connection with someone else's complaint of discrimination

- alleged that the employer has committed an act that would contravene one of the discrimination statutes (this provision would include, for example, the making of an internal complaint about the employer's actions so long as the complainant is alleging that the employer has committed an act that contravenes discrimination law)

- done anything in relation to anti-discrimination legislation (this is a catch-all provision)

- intended to do any of the above.

The above list is collectively known as the 'protected acts'. The victimisation provisions also apply to situations where the employer suspects that the employee has done one of the protected acts, or knows or suspects that they intend to do a protected act.

The purpose of the victimisation provisions in the legislation is to afford protection to people against retaliation on the part of their employer in the event that they raise a genuine complaint that the employer has done something in breach of discrimination legislation.

The victimisation provisions also cover the situation where an employee is penalised by their employer on account of complaining that someone else has discriminated against them. For example, if an employee was to bring proceedings in an ordinary civil court alleging sex or race discrimination against a bank, building society or hotel (for example), and if their employer disapproved of such action and responded by subjecting the employee to some detriment as a result, then a claim of victimisation could be brought against the employer.

Similarly, if an individual who has brought discrimination proceedings against a previous employer (irrespective of the outcome of such proceedings) is rejected in their application for new employment with a different employer (perhaps because the potential new employer takes the view that the individual might be a trouble-maker), the person could take victimisation proceedings against the new employer. The argument would be simply that the reason for the new employer's rejection of the individual was that they had previously made a complaint to a tribunal alleging discriminatory treatment.

Types of treatment that may amount to victimisation

Any type of detrimental treatment of an individual on the grounds that they have done one of the protected acts will be covered – for example, refusal to employ or promote, denial of a benefit, unpleasant or abusive personal remarks, dismissal etc.

Causal link

In order to succeed in a complaint of victimisation, the employee alleging victimisation must be able to show that their treatment was caused by or motivated by their involvement in a complaint of discrimination. If there is no causal link between the employee's original complaint of discrimination (or involvement in someone else's complaint) and the less favourable treatment complained of, a claim for victimisation will not be able to succeed. Clearly, if an employer can show to a tribunal's satisfaction that they did not know that the employee had done a protected act, then the employee's case will fail. However, following the case of *Nagarajan v London Regional Transport* (see below), the

[1999] IRLR 572

principle was established that a claim for victimisation can succeed even where the employer's motive in treating the employee unfavourably was a subconscious one.

[1988] IRLR 204

In *Aziz v Trinity Street Taxis Ltd & ors*, the Court of Appeal identified three elements that a complainant must prove if they are to succeed in a claim for victimisation. The complainant must:

- show that they have done one of the protected acts

- provide evidence that they have been treated less favourably than others in the relevant circumstances

- prove on the balance of probabilities that the less favourable treatment was by reason of their doing one of the protected acts.

[2002] IRLR 776

Case Examples of Victimisation

In *Commissioners of Inland Revenue & anor v Morgan*, the EAT held that the employer had victimised a black barrister because she had recently brought a race discrimination claim against them in relation to unsatisfactory career progression. The treatment that gave rise to a finding of victimisation was the circulation of a memo informing colleagues that the employee had brought a race discrimination claim against the organisation and warning them that some of their personal details might have to be disclosed to the complainant and to the public in relation to the disposal of her race discrimination complaint. The circulation of the memo, the EAT held, had a detrimental effect on the attitude of the employee's colleagues towards her, and hence constituted victimisation.

[1999] IRLR 572

In *Nagarajan v London Regional Transport*, the employee had previously brought various complaints of race discrimination against his employer. When at a later date he re-applied for employment, he was turned down, an action which he believed constituted victimisation. The House of Lords upheld the employment tribunal's decision that, in making the selection for the post, those responsible for the recruitment decision had been consciously or subconsciously influenced by the employee's earlier complaints. So long as the principal cause, or an important cause, of the unfavourable treatment was the fact that the complainant had done a protected act, the case could be upheld.

[2000] EAT 1107/99 and 1108/99

In *Tchoula v ICTS (UK) Ltd*, a black security officer failed in his original claim for race discrimination but later succeeded in three claims for victimisation following his unfair treatment and dismissal, which, the EAT judged, occurred because of the original race discrimination complaint.

Continued

Continued

In *McGuigan v T G Baynes & Sons EAT*, an employee who was on maternity leave was considered for redundancy. She had previously voiced criticisms of her employer's attitude to women. For this reason she was marked down two points in the employer's redundancy scoring exercise. The EAT held that this amounted to victimisation, even though the employee might have been made redundant in any event.

EAT 1114/97

In *Chief Constable of West Yorkshire Police v Khan [2001] IRLR 830*, a police officer who had applied to another police force for a job was refused a reference. The reason for this was that the officer had brought race discrimination proceedings against the Chief Constable that were still outstanding, and the Chief Constable feared that the provision of a reference could prejudice the defence of the claim. The House of Lords held ultimately that, although the refusal of the reference amounted to less favourable treatment, the reason for the treatment was not the bringing of the race discrimination complaint, but rather the Chief Constable's legitimate desire not to compromise the handling of the race discrimination proceedings. Thus the police officer's complaint of victimisation failed.

[2001] IRLR 830

Harassment as discrimination

Until recently, the concept of harassment was not mentioned anywhere in UK anti-discrimination legislation. Neither the SDA 1975 nor the RRA 1976 (before it was amended) contained any provision that sexual or racial harassment would amount to unlawful discrimination. The DDA 1995 fared no better. Despite this erstwhile lacuna in the wording of the statutes, over the years courts and tribunals have consistently held that harassment on grounds of sex, race or disability in an employment context will constitute direct discrimination, as it will fall under the heading of 'any other detriment' (a phrase used in all three statutes mentioned above).

Finally, in 2003 race discrimination legislation was the first to be amended, at least in part, to incorporate a statutory definition of harassment, but this provision is not yet included across all discrimination statutes. The SDA 1975, for example, has not yet been amended to incorporate any statutory definition of harassment, although this is planned for the future (October 2005). Similarly, the DDA 1995 does not yet contain a definition of harassment, and so any case of harassment brought under this Act will fall to be interpreted according to case precedent (ie under the 'any other detriment' provisions). Regulations amending the DDA 1995 in this respect have been drafted and are due for implementation in October 2004.

The newer Regulations governing discriminatory treatment on grounds of religion or belief and on grounds of sexual orientation do contain a definition of harassment consistent with the definition in the amended RRA 1976 applicable to race, ethnic or national origins. Thus harassment is described (for example) in the following terms:

> A person subjects another to harassment where, on the grounds of that other's race or ethnic or national origins, he engages in unwanted conduct which has the purpose or effect of –
>
> (a) violating that other's dignity, or
>
> (b) creating an intimidating, hostile, degrading, humiliating or offensive environment for that other.
>
> Conduct shall be regarded as having the effect specified in paragraphs (a) and (b) if, and only if, having regard to all the circumstances, including, in particular, the perception of that other, it should reasonably be considered as having that effect.

The subject of harassment as a form of unlawful discrimination is dealt with fully in Chapter 7.

The Equal Pay Act

The Equal Pay Act 1970 requires equality of treatment in pay and contractual terms (including pension benefits) as between men and women. Both men and women are protected equally by the legislation, although in practice most claims are brought by women. For a claim to get off the ground, the applicant must compare their treatment with someone of the opposite sex who is doing:

- 'like work' (the same or a similar job), or

- work rated as equivalent (as a result of a job evaluation scheme), or

- work of equal value (equal in terms of the demands made – for example, effort, skill and decision-making).

All workers, including contractors, are protected by the equal pay legislation. The right to bring an equal pay claim is not dependent on the employee's having any minimum length of service. The timescale for bringing a claim to tribunal is, in most cases, six months; thus an employee may bring a claim at any time during employment or within six months of termination. An amendment to the Equal Pay Act implemented in July 2003 provided that, where an employer has deliberately concealed relevant facts from an employee with respect to pay, then the employee may bring an equal pay claim to an employment tribunal at any time within six years of the date they discover the concealed facts.

Facing a tribunal claim for unlawful discrimination

Claims for unlawful discrimination in employment are brought before employment tribunals, which sit in most major towns and cities throughout Britain. As discussed earlier, employees, workers, job applicants and in some cases ex-employees are eligible to bring a claim of unlawful discrimination to an employment tribunal. Management can benefit from developing an awareness of how employment tribunals function and the potential costs involved in the event of a case of discrimination against their employer succeeding.

Timescale for a claim to be brought before a tribunal

Claims must be lodged with the tribunal service within three calendar months of the discriminatory treatment complained of (except for claims of equal pay, for which there is a six-month time limit). Tribunals have discretion to waive the three-month time limit for discrimination claims if, in their view, it is just and equitable to do so, taking into account the circumstances of the individual case.

If discrimination against an employee has persisted over a period of time rather than consisting of a single incident, the employee may bring an aggregated complaint to a tribunal, so long as the application is registered with the tribunal within three months of the most recent discriminatory incident. This is because the legislation allows for claims to be brought based on an 'act of discrimination extending over a period'. This provision could apply, for example, in a case where an employee was being regularly subjected to discriminatory harassment, but the incidents, when viewed individually, were relatively minor. The employee could argue that their employer's treatment of them constituted a course of conduct extending over a period of time and that the incidents, when viewed collectively, represented a detriment.

In *Hendricks v Commissioner of Police for the Metropolis*, the Court of Appeal interpreted the phrase 'act of discrimination extending over a period' broadly, and held that it could include any ongoing situation or continuing state of affairs in which female or ethnic minority officers were subjected to linked incidents of discrimination. By contrast, if an employee was subjected to a succession of unconnected incidents, this would not represent an act extending over a period. Any claim for unlawful discrimination would therefore be limited to complaining about incidents that had occurred within the three months preceding the date the claim to tribunal was made. [2003] IRLR 96

In future, once the dispute resolution measures contained in the Employment Act 2002 are implemented (expected in October 2004), any employee wishing to take a complaint of unlawful discrimination to an employment tribunal will first have to submit a written grievance to their employer and allow a 28-day period for the employer to respond. At the same time the three-month time limit for lodging a complaint is to be extended to six months to allow internal procedures that have commenced to be completed.

Compensation for unlawful discrimination

Where a complainant succeeds in a case of unlawful discrimination at an employment tribunal, the usual outcome is that they are awarded compensation. Tribunals will calculate compensation under some or all of the following headings:

- loss of earnings to date

- future loss of earnings (where relevant)

- injury to feelings (not available under the Part-Time Workers (Prevention of Less Favourable Treatment) Regulations or the Fixed-Term Employees (Prevention of Less Favourable Treatment) Regulations)

- injury to health (not available under the Part-Time Workers (Prevention of Less Favourable Treatment) Regulations or the Fixed-Term Employees (Prevention of Less Favourable Treatment) Regulations)

- (in England and Wales only) aggravated damages.

There is no ceiling on the amount of compensation that can be awarded following a successful complaint of discrimination. Tribunals have the flexibility to award an amount they consider just and equitable in accordance with the particular circumstances of the individual case. According to the most recent survey conducted by *Equal Opportunities Review*, the median award for sex discrimination claims during 2002 was £5,000, for race discrimination claims £7,500, and for disability discrimination cases £5,666 (*IRS Equal Opportunities Review No. 124, December 2003*). To date, the highest award for unlawful sex discrimination has been £1.37 million (*Bower v Shroder Securities Ltd*), for race discrimination £762,000 (*Chaudhary v British Medical Association*), and for disability discrimination £279,000 (*Newsome v The Council of the City of Sunderland*). The Chaudhary case is, however, subject to an appeal to the EAT.

[2001]; 08 February 2002 case number 3203104/99; [2002] case number 2401502/00; [2001] case number 6403592/99, [2002] case number 2401502/00; [2001] case number 6403592/99

Compensation for any financial loss that the complainant has experienced as a result of discriminatory treatment is calculated and awarded on a net basis.

Injury to feelings

For injury to feelings, tribunals have a wide discretion when deciding how much to award, and awards can vary greatly. In one race discrimination case (*Doshoki v Draeger Ltd*) the EAT decided that the minimum amount that it was appropriate to award for injury to feelings was £750. In *Vento v Chief Constable of West Yorkshire Police* (a sex discrimination case) the Court of Appeal set down three recommended bands of compensation for injury to feelings:

[2002] IRLR 340

[2002] EWCA Civ 1871

1. a band of between £500 and £5,000 for 'less serious' cases, for example an incident of discrimination that was a one-off occurrence

2. a band of between £5,000 and £15,000 for middle to serious cases

3. a band of between £15,000 and £25,000 for serious cases. This band would be applicable to the most severe types of case, such as those involving a lengthy and malicious campaign of serious discriminatory harassment against an individual.

The sum of money awarded will depend on the tribunal's assessment of the level of genuine upset and distress that the complainant has suffered as a result of the discriminatory treatment inflicted on them.

Injury to health

In cases where the employee has become ill as a result of discrimination or harassment at work, tribunals also have the authority (in appropriate cases) to award a separate sum of money in respect of injury to health (also referred to as 'personal injury' or 'psychiatric injury'). In the *Lincolnshire Police v Stubbs* case (above), the employment tribunal distinguished between injury to feelings and injury to health. They described the concept of injury to feelings as dealing with 'emotions such as anger, frustration, humiliation and loss of confidence', whereas injury to health was viewed as a 'specie of personal injury which should attract a separate award'.

An award for injury to health could be made in a case where the complainant could demonstrate that their mental health had been damaged as a direct result of the discriminatory treatment they experienced, in other words that the discrimination caused them to develop a mental illness. Medical evidence would, of course, be required to convince a tribunal that such compensation was appropriate, and such a claim would also depend on there being evidence that the employee's illness was caused by factors in the workplace (and not, for example, by external factors).

Aggravated damages

In very serious cases, an additional sum of money may be awarded to the complainant for aggravated damages. This could occur where the employer (in the tribunal's view) has acted in a 'high-handed, malicious, insulting or oppressive manner' towards the employee (a phrase coined in the case of *Alexander v Home Office*). Aggravated damages may also, for example, be awarded in a case where the employer has persistently refused to take any action to support an employee who has complained internally of discrimination or to resolve the problem.

[1988] IRLR 190

Compensation following a successful equal pay claim

If a claim for equal pay succeeds, the employee will be entitled to have their pay and/or contractual terms raised to a level equivalent to the level of their comparator's pay and conditions, with each term of the contract being considered individually. It is not open to the employer to solve the matter by reducing the pay package of the comparator.

There may also be compensation consisting of arrears of pay and/or damages for up to a maximum of six years in England and Wales and five years in Scotland. This will be based on the date that proceedings were lodged. However, in a case where there has been a deliberate concealment of relevant facts from the employee, up to 20 years' arrears of pay may be recovered.

Further information about equal pay in practice is given in Chapter 4.

The burden of proof in discrimination cases

The general principles with respect to the burden of proof in a claim for unlawful discrimination are these:

- Tribunals do not require proof beyond reasonable doubt, but instead work to the 'balance of probabilities' test.

- Once the complainant has established facts that indicate less favourable treatment, the burden of proof shifts to the employer to show that the reason for the treatment had nothing to do with gender, race etc – ie that they did not discriminate.

- This means that, unless the employer can provide an alternative, credible explanation for their treatment of the complainant, the complainant will win the case.

The position is, however, slightly different in cases of race discrimination founded on colour or nationality and in cases of disability discrimination – see below.

Even though there are currently different approaches to the burden of proof in different statutes, the difference in interpretation is not substantial. The different approaches can be summed up as follows:

- In cases of discrimination on grounds of gender, marital status, race, ethnic and national origins, sexual orientation and religion, the burden of proof shifts to the employer once the applicant has shown facts that indicate less favourable treatment. If the employer cannot provide an alternative, non-discriminatory reason for their treatment of the applicant that the tribunal finds credible, the tribunal is bound to find in favour of the applicant.

- In cases of discrimination on grounds of colour or nationality, the burden of proof is technically on the applicant to prove – on the balance of probabilities – that they were treated unfavourably on the stated grounds. Because proof of discrimination is rarely available, tribunals may in practice (if they consider it appropriate to do so) draw an inference from all the facts of the case that the treatment of the applicant was racially discriminatory. Tribunals will normally do this in cases where they are satisfied the applicant has suffered a detriment and the employer's explanation of their actions is unsatisfactory. It is up to the tribunal to make the decision whether it is appropriate to draw an inference of discrimination, as they are not bound to do so.

- In cases of equal pay, the applicant must show that they were being paid less (or afforded less favourable contractual terms) than a comparator of the opposite sex who was engaged in like work, work rated as equivalent or work of equal value. Once this is established, the burden of proof is on the employer to show that there was a material factor that justified paying the applicant a lower rate of pay. If they cannot do this, the applicant will win the case.

- In cases of disability discrimination, it is for the applicant to show that their condition meets the statutory definition of disability contained in the DDA 1995, and that they were treated unfavourably on grounds related to their disability. If the complainant succeeds in doing this, the burden of proof will then be on the employer to demonstrate to the tribunal's satisfaction that they fulfilled their duty to make 'reasonable adjustments' as required under the Act, and that their treatment of the complainant was justified on grounds that were material and substantial (see Chapter 11 for a discussion of the provisions of the DDA 1995).

- In cases of discrimination against an employee on grounds of their fixed-term or part-time status, the employee must first show that they suffered less favourable treatment than a valid comparator. The burden of proof will then be on the employer to justify any less favourable treatment, ie to show to the tribunal's satisfaction either that the fixed-term or part-time employee was not in fact treated less favourably than the comparator, if they were less favourably treated, or that there was a valid reason that justified their treatment.

Points to note

- Legislation in Britain protects workers against discrimination on grounds of gender, trans-gender status, marital status, sexual orientation, colour, race, nationality, ethnic or national origins, religion or belief, disability, part-time status and fixed-term status.

- Any worker who is engaged to perform work for an employer on a personal basis (ie the individual performs the work personally rather than organising others to do the work or delegating the work) is protected against discriminatory treatment on the prohibited grounds.

- Employers may be held liable in law for discriminatory treatment perpetrated by one employee against another in the course of employment irrespective of whether there was any intention to discriminate.

- Discrimination may be direct (ie targeted at an individual) or indirect (ie where a provision criterion or practice applied by the employer has an adverse impact on the group to which the individual belongs, places them personally at a disadvantage and cannot be justified).

- Victimisation provisions in the legislation afford protection to workers against retaliation on the part of their employer in the event that they raise a genuine complaint that the employer has done something in breach of discrimination legislation.

- Employees and other workers are protected against harassment on a range of protected grounds either by dint of statute or because harassment has been deemed by courts and tribunals to constitute a detriment.

- There is no ceiling on the amount of compensation that can be awarded following a successful complaint of discrimination, and tribunals have flexibility to award an amount that they consider just and equitable in accordance with the particular circumstances of the individual case.

- In order to succeed in a claim of unlawful discrimination at tribunal, the applicant does not require proof beyond reasonable doubt, as tribunals work to the 'balance of probabilities' test.

Action points

- Develop an understanding of the key legal principles and the scope of discrimination legislation in order to ensure that equality and diversity can be managed effectively and discrimination avoided.

- Incorporate a clause into employees' contracts or an equal opportunities policy advising staff that the principles contained in the policy apply not only during all working time, but also at all work-related events.

- Review any practices that involve requiring employees to work long or unsocial hours or travel away from home on business to ensure that they can be objectively justified based on the needs of the job (otherwise they will discriminate indirectly against female staff).

- Develop an awareness of how employment tribunals function and the potential costs involved for the organisation if a case of discrimination is successful.

- Ensure, when facing a claim of unlawful discrimination at an employment tribunal, that there is a credible explanation for the particular treatment of the complainant that is unrelated to gender, race etc, otherwise the complainant is likely to win the case.

Reference

IRS Equal Opportunities Review. No. 124 December 2003.

CHAPTER 11

GROUNDS FOR DISCRIMINATION

This chapter aims to provide interpretation of the various grounds on which discrimination is unlawful in Great Britain. The text will alert readers to areas of potential risk and provide a clear understanding of the various areas in which equality and diversity need to be pro-actively managed.

Summary of the grounds on which discrimination is prohibited

Sex discrimination is prohibited by the Sex Discrimination Act (SDA) 1975, and means unfavourable treatment on grounds of gender. The Act protects men and women equally.

Trans-gender status or **gender re-assignment** (covered by the SDA 1975) means the process by which an individual changes their gender (male to female or female to male) under medical supervision. Protection against discriminatory treatment is available as soon as it is known that a worker intends to go through the process of sex change.

Sexual orientation discrimination is prohibited by the Employment Equality (Sexual Orientation) Regulations 2003. These Regulations protect workers (and job applicants) against discriminatory treatment on the grounds that they are, or are perceived to be gay, lesbian, bisexual or heterosexual. Discrimination on account of another person's sexual orientation is also prohibited.

Marital status is covered by the SDA 1975, although only discrimination on grounds of married status is prohibited, and not discrimination on the grounds that a worker is single.

Pregnancy and maternity discrimination is not dealt with in any of the UK's anti-discrimination statutes but has consistently been deemed unlawful by UK

Continued

courts and tribunals and by the European Court of Justice (ECJ). Any unfavourable treatment of a woman on any grounds related to pregnancy, childbirth or maternity leave is unlawful.

Discrimination against parents may occur if an employee who is the parent or carer of a child under the age of 6 is refused a request for flexible working under the Flexible Working (Procedural Requirements) Regulations 2002 and there is no proper business reason for the refusal.

Part-time workers are protected against unfavourable treatment on grounds of their part-time status under the Part-Time Workers (Prevention of Less Favourable Treatment) Regulations 2000. The Regulations confer the right to equality of treatment for part-time workers as compared with equivalent full-time workers engaged on the same type of contract, unless less favourable treatment can be justified.

Fixed-term employees are protected against unfavourable treatment on the grounds of their fixed-term status by the Fixed-Term Employees (Prevention of Less Favourable Treatment) Regulations 2002. The Regulations confer the right to equality of treatment to fixed-term employees as compared with equivalent permanent employees with the same length of service, unless less favourable treatment can be justified.

Race discrimination (prohibited by the Race Relations Act 1976) – means unfavourable treatment on grounds of colour, race, nationality, ethnic origins or national origins. Everyone is protected equally whatever their race or racial origins. Discrimination on account of another person's race is also prohibited.

Religion or belief is covered by the Employment Equality (Religion or Belief) Regulations 2003, which prohibit discrimination on grounds of a worker's actual or perceived religion, religious belief or similar philosophical belief. Discrimination on account of another person's religion or belief is also prohibited.

Disability discrimination (prohibited by the Disability Discrimination Act 1995) covers discrimination that is in any way related to a worker's disability. The Act also imposes a duty on employers to make reasonable adjustments to working arrangements and premises to accommodate the needs of job applicants and workers who are disabled. At the time of writing, the Act applies only to employers with 15 or more workers, but the threshold of 15 is set to be removed in October 2004.

Age discrimination is not, at the time of writing, prohibited by UK law, but legislation banning age discrimination in employment is set to be implemented in October 2006. This legislation will cover workers and job applicants of all ages.

Gender

Gender discrimination is prohibited in the UK under the SDA 1975 and the Equal Pay Act 1970. These Acts together form a comprehensive package providing substantial protection to all workers and job applicants against all forms of gender discrimination. In general, the Equal Pay Act 1970 covers pay and all other terms of employees' contracts of employment, whilst the SDA 1975 protects individuals from discrimination in:

- all stages of recruitment and selection (see Chapters 1 and 2)

- terms and conditions of employment (see Chapter 3)

- benefits, facilities and services offered to employees (see Chapter 3)

- opportunities for promotion, transfer and training (see Chapter 6)

- dismissal, including redundancy (see Chapter 8)

- post-employment discrimination (see Chapter 8)

- any other detriment.

The SDA 1975 prohibits both direct and indirect discrimination, and also victimisation. Sexual harassment is also unlawful on account of consistent findings by courts and tribunals that it constitutes a form of detriment.

The SDA 1975 affords protection equally to men and women. Although the Act was implemented primarily to redress the problem of discrimination against women, men have exactly the same rights and entitlements as women under the Act. The same principle applies to the Equal Pay Act 1970, although in practice far more women than men bring claims under both Acts.

Certain limited exemptions exist to the general principle that is unlawful to take an individual's gender into account when deciding whom to recruit, transfer or promote. These are explored fully in Chapter 1 under 'Genuine occupational requirements and qualifications', page 5).

The SDA 1975 covers not only unfavourable treatment on grounds of gender, but also discrimination on grounds of marital status and gender re-assignment. These two areas are dealt with separately below.

The effect of EU law on the Sex Discrimination Act (SDA) 1975

The UK's laws on sex discrimination are governed by European law, which means that the SDA 1975 and the Equal Pay Act 1970 must be consistent with, and must fully implement, the relevant EU Directives, which are the Equal Treatment Directive (Council Directive 76/207) and the Equal Pay Directive (Council Directive 75/117). Article 141 of the Treaty of Rome also applies.

The European Court of Justice (ECJ), which sits in Luxembourg, is the supreme court for all EU member states, with responsibility for interpreting EU law and ensuring that it is observed throughout the Community. Cases of sex discrimination can, in certain circumstances, be appealed to the ECJ where the scope of the national courts/tribunals has been exhausted without a satisfactory remedy. Tribunals and appeal courts may also refer matters to the ECJ for guidance.

Trans-gender

In 1999, the SDA 1975 was amended by the Sex Discrimination (Gender Reassignment) Regulations 1999. As a result, the SDA 1975 now expressly provides that it is discriminatory and unlawful to treat an employee or job applicant unfavourably on the grounds that they:

- intend to undergo gender re-assignment

- are in the process of undergoing gender re-assignment

- have undergone gender re-assignment.

'Gender re-assignment' is defined as 'a process which is undertaken under medical supervision for the purpose of reassigning a person's sex by changing physiological or other characteristics of sex, and includes any part of such a process'. Thus, protection against unfavourable treatment kicks in as soon as an employee makes it known that they intend to go through the process of changing their sex. The SDA 1975 does not, however, offer protection to individuals who are transvestites, ie cross-dressers.

It is important for employers to be aware that an individual who indicates that they intend to go through the process of sex change is protected against all forms of discrimination, including harassment, and to take appropriate measures to support the employee. This will include allowing a reasonable amount of time off work for the employee to undergo the necessary medical or surgical treatment. It would be unlawful to penalise an employee for taking time off work for this purpose if the employer would allow a similar amount of time off for reasons associated with sickness or injury.

There are limited exceptions to the principle that an individual's trans-gender status must not be taken into account when deciding whom to recruit or promote into a particular post. These are covered in Chapter 1 under 'Genuine occupational requirements and qualifications', page 5.

Practical issues associated with trans-gender employees

In order to manage the practical matters that may arise when an employee announces that they intend to undergo a sex change, the employer should first and foremost talk to the employee confidentially and establish how they would prefer the matter to be handled in terms of communication with colleagues, customers etc, and how certain practical matters are to be dealt with. The following matters will need to be addressed:

- the expected timescales for the employee's transition to the opposite sex and how much time off for medical or surgical treatment will be required

- at what point the sex change will be complete, thus necessitating changes to the employee's records to give recognition to their new gender identity

- whether the employee wishes to remain employed in their current post or to be considered for a transfer to another department or another part of the organisation

- at what point in time colleagues and others (eg customers) are to be informed of the employee's intentions and what precisely is to be communicated. People seeking to undergo gender re-assignment are required to undergo a 'real-life test', ie to live exclusively as a member of the opposite sex, before any medical treatment or surgery is undertaken. Clearly management should ensure that communication about the employee's plans takes place at or before this stage

- who is to inform the employee's colleagues and others about the sex change, ie whether the employee would prefer to do this themselves or have the employer make the announcement on their behalf

- whether any briefing, coaching or training might be required for the employee's colleagues, in particular to help them understand that no harassment or other detrimental treatment of the employee must take place

- agree a procedure for the employee's adherence to any dress code, or the point in time when the employee will begin wearing the opposite sex's version of the staff uniform – allowing flexibility where necessary

- agree when the employee will commence using single-sex facilities (such as toilets) as a member of their new gender.

Court of Appeal [2003]
EWCA Civ 1045

The question of which toilets an employee going through the process of sex change should use can be problematic. Useful guidance was provided by the Court of Appeal in *Croft v Royal Mail Group plc*:

Case Example

In *Croft v Royal Mail Group plc Court of Appeal*, the Court of Appeal upheld the finding that an employer had not discriminated unlawfully against a male-to-female trans-sexual by refusing to allow her to use the female toilet facilities prior to gender re-assignment surgery. The employee, who had worked for Royal Mail for 10 years as a man, had begun taking female hormones as part of the process of gender re-assignment.

Having sought advice, the employer informed staff that the employee should be treated as a woman and emphasised the organisation's anti-harassment policy. They suggested to the employee that she should use a unisex disabled toilet on a temporary basis until the completion of gender re-assignment surgery. The employee was unhappy with this arrangement, however, and subsequently resigned and claimed sex discrimination and constructive dismissal.

The Court held that, because the employee was still a man in law at the time in question, she had no right to insist on using the female toilets until after the process of gender re-assignment was complete, and the employer's action in asking her to use the unisex disabled toilet for a period of time had been appropriate in the circumstances and lawful.

It will be very important, if an employer is to avoid liability for sex discrimination, to ensure that the organisation's equal opportunities and anti-harassment policies and procedures include trans-gender people. If and when a case arises, the employer should, as in the *Croft* case above, seek to balance the rights of the individual not to suffer discrimination against the legitimate interests of other employees.

The UK's position on trans-gender status

In another important case that reached the European Court of Human Rights (*Goodwin v UK*), it was held that, once an individual has completed the process of gender re-assignment, they have the right to be treated in every respect as legally belonging to their acquired sex. The Court held that the UK's lack of recognition of trans-sexual people's new gender identity for legal purposes represents a breach of Article 8 of the European Convention on Human Rights (the right to respect for private life) and Article 12 (the right to marry). It is important to note that this decision only affects post-operative trans-gender people, ie those who have completed all the relevant medical and surgical processes.

[2002] IRLR 664

At the time of writing, the Government has not yet implemented changes to UK law to apply the *Goodwin* decision, but it is expected that they will do so in the near future. It will thus be essential for employers to treat trans-gender people in the same way as all other employees of their acquired gender in every respect once the process of the sex change is complete. This will affect occupational pension schemes and other fringe benefits. During the period of time that the employee is undergoing the 'real-life test', the employer should handle such practical matters with sensitivity. If it possible to do so, it would be preferable to permit the employee to use a designated unisex toilet (preferably not the disabled toilet) during this time, and to allow flexibility with regard to any dress code.

Sexual orientation

Until recently, protection against discrimination on grounds of an individual's sexual orientation was not provided by UK law. Numerous attempts had been made to assert that the SDA 1975 should be interpreted so as to encompass discrimination on grounds of sexual orientation, but these arguments consistently failed both in the UK courts and at the ECJ. The word 'sex' in the SDA 1975 clearly means 'gender', and not 'sexual orientation' or 'sexual preference'.

The position was changed in December 2003 with the implementation of the Employment Equality (Sexual Orientation) Regulations 2003. The Sexual Orientation Regulations, which implement the EU Framework Directive for Equal Treatment, provide that unfavourable treatment on grounds of an individual's sexual orientation during recruitment, employment, at termination of employment and post-employment will be unlawful. The Regulations prohibit direct discrimination, indirect discrimination, victimisation and harassment, which is defined as a distinct form of discrimination (see Chapter 7). 'Sexual orientation' is defined in the Regulations as a sexual orientation towards:

Council Directive 2000/78

- persons of the same sex (this covers gay men and lesbian women)

- persons of the opposite sex (this covers heterosexual men and women)

- persons of the same sex and of the opposite sex (this covers people who are bisexual).

The Sexual Orientation Regulations are in the spirit of true equality, as they protect everybody equally. They do not, however, protect people on account of an involvement in sexual practices, preferences or fetishes such as (for example) sado-masochism. Equally, an orientation towards children would not entitle a paedophile to protection under the Regulations.

People who have changed their sex (trans-gender people) are not covered by these Regulations, as trans-gender people are expressly protected by the SDA 1975 (see above).

Protection is also available under the Regulations to employees treated unfavourably on account of a perception that they are gay, lesbian, bisexual or heterosexual, whether or not that is their actual sexual orientation. For example, harassment based on an incorrect assumption that a particular individual was gay could give rise to a legitimate claim for unlawful discrimination. Furthermore, if an employee is treated unfavourably in any way (for example, being taunted or teased) because they associate with someone of a particular sexual orientation (for example, if they have a gay brother or lesbian daughter), or because they refuse to carry out an instruction to discriminate against gay or lesbian people, that will constitute unlawful treatment.

One exception to the general principle that employees must not be subjected to any disadvantage in employment on grounds of their sexual orientation is in the provision of benefits to employees' partners. The Regulations contain a clause that expressly permits employers to offer benefits (for example, pension and insurance benefits or access to discounted goods or services) by reference to marital status, if they wish to do so. Thus, schemes that offer benefits only to employees' married (but not unmarried) partners are lawful, even though on the face of it this type of arrangement discriminates indirectly against gay and lesbian people, who of course cannot marry. Where, however, an employer elects to offer benefits to their employees' *unmarried* heterosexual partners, they must provide equivalent benefits to employees who have same-sex partners.

The Sexual Orientation Regulations also contain two 'genuine occupational requirements' or GORs that are relevant to decisions to recruit, transfer, promote or dismiss an employee on grounds of their sexual orientation in certain narrowly defined circumstances. The first GOR relates to the situation where a particular sexual orientation is a genuine and determining requirement for the post in question, whilst the second may apply where the employment is 'for the purposes of an organised religion', for example where an organisation such as a church is opposed to employing gay or lesbian people for reasons rooted in the doctrines of the particular religion. These issues are dealt with in Chapter 1 under 'Genuine occupational requirements and qualifications', page 5.

Practical issues associated with employees' sexual orientation

In many cases, an employer may not know the sexual orientation of their employees, and arguably there is no reason why they should know, since the Regulations do not place an obligation on individuals to disclose their sexual orientation, even in a court or tribunal hearing. Evidence suggests, however, that gay and lesbian employees are particularly likely to be the victims of stereotyping, prejudice and harassment in the workplace (see also Chapter 7). Many will conceal their sexual orientation for fear of unfavourable treatment by colleagues or by the employer generally. Myths and stereotypes about gay and lesbian people abound, including the false assumptions that they:

- are promiscuous

- are a risk to children

- are HIV-positive

- are 'effeminate' (gays) or 'butch' (lesbians).

These views are completely false, and any such negative attitudes or assumptions in the workplace should of course be guarded against by employers and speedily redressed if they manifest themselves in any way. Policies and procedures should clearly identify sexual orientation as a ground entitling employees to equality of treatment and freedom from all forms of harassment. Employers should in particular be alert to any instances of banter, taunts or jokes based on sexual orientation (see Chapter 7 for a full discussion of different forms of harassment) that could create an uncomfortable working environment for a particular employee (whatever their sexual orientation) and thus constitute unlawful harassment.

Marital status

The SDA 1975, as well as outlawing discrimination on the grounds of gender and trans-sexual status, also covers discrimination against employees on grounds of marriage. Specifically, the Act states that married employees (of either sex) must not be treated less favourably than unmarried employees on grounds of their marital status.

Curiously, the Act does not afford similar protection to single people, and so it would appear on the face of it that discrimination against single employees on grounds of their being single would not be unlawful (although such treatment would not, of course, be in the spirit of equality and is not therefore to be recommended!).

Policies and rules on married partners not working together

[2002] IRLR 239

One example of a case in which an employee was held to have suffered discrimination on grounds of marriage was *Chief Constable of Bedfordshire Constabulary v Graham* (discussed fully in Chapter 6 under 'Ensuring any criteria or conditions for promotion are not indirectly discriminatory', page 111). It was ruled in this case that the revoking of a police officer's appointment to a division commanded by her husband was both directly and indirectly discriminatory.

This does not mean, however, that employers can never impose a rule that people related by marriage or living together as partners should not be employed in the same department or section. However, before applying such a policy or rule, the employer should analyse:

- whether any real risk or practical difficulty is likely to arise if people in close relationships work together

- whether a policy or rule banning people in close relationships from working in the same department or section can be justified on business-related grounds

- whether such a policy or rule, if it is thought to be necessary, needs to be applied throughout the organisation or only in certain areas, or in certain defined circumstances (for example, where an employee would be the manager or supervisor of their partner, son, daughter etc).

If it is established that a policy or rule of this type would be necessary and appropriate in relation to a genuine business need, then the employer may be able to apply the policy without being in breach of anti-discrimination legislation. It is advisable, however, to ensure avoidance of marital discrimination, to apply any policy or rule on this matter to both married and unmarried partners and also to other close personal relationships such as siblings, parents and sons/daughters.

Pregnancy and maternity

The Employment Rights Act 1996 contains provisions that make it unlawful to dismiss a woman on any grounds related to pregnancy, childbirth or maternity or to subject her to a detriment on any of these grounds. In order to bring a claim for unfair dismissal on account of a dismissal on pregnancy-related grounds, the employee is not required to have any minimum period of qualifying service.

The SDA 1975 does not deal with discrimination on grounds of pregnancy or maternity leave. Nevertheless, courts and tribunals have over the years interpreted discrimination on pregnancy/maternity grounds as sex discrimination, on the basis that such treatment is 'gender-specific'. One of the earliest cases of its kind was *Dekker v Stichting Vormingscentrum voor Jonge Volwassen*, in which the ECJ held that a refusal to appoint a pregnant job applicant who was the most suitable candidate for a particular job amounted to direct sex discrimination. The ECJ held that any discrimination based on pregnancy or on the consequences of pregnancy (eg the employee's inevitable absence from work on maternity leave) will be direct sex discrimination (for details of the *Dekker* case, see Chapter 2 under 'Ensuring fair treatment of an applicant who is pregnant', page 39). [1991] IRLR 27

In a subsequent case, *Webb v EMO Air Cargo (UK) Ltd*, the ECJ held that the dismissal of a woman for reasons connected with pregnancy will always amount to direct sex discrimination simply because only women (and not men) can be [1994] IRLR 482 pregnant. It was also held in this case that the fact an employee's presence at work at a particular time is essential to the employer's business is not a defence. A woman has an absolute right not to suffer pregnancy discrimination, and this right cannot be dependent upon the particular circumstances of the employer at the time.

The basic principle is that any unfavourable treatment of a female job applicant, existing employee or ex-employee on the grounds that she is (or was) pregnant or took maternity leave will constitute direct sex discrimination. This principle has the advantage of being absolutely clear, unlike some areas of employment law! Employers who subject an employee who is pregnant or who has taken maternity leave to any form of detriment on grounds that are related in any way to pregnancy, childbirth or maternity leave will be liable for sex discrimination. It is important to bear in mind that, where unfavourable treatment of a pregnant woman is caused by the consequences of her pregnancy (rather than the pregnancy itself), this will also constitute unlawful sex discrimination. Consequences of pregnancy might, for example, include pregnancy-related illness leading to absence from work (see Chapter 3 under 'Sickness absence on account of a pregnancy-related condition', page 62), or tiredness at work leading to inferior job performance. It is essential that a pregnant employee is not penalised for reasons of this nature.

It may be helpful for employers to devise guidance notes for managers to highlight their responsibilities towards employees who are pregnant, and also a general guide for pregnant employees to outline their rights and the employer's policy and procedures in respect of pregnancy and maternity leave.

Examples of unfavourable treatment that could constitute sex discrimination during pregnancy or maternity leave (unless there is a different and valid reason for the employer's action) would include:

- excluding a woman from training just because she is pregnant

- denying a woman a promotion because she is about to go on maternity leave (or is currently on maternity leave) and will not be available immediately to take up the position

- moving a pregnant employee to another job to avoid her coming into contact with customers or clients

- carrying out disciplinary proceedings against a pregnant employee when she is unable, owing to an illness resulting from pregnancy, to attend a disciplinary hearing

- denying a woman a full and fair appraisal on grounds of her absence on maternity leave, especially if appraisal is linked to pay and/or promotion opportunities

- failing to consult an employee over proposed redundancies on the grounds that she is absent on maternity leave

- dismissing a pregnant employee on account of time off work for a pregnancy-related illness (see *Brown v Rentokil* case in Chapter 3 under 'Sickness absence on account of a pregnancy-related condition', page 62)

- denying the woman the right to occupational sick pay if she is absent from work with a pregnancy-related condition where other employees would have been granted this benefit.

Risk assessments in relation to pregnancy

Employers should bear in mind the important requirement to conduct risk assessments in relation to pregnancy, and to take action to reduce or eliminate any risks to new or expectant mothers that are identified. It is equally important to note that the duty to conduct such risk assessments arises as soon as a woman of child-bearing age is employed, and not just after an employee has become pregnant. In *Hardman v Mallon*, the Employment Appeal Tribunal (EAT) held that a failure to carry out a proper risk assessment in relation to a pregnant employee was direct sex discrimination.

[2002] IRLR 516

Further information on pregnancy discrimination is available in Chapter 2 ('Ensuring fair treatment of an applicant who is pregnant', page 39), Chapter 3 ('Sickness absence on account of a pregnancy-related condition', page 62), and Chapter 8 ('Redundancy selection in relation to an employee on maternity leave', page 149).

Discrimination against parents

Discrimination against parents may occur in certain circumstances if a valid request for flexible working is received and the employer either fails to follow the procedure prescribed for dealing with the request in the Flexible Working (Procedural Requirements) Regulations 2002, or refuses the request without having a valid business reason for doing so.

Eligibility to request flexible working

Under the Flexible Working (Eligibility, Complaints and Remedies) Regulations 2002, employees (but not other workers) who have a child under the age of 6 may submit a formal request for flexible working to their employer. The employer is not under an obligation to agree automatically to such a request, but must follow a prescribed procedure for considering the request seriously (see below).

The entitlement to request flexible working extends to any employee (male or female) who is the parent, adoptive parent, foster parent or guardian of a child, or the partner of any of these (including a same-sex partner), provided the employee has a minimum of six months' service. If an employee has a disabled child, a request may be submitted up until the child's 18th birthday. To be valid, the employee's request must be made for the purpose of caring for a child. Requests cannot be made more often than once a year.

Irrespective of the statutory right for employees who are the parents of young children to request flexible working, employers may prefer to extend such a policy to all employees, and not just those who are the parents or carers of children under the age of 6.

The meaning of 'flexible working'

The right to request flexible working includes the right for employees to request changes to:

- the number of hours they work

- the times they work, ie the days worked and start/finish times

- the place of work, ie the employee may submit a request to do some or all of their work from home.

Requests could, for example, include requests for part-time working, job-sharing, compressed hours, staggered hours, shift working (or removal from shift working), flexitime, tele-working, term-time working, annualised hours etc.

How an employee should submit a request

An employee who wishes to use the statutory procedure for making a request for flexible working must do so in writing (otherwise the request will not be valid). The request should state:

- that it is a request for flexible working for the purpose of caring for a child

- whether the employee has previously submitted any request for flexible working, and if so when

- the change(s) to working arrangements that the employee is seeking

- the date on which the employee proposes the change(s) should take effect

- the effect (if any) that the employee thinks the change(s) will have on the employer, and how any such effect might be dealt with.

Any request that does not fulfil these criteria will not, technically, be valid. However, if an application for flexible working does not contain all the required information, the employer should not simply reject it but, instead, should inform the employee of the omission(s) and ask them to resubmit the application with all the relevant information.

Irrespective of the legislative requirements governing employees and employers in respect to statutory requests for flexible working, there is nothing to stop an employer from applying a more informal approach to requests to changes in working hours and dealing with requests irrespective of the manner in which they are submitted.

Dealing with requests for flexible working

An employer who is in receipt of a statutory request for flexible working is not obliged to agree to it automatically, but must follow a defined statutory procedure. If, however, the employer elects to agree to the employee's request at the outset, the only requirement will be to notify the employee in writing of the changes to their terms of employment and the date on which they are to take effect.

Under the statutory procedure, the employer must:

- hold a meeting with the employee who has made the request within 28 days in order to explore how the request might be made to work (and, if appropriate, seek compromises)

- allow the employee to be accompanied at the meeting by a colleague, if they wish

- provide a written reply to the request within 14 days of the meeting which must, if the request is rejected, explain the specific business grounds for the refusal and why these are relevant to the employee's case

- grant a right of appeal within 14 days if the request is refused, hear the appeal within another 14 days and communicate the outcome within yet another 14 days.

If an employee's request is granted, the change to their pattern of working will be regarded as a permanent change to the terms of their contract (unless expressly agreed otherwise). It follows that the employee will have no automatic right to revert to their previous pattern of working at a future date. Similarly, the employer will not be able to insist that the employee reverts to the previous working arrangements when the child reaches the age of 6.

Trial periods

Despite this rule, there is nothing to stop an employer and employee from agreeing to a trial period in respect of any new working arrangement. A trial period would give both parties a clear insight into the viability of the new arrangement and would allow the employer to see whether it was likely to cause any real problems for the organisation. At the end of the trial period, the employer could decide whether or not to agree to make the arrangement permanent. One advantage of this approach is that, if the request ultimately has to be refused, the employer will have some evidence to back up the assertion that the employee's request was not workable for one of the permitted reasons (see below).

If a trial period is agreed, it will be very important to document clearly that the new working pattern represents a temporary variation to the terms of the employee's contract, and that the employer reserves the right to require the employee to revert to their previous pattern of working at the end of the stated period if, in their view, the new working arrangements have not worked successfully. The start and end date of the trial period should be clearly stated, and the document should be signed by both parties.

When refusing a request for flexible working is permitted

s80G ERA 1996

If a request for flexible working is refused, there must be a specific business reason for the refusal. Valid reasons are contained within the legislation and are as follows:

- burden of additional costs

- detrimental effect on ability to meet customer demand

- detrimental impact on quality or on performance

- inability to reorganise work among existing staff, or recruit additional staff

- insufficiency of work during the periods the employee wishes to work

- planned structural changes.

This represents an exhaustive list, and employers are not entitled to invent their own reasons for refusing an employee's request for flexible working, whatever their motives.

Checklist for the effective management of requests for flexible working

- Put procedures in place to deal with requests, and decide who will be responsible for dealing with them and who will hear any appeals.

- Consider extending the right to request flexible working to all staff, and not just those who are the parents of young children.

- Train line managers to deal with requests.

- Communicate the right to request flexible working to employees through the appropriate channels, for example staff handbooks.

- Where an employee is on maternity leave, keep in touch with her to establish whether she might wish to switch to part-time working on her return to work, and if so, encourage her to make the request early.

On receipt of a request for flexible working, managers should:

- Check that the employee is eligible (ie that they are the parent or carer of a child under 6 and have at least six months' service).

- Ensure a meeting is arranged within the prescribed timescale (28 days).

- Encourage the employee to suggest more than one alternative pattern of working.

- Encourage the employee (at the meeting) to offer suggestions based on their experience as to how the working pattern they are seeking could be made to work, for example how a job could be divided up so as to facilitate a job-share arrangement.

- Be prepared to consider the request with an open-minded attitude, and consider alternatives.

- If in doubt, agree a trial period, and ensure the agreement to take this course of action is properly documented.

- Before refusing the request, be certain there is a proper reason to refuse, and clear evidence to support the reason for the refusal (as opposed to the manager's personal opinion of the matter).

- Agree variations to the employee's contractual terms in writing.

Information about employees moving from full-time to part-time work is available in Chapter 5 under 'Moving to part-time work', page 85.

Discrimination against part-timers

Under the Part-Time Workers (Prevention of Less Favourable Treatment) Regulations 2000, part-time workers are protected against all forms of discriminatory treatment on grounds of their part-time status, unless the treatment can be justified in the particular circumstances. The Regulations cover pay, terms and conditions of employment, access to and benefits from occupational pension schemes, and non-contractual issues such as training, appraisal, and opportunities for promotion and transfer.

The Regulations define a part-time worker as someone who 'is paid wholly or in part by reference to the time he works and, having regard to the custom and practice of the employer ... is not identifiable as a full-time worker'. This none-too-helpful definition essentially means that a part-time worker is someone who works fewer hours per week or month than the organisation's standard full-time hours. There is no legal definition of full-time hours, and each employer is therefore entitled to make their own decision as to the number of hours per week that they regard as full-time.

Although the Part-Time Workers Regulations do not confer a right for employees to switch from full-time to part-time working, courts' and tribunals' interpretation of sex discrimination legislation has led to the principle that a refusal to allow a woman with caring responsibilities to reduce her hours may amount to indirect sex discrimination. The general principle, upheld consistently over many years, is that fewer women than men can comply with a requirement to work full-time hours owing to child-care responsibilities, and that women are therefore more likely than men to be disadvantaged by an employer's insistence on full-time working. A claim for indirect sex discrimination from a female employee with child-care responsibilities on account of being required to work full-time hours will succeed unless the employer can show that the hours requirement was objectively justified in the particular case (see also Chapter 10 under 'Indirect discrimination', page 181).

The rights of part-time staff are dealt with fully in Chapter 5 (see, for instance, page 83).

Discrimination against fixed-term employees

Under the Fixed-Term Employees (Prevention of Less Favourable Treatment) Regulations 2002, employees engaged on fixed-term contracts must not be treated less favourably than comparable permanent employees, unless there is an objective reason for the different treatment of fixed-term staff, or there is some other reason that provides objective justification for less favourable treatment. As in the Part-Time Workers Regulations, protection against discrimination covers all terms and conditions of employment, including pay and pension benefits, and also general treatment at work.

A fixed-term contract is defined in the Fixed-Term Employees Regulations as a contract that is set up to:

- last for a specified period, ie the contract has a predetermined termination date, or

- continue until a particular task or project is complete, or

- continue until the occurrence (or non-occurrence) of a specified event.

The rights of fixed-term staff are dealt with fully in Chapter 5.

Race

The RRA 1976 prohibits discrimination on grounds of:

s80G ERA 1996

- colour

- race

- nationality (see below under 'The distinction between "nationality" and "national origins"', page 214)

- ethnic origins (see below under 'The meaning of "ethnic origins"', page 214)

- national origins (see below under 'The distinction between "nationality" and "national origins"', page 214).

The RRA 1976 affords equal protection to everyone, whatever their race or racial origins. Although the Act was originally designed to outlaw detrimental treatment of people from ethnic minority groups, it applies equally to all. Thus a white, British employee is protected against race discrimination in the same way as (for example) a black employee of Nigerian nationality.

Like the SDA 1975, the RRA 1976 protects individuals from discrimination in:

- all stages of recruitment and selection (see Chapters 1 and 2)

- terms and conditions of employment (see Chapter 3)

- benefits, facilities and services offered to employees (see Chapter 3)

- opportunities for promotion, transfer and training (see Chapter 6)

- dismissal, including redundancy (see Chapter 8)

- post-employment discrimination (see Chapter 8)

- any other detriment.

Certain limited exemptions exist to the general principle that is unlawful to take an individual's race into account when deciding whom to recruit, transfer or promote (or, in certain cases, dismiss). These are explored fully in Chapter 1 under 'Genuine occupational requirements and qualifications', page 5).

The distinction between 'nationality' and 'national origins'

The distinction between 'nationality' and 'national origins' can sometimes be blurred. 'Nationality' includes citizenship, and is a legal concept that a person can change after birth. A person may even choose to have dual nationality. A person's 'national origins', on the other hand, subsist at birth and depend largely on the person's ancestry. For example, a British citizen may have Polish national origins if their parents (or even grandparents) emigrated from Poland to Britain. Another guideline comes from the House of Lords, which ruled many years ago (in *Ealing London Borough Council v Race Relations Board)* that national origins means 'nation' in the broad sense of race and not in the legal sense of citizenship.

[1972] AC 342

[2001] IRLR 150

In a more recent case, *BBC Scotland v Souster [2001] IRLR 150*, it was held that for the purposes of the RRA 1976, the Scots and the English are separate racial groups by reference to their national origins. The Scottish Court of Session upheld the principle that the English, Scots, Welsh and Northern Irish are all British in nationality because they are citizens of the United Kingdom, but ruled that national origins is a separate concept from that of nationality, involving such issues as history and geographical separation. Since Scotland and England were once separate nations, it was clear to the Court that the Scots and the English are distinct groups in terms of national origins. This decision means in effect that it is just as unlawful to refuse (for example) to appoint someone because they are Scottish (or English, as the case may be) as it would be to refuse to appoint someone because they are black.

The meaning of 'ethnic origins'

'Ethnic origins' is not defined in the RRA 1976 but has been interpreted by courts and tribunals as meaning 'a group with certain defined characteristics'. In *Mandla & anor v Lee & ors*, the House of Lords held that for a group to be of separate ethnic origins, it has to have the following characteristics:

[1983] IRLR 209

- a long-shared history, distinguishable from other groups, the memory of which it keeps alive

- a cultural tradition of its own, including family and social customs and manners, often but not necessarily associated with the group's religious observance.

Over and above these essential characteristics, there might be other characteristics which, although not essential, may be relevant to the question of whether a particular group is of separate ethnic origins when compared with the surrounding community. These further characteristics are:

- a common geographical origin or descent from a small number of common ancestors

- a common language (which need not be peculiar to the group)

- a common literature peculiar to the group

- a common religion different from that of other neighbouring groups or from the general community surrounding it

- being a minority or oppressed group, or being a dominant group within a larger community.

It has been established that, for the purposes of the RRA 1976, Sikhs, Jews and Gypsies (ie genuine Romany people) are groups of separate ethnic origins. Sikhs and Jews are also protected against discrimination under the Employment Equality (Religion or Belief) Regulations 2003 (see below).

In contrast, Muslims are not, in law, deemed to be a group with separate ethnic origins (although Muslims are of course protected by the Religion or Belief Regulations – see below).

Discrimination on account of another person's race

As well as affording protection to employees against discriminatory treatment on grounds of their race, the RRA 1976 also affords protection to individuals treated unfavourably on grounds related to another person's race. In *Showboat Entertainment Centre Ltd v Owens*, the EAT expressly held that, to succeed in a claim for race discrimination, the complainant only had to show that the detrimental treatment they had suffered was based broadly on racial grounds, and such grounds could apply to either their own racial characteristics or to the racial characteristics of another person.

[1984] IRLR 7

Similarly, in *Weathersfield Ltd t/a Van & Truck Rentals v Sargent*, the Court of Appeal held that giving an employee instructions to carry out a racially discriminatory policy or practice will amount to discrimination on racial grounds irrespective or the racial group of the person given the instruction. The Court also commented that this type of instruction will place the person in an 'outrageous and embarrassing position'. As a result of this case, employers should be aware that any company policy or procedure that in any way requires employees to carry out racially discriminatory practices may result in claims of direct race discrimination from an employee who is expected to comply with the policy or

[1999] IRLR 94

procedure against their will. It is also likely that such instructions would give an employee with one year's service (or more) grounds to resign and claim constructive dismissal.

Segregation

The RRA 1976 contains a provision that specifically makes it unlawful to segregate persons on racial grounds. Thus, any practice of keeping employees of a particular racial group apart from those of another racial group will amount to unlawful race discrimination, no matter what the motive behind it might be.

Specific duties imposed on public authorities

The Race Relations Amendment Act 2000, which was brought into force in April 2001, imposes a duty on all public authorities to eliminate race discrimination and positively promote racial equality in the exercise of their public functions. Although most of the Act does not relate specifically to employment, the Act and the accompanying RRA 1976 (Statutory Duties) Order 2001 impose on public-sector employers a duty to prepare and publish a 'race equality scheme', ie a document setting out the organisation's processes for fulfilling their general and specific duties under the Act and the Order.

The Act also imposes certain duties on public-sector employers to have systems in place to monitor the ethnic balance of staff, job applicants and applicants for training and promotion. Furthermore, where a public authority employer has 150 or more full-time staff (or the equivalent number, taking into account any part-timers), there is a duty to monitor the number of staff (in terms of ethnic background) who receive training, who benefit or suffer detriment as a result of performance assessment, who raise formal grievances, who are the subject of disciplinary action and who leave employment.

Although the duty to monitor means simply collecting information, under the general duty to promote racial equality, public authorities would then be under a duty to use this information to investigate and resolve any possible unfairness of treatment or discrimination on racial grounds.

The effect of EU law on the Race Relations Act (RRA) 1976

Council Directive 2000/43

The RRA 1976 prohibits direct and indirect discrimination, victimisation and harassment if the treatment of the individual is on grounds of colour, race, nationality, ethnic origins or national origins. However, the Act was amended in July 2003 by dint of the RRA (Amendment) Regulations 2003 to bring it into line with the EU Race Directive. Since then, the definition of indirect discrimination and the interpretation of what constitutes harassment differ slightly depending on the sub-heading under which a claim for discrimination is brought.

This rather unsatisfactory state of affairs has come about because of the way in which the UK Government chose to implement the EU Race Directive. Whilst the UK's RRA 1976 covers discrimination on grounds of colour, race, nationality, and ethnic and national origins, the EU Directive only required protection from discrimination on grounds of race, and ethnic and national origins. The UK Government implemented the Directive by means of Regulations, rather than by primary legislation, with the result that only the measures contained in the Directive could be implemented (and not any wider or additional measures).

The position now is therefore as follows:

- Discrimination on grounds of race, ethnic origins and national origins is governed by EU law.

- Discrimination on grounds of colour or nationality is not governed by EU law.

- Depending upon which ground a claim for discrimination is founded on, the definition of indirect discrimination, the circumstances in which indirect discrimination can be justified and the interpretation of what constitutes harassment will be different. The EU Race Directive imposed a new statutory definition of indirect discrimination, and also made harassment a distinct form of unlawful discrimination.

These issues are explained fully in Chapter 10 ('Indirect discrimination', page 181, 'Harassment as discrimination', page 187 and 'The burden of proof in discrimination cases', page 192) and Chapter 7 ('Racial harassment', page 119).

Religion or belief

In December 2003, the Employment Equality (Religion or Belief) Regulations 2003 were brought into force in order to implement the EU Framework Directive for Equal Treatment. The Regulations provide that unfavourable treatment on grounds of an individual's religion or belief during recruitment, employment, at termination of employment and post-employment will be unlawful. The Regulations prohibit direct discrimination, indirect discrimination, victimisation and harassment, which is defined as a distinct form of discrimination (see Chapter 7).

Council Directive 2000/78

The Regulations define 'religion or belief' as 'any religion, religious belief or similar philosophical belief'. This definition is wide enough to cover fringe or cult religions, and a range of other philosophical beliefs. For example, someone who was an animal rights activist might be able to argue successfully that their beliefs fell within the definition. Political belief is, however, not included within the scope of the definition, unless the belief in question is similar to a religious belief. The distinction between a religious belief and a political belief is not always clear, however, as there can be a crossover between politics and religion. For instance, the Islamic Party of Britain, Communism, National Socialism (Nazism) and Pacifism could all be said to be belief systems that affect an individual's view of the world, with the result that members of any of these groups would be protected against discriminatory treatment.

What is inconveniently unclear from the wording of the Regulations is whether an employee who is discriminated against because they do not have any religious beliefs would be protected. Ultimately, this will remain unclear until an EAT or higher court makes a decision on this specific point.

The Guidance Notes of the Department of Trade and Industry (DTI) on the Regulations (which are not legally binding) state that courts and tribunals may consider a number of factors when deciding whether an individual's beliefs fall within the scope of the Regulations. As examples, they cite collective worship, a clear belief system and a profound belief affecting one's way of life or view of the world. However, there is no requirement for a religion or belief to have a minimum number of followers for it to qualify as a religion under the Regulations.

Protection is also available under the Regulations to employees who are treated unfavourably on account of a perception that they are of a particular religion or hold certain religious beliefs, whether or not that perception is accurate. For example, harassment of an employee based on an incorrect assumption that they were Muslim could give rise to a legitimate claim for unlawful discrimination. Furthermore, if an employee is treated unfavourably in any way (for example, being taunted or teased) because they associate with someone of a particular religion (for example, if their partner is Catholic), or because they refuse to carry out an instruction to discriminate against, say, Muslims, that will constitute unlawful treatment.

The Religion or Belief Regulations also contain two 'genuine occupational requirements' (GORs) that are relevant to decisions to recruit, transfer, promote or dismiss an employee on grounds of their religion or belief in certain narrowly defined circumstances. The first GOR relates to the situation where a particular religion or belief is a genuine and determining requirement for the post in question, whilst the second may apply where the employment is in an organisation with an ethos based on a particular religion or belief, such as a church or religious school. These issues are dealt with in Chapter 1 under 'Genuine occupational requirements and qualifications', page 5.

Practical issues associated with employees' religious beliefs

This strand of discrimination law gives rise to particular difficulties, in that the majority of employers will have little knowledge of different religions and the beliefs and practices of their followers.

In order to promote equality of opportunity amongst employees of different religions, and avoid unlawful discrimination, employers should:

- review all their policies and procedures to ensure that none of their provisions could place employees of a particular religion or belief at a disadvantage

- consult employees and ask them what their needs are with respect to religion and belief or (where appropriate) set up an employee body to advise on religion and belief so that employees' needs can be identified and accommodated where possible

- review any dress codes, rules on dress and appearance or staff uniform requirements, and ensure that these allow for modes of dress that are linked to religious beliefs wherever possible (see Chapter 3, 'Dress codes and when they may discriminate or breach human rights', page 56)

- review policies on time off and holidays to ensure these are sufficiently flexible to allow employees of different faiths to be granted time off on days or dates that are significant to them on grounds of their religion or belief (see Chapter 3, 'Time off for religious holidays and when a refusal may be discriminatory or in breach of the individual's human rights', page 52)

- check that anti-harassment policies and procedures cover harassment on grounds of religion or belief, and ensure that these provisions are drawn to the attention of all staff

- train managers on how to deal with workplace issues that may arise as a result of employees' religious beliefs.

Conflicting rights

Some employers will inevitably be faced with the challenge of how to resolve conflicting legal rights. An individual's religion or belief may lead to discrimination against other people on grounds of:

- gender

- sexual orientation

- race

- disability.

The issue of conflicting rights is not dealt with directly in the legislation, but what is certain is that if a clash of rights should arise relating to an individual's religious beliefs, the employer would need to handle the matter very carefully and with great sensitivity. For example, if a male employee refused to follow instructions from a female supervisor because his religious beliefs involved a strong view that women are inferior, the employer would face the rather daunting task of having to try to reconcile the situation without discriminating unlawfully against either employee. Doing nothing would constitute sex discrimination against the female supervisor, as she would be able to claim that her employer's failure to support her occurred because she was a woman. To reprimand the religious employee for his refusal to follow his supervisor's instructions might give rise to a claim for religious discrimination.

Another example could be if an employee who, on account of religious beliefs, held strongly censorious views about homosexuality and persisted in imposing his views on a gay colleague to the extent that the colleague found the behaviour offensive. Again, if the employer did nothing to protect the gay employee, this could lead to a claim for sexual orientation harassment, whilst instructing the religious employee to desist from his behaviour might lead to a claim for religious discrimination (or even an argument that the individual's human rights had been breached under the right to freedom of thought, conscience and religion).

Employers may take some heart in the general principle that to apply a requirement to an employee to follow reasonable instructions, or to require them not to harass a colleague, would normally be viewed as appropriate where the purpose of the instruction was clearly to promote equality and prevent the employee from breaking the law. In the second example, the instruction to the religious employee would not, arguably, be on grounds of their religion or belief, but rather on the grounds that all employees are required to adhere to the employer's equal opportunities policy and/or anti-harassment policy. Even if the employer's actions were deemed to be indirectly discriminatory on grounds of religion, the employer would be able to show that such actions were proportionate to the achievement of a legitimate aim, and thus not unlawful. It is well established in both domestic and EU law that employees have the right to work in an environment in which equality and dignity are respected, and this right is unlikely to be overridden by the religious interests of individual employees. Chapter 10 ('Indirect discrimination', page 181) provides a full discussion of indirect religious discrimination.

Further information is available in Chapter 1 ('Religion – genuine occupational requirements', page 10), Chapter 2 ('Questions at interview', page 28), Chapter 3 ('Time off for religious holidays and when a refusal may be discriminatory or in breach of the individual's human rights', page 52, and 'Dress codes and when they may discriminate or breach human rights', page 56), Chapter 7 ('Religious harassment', page 120) and Chapter 10 ('Indirect discrimination', page 181 and 'The burden of proof in discrimination cases', page 192).

A useful source of information about Britain's main religions is available in ACAS's *Guidance on Religion or Belief and the Workplace (Appendix 2)*, available on the ACAS website: www.acas.org.uk. Other useful sources are www.bbc.co.uk/religion/ and www.bbc.co.uk/worldservice/people/features/world_religions/index.shtml.

Disability

At present the DDA 1995 applies only to employers who have 15 or more staff. As from October 2004, the small-employer exception will be removed and employers will come into scope whatever their size.

The number 15 must be calculated to incorporate the total number of workers at all the employer's branches and locations, rather than each individual workplace being calculated separately. All workers must be included – for example, temporary workers, part-timers and contract staff must be counted. Employees of associated companies need not, however, be included in the calculation of the number.

In *Burton v Higham t/a Ace Appointments*, the EAT held that an employment agency which engaged temporary staff who were then assigned to work for their clients had to include these temporary workers in their headcount for the purposes of establishing whether or not the threshold of 15 in the DDA 1995 applied to them.

[2003] IRLR 257

Key provisions under the Disability Discrimination Act (DDA) 1995

The key provisions of the DDA 1995 are that employers:

- should not, for a reason that relates to an individual's disability, treat that person less favourably than they treat or would treat others to whom the reason does not or would not apply, unless it can be shown that the treatment in question is justified (see below under 'When disability discrimination may be justified', page 227)

- make reasonable adjustments to working arrangements, working practices and premises in order to accommodate the individual needs of disabled workers.

Definition of disability

The DDA 1995 defines a disabled person as one who 'has a physical or mental impairment which has a substantial and long-term adverse effect on his ability to carry out normal day-to-day activities'. This definition is very broad, and employers should note the following points:

- The Act covers both physical and mental impairments.

- 'Long-term' is defined as 12 months or more, ie an individual who has been disabled for at least 12 months, or whose condition is reasonably expected to last 12 months or more, is protected by the Act. Thus someone who becomes disabled suddenly (for example as a result of an accident) would fall within the ambit of the Act immediately.

- 'Normal day-to-day activities' means 'life' activities and not the duties of the individual's job. Thus, the question as to whether an employee's impairment amounts to a disability will depend on the extent to which it affects the sorts of activities that most people carry out fairly regularly and frequently as part of their day-to-day lives. For example, lifting heavy weights is not a normal activity for most people in their everyday lives, and so the fact that a particular individual cannot lift heavy weights as part of their job does not qualify them as a disabled person in law. A 'normal' day-to-day activity might be to lift and carry a bag of shopping, or lift and carry a small pile of books or files. Equally, highly specialised activities such as playing a musical instrument to a professional standard or running three miles to the office would not be classed as normal day-to-day activities.

- The cause of a person's impairment is not relevant to the determination of whether or not it will be classed as a disability under the Act. Thus, for example, someone who has developed lung cancer as a result of heavy smoking will be able to claim protection under the Act on account of the lung cancer.

- If a disabled person's condition is controlled by medication or other forms of support such that they are able to carry out normal day-to-day activities, they may nevertheless be regarded as disabled in law if they would be impaired without the medication or support. For example, if an employee with epilepsy is symptom-free as a result of prescribed drugs, but would, without the drugs, be substantially impaired, they are regarded as disabled in law. Similarly, if an employee with a hearing impairment can hear near-normally by using a digital hearing aid, but would be substantially deaf without the aid, they are protected by the Act. (The only exception to this general principle is poor eyesight – if a person's eyesight is correctable by the wearing of spectacles or contact lenses, they are not considered to be disabled under the Act.)

- Employers should beware of assuming that an employee is not disabled on account of the employee's appearance or visible behaviour, and should bear in mind that an individual may have developed coping strategies that make their disability less obvious to others.

An impairment will only be taken to amount to a disability if it has a substantial and long-term adverse affect on one or more of the following: mobility, manual dexterity, physical co-ordination, continence, the ability to lift, carry or otherwise move everyday objects, speech, hearing or eyesight, memory or the ability to concentrate, learn or understand, or perception of the risk of physical danger. A person with a severe disfigurement is also classed as disabled under the Act. Each of these is explained below:

Mobility

This covers a person's ability to walk, move about generally, change position, reach up and down, turn around etc. Normal day-to-day activities that involve mobility would include walking, climbing or descending stairs, getting in and out of a car, reaching up to a high shelf or bending down to pick an object up from the floor.

Manual dexterity

This means the ability to use the hands and flex the fingers normally, and to co-ordinate the use of both hands to perform a single task. Activities that involve this ability would include (for example) picking up a cup of coffee, using a pen to write, applying make-up or shaving.

Physical co-ordination

This category covers a person's ability to balance and co-ordinate the movements of different parts of the body. Examples of the effects of such an impairment could include an inability to co-ordinate the movements of hands and feet when driving a car, difficulty in pouring hot water from a kettle into a cup without spillage, or an inability to carry out more than one task at the same time without serious difficulty.

Continence

This heading covers a person's ability to control the functioning of their bladder and bowels normally.

Ability to lift, carry or otherwise move everyday objects

This category covers a wide range of activities involving lifting and moving objects around. An employee may be disabled under this heading if they are unable to pick up with one hand ordinary objects such as a carrier bag containing grocery shopping, hold ordinary objects firmly without hand-shake or carry a tray with a moderate load of filled coffee cups steadily.

Speech, hearing or eyesight

An impairment could be classed as a disability if it adversely affects the person's ability to articulate ordinary words, hear what is being said at a meeting in a moderately noisy environment (without a hearing aid) or read a newspaper at a normal distance even when wearing prescribed spectacles or contact lenses.

Memory or ability to concentrate, learn or understand

This category potentially includes a wide range of physical and mental conditions and illnesses that might give rise to inherent difficulties in concentration, comprehension or learning. Examples of difficulties in normal day-to-day activities could include an inability to understand or follow simple instructions owing to learning difficulties, an inability to concentrate on routine tasks for more than a very short period of time, and behavioural problems caused by mental illness or brain damage.

Perception of the risk of physical danger

This covers both the over- and underestimation of risks to the safety, health or well-being of self or others. Someone with such an impairment might not understand the importance of following safety instructions when carrying out tasks and might inadvertently put others at risk, not fully understand the risks involved in reckless behaviour such as horse-play, or neglect physiological needs such as eating or keeping warm.

Severe disfigurement

Severe disfigurements could include large visible scars or birthmarks, severe burn marks, visible skin diseases, limb deformities and the like.

Types of condition that may be disabilities

The range of conditions that can come within the scope of the DDA 1995 is very wide indeed. The following may all be covered, provided their effects on the individual's normal, day-to-day activities are long-term and substantial:

- the full range of physical illnesses

- progressive illnesses, such as cancer and multiple sclerosis as soon as they are diagnosed and have some effect on the person, even if the effect is not, in the beginning, substantial (however, a medical diagnosis of a progressive condition which as yet causes no symptoms will not qualify the person as disabled under the Act)

- AIDS and symptomatic HIV

- conditions that occur intermittently (for example, rheumatoid arthritis) provided that, when the condition does occur, it has a substantial adverse effect on the individual. In this case the person is protected by the Act at all times, including periods when the condition is in remission.

- conditions that fluctuate such that at times the effects are substantial and at times they are not, in which case the person retains protection under the Act throughout

- clinically recognised mental illnesses such as schizophrenia and bipolar disorder (also known as manic depression)

- conditions such as severe dyslexia, myalgic encephalomyelitis (ME) and some stress-related illnesses, so long as the effects are substantial and long-term. Although stress alone is not regarded as a disability under the Act, stress can lead to an illness (for example, depression or post-traumatic stress disorder) that could amount to a disability. Employers in doubt about this in relation to a particular employee should obtain professional medical advice regarding the employee's condition, how it affects them and what supportive action would assist the employee to function effectively in the workplace.

- learning disabilities or difficulties.

It is important to note also that if an employee had an illness in the past which at the time amounted to a disability (or would have counted as a disability if it occurred before the Act was implemented), then they retain permanent protection against discrimination for a reason related to that disability (see Chapter 2, 'Past disabilities', page 34).

Excluded conditions

Certain conditions are excluded from the scope of the DDA 1995. These are:

- addiction to nicotine, alcohol or drugs (other than prescribed drugs)

- hay fever

- tattoos that have not been removed

- any type of body-piercing

- certain mental conditions, including a tendency to set fires, a tendency to steal, a tendency to physical or sexual abuse of other persons, exhibitionism and voyeurism

- a genetic predisposition towards a particular illness.

Employers should bear in mind, however, that although the above conditions are excluded from the DDA 1995, if they are symptoms of another condition then that other condition may amount to a disability. For example, an employee with a clinically recognised mental illness may exhibit a tendency to abuse other persons as a symptom of their illness. Such a person would be disabled within the meaning of the Act on account of their mental illness.

A further point to bear in mind is that although addictions to alcohol and drugs are excluded from the scope of protection under the Act, an individual with such an addiction may become disabled as a consequence of it. For example, an alcoholic may develop liver disease as a consequence of persistent, heavy drinking and thus become disabled. The cause of a person's disability is irrelevant to the question as to whether or not they qualify for protection under the DDA 1995.

Direct discrimination

The duty under the DDA 1995 not to directly discriminate against disabled job applicants and existing workers mirrors to a great extent the direct discrimination provisions in the SDA 1975 and the RRA 1976 (see Chapter 10 for a discussion on direct discrimination, page 129). Like the other statutes, the DDA 1995 prohibits direct discrimination during all stages of recruitment, throughout employment, at termination of employment and post-employment. One key difference, however, between the direct discrimination provisions of the DDA 1995 and those of the sex and race legislation is that employers may discriminate on grounds related to a worker's disability if the particular treatment of the worker can be justified (see below).

Discrimination may be on grounds of a job applicant's or employee's disability, but it may also be on grounds of the *effects* of the person's impairment. Effects can, for example, include reduced job performance, an inability to perform certain tasks or absence from work (if the disability consists of an illness or results from an accident). Discrimination on grounds of any of these effects will be unlawful, unless justified. A disabled worker will be able to succeed in a claim for disability discrimination provided they can show:

- that they were subjected to some form of unfavourable treatment, and

- that the reason for their treatment was a reason related to their disability.

The duty to make reasonable adjustments

The duty to make reasonable adjustments replaces the indirect discrimination provisions that occur within the other statutes. The employer is under a duty, whenever they know (or ought reasonably to know) that an employee is disabled, to take the initiative and identify any measures that will assist or support the disabled employee in the workplace. This will involve identifying changes to any working arrangements, working practices or premises that cause the disabled employee a substantial disadvantage on account of their disability. Measures should be sought that will have the effect of removing or reducing the employee's difficulties. The employer is, however, required to do only what is 'reasonable' in all the circumstances. What is reasonable will, in turn, depend on a range of factors such as the cost (if any) of the proposed adjustment, the size and resources of the business, the degree of disruption that any adjustment might cause, the likely effect on colleagues or customers and any other legitimate interests of the employer (such as safety).

The 'Code of Practice for the elimination of discrimination in the field of employment against disabled persons' provides useful guidance to employers on a wide range of matters relevant to disabled workers. In relation to reasonable adjustments, the Code states that an employer should do all they 'could reasonably be expected to do to find out whether' an employee is disabled and thus disadvantaged by the employer's working arrangements or premises. For example, if an employee has had a substantial period of sickness absence (whether in one block or as several separate periods of absence), the employer should make enquiries of the employee to establish whether their condition might amount to a disability and whether there are any adjustments that could be made to help the employee.

The subject of making reasonable adjustments is fully covered in Chapter 3, 'Making reasonable adjustments for disabled employees', page 64.

When disability discrimination may be justified

Treating someone unfavourably on grounds related to disability is capable of justification under the DDA 1995, provided the reason for the treatment of the employee is both material to the circumstances of the case and substantial. One key feature of this provision, however, is that discriminatory treatment will never be capable of justification unless the employer has first made all possible reasonable adjustments to assist and support the employee (or job applicant). If there are no reasonable adjustments that would help, or if all reasonable adjustments have already been made, the employer may then be able to justify discriminatory treatment. For example, it may be justifiable to:

- dismiss an employee where it has become impossible, extremely difficult or highly impracticable for them to do their job and there are no adjustments that would improve the situation

- refuse to employ a job applicant on the grounds that the employer operates in an area which is unsuitable for a person with a particular disability.

Dealing with negative attitudes towards disabled people

There are many stereotypes and prejudices against disabled people, including the false assumptions that they:

- are ill

- will inevitably be off sick a lot

- are unreliable

- pose significant safety risks to themselves and others in the workplace

- are less productive than non-disabled employees

- will need a lot of supervision or constant support in the workplace.

Such negative (and almost always false) assumptions act against the interests of disabled people and fly in the face of both diversity and effective management. The majority of disabled people are neither ill nor unsafe, and evidence suggests that they are likely to be more reliable, and have lower absence rates, than the average of the workforce at large.

Checklist for reasonable treatment of a disabled employee

Employers should:

- treat disabled job applicants and employees with dignity and respect

- ensure that any language used in relation to the employee's condition is not derogatory or negative (if in doubt about language, ask the employee)

- recognise and reject any negative assumptions about the person's abilities

- ensure a disabled employee is given meaningful work to do, thus enabling them to use their skills and talents fully

- discuss with the disabled employee what, if any, adjustments to working arrangements would help them perform at their best or overcome any difficulty that they are experiencing or might experience

- adopt a positive and flexible attitude to the question of reasonable adjustments

- ensure discussions about the effects of an employee's (or job applicant's) disability are focused on their *ability* to perform the relevant work, and not just on their disability

- take active steps to integrate any disabled worker into the team, where appropriate

- be supportive towards disabled employees in a general sense.

Further information relating to disability discrimination appears in Chapter 1 ('Positive action in relation to disabled job applicants', page 15 and 'Ensuring short-listing is done against objective criteria', page 23), in Chapter 2 ('Interviewing disabled job applicants', page 31), Chapter 3, 'Making reasonable adjustments for disabled employees', page 65, and 'Managing sickness absence in respect of a disabled employee', page 68), Chapter 6 ('Making adjustments for a disabled employee in training', page 102), Chapter 7 ('Disability harassment', page 122), Chapter 8 ('Dismissing a disabled employee on grounds of lack of capability', page 142, 'Avoiding disability discrimination during the redundancy selection process', page 150, and 'The duty to offer disabled employees available alternative employment', page 151) and Chapter 10 ('Direct discrimination', page 179, and 'The burden of proof in discrimination cases', page 192).

Age

At present there is no age discrimination legislation in the UK. As a result of the EU Framework Directive (Council Directive 2000/78), however, the UK (and other EU member states) will be obliged to implement age discrimination legislation by October 2006. The Framework Directive obliges all member states to introduce legislation banning direct and indirect age discrimination, victimisation and harassment. The Directive does, however, allow different treatment on grounds of age in certain circumstances.

Council Directive 2000/78

The Government has already consulted widely on the matter of age discrimination and it is likely that the legislation, when it is enacted, will:

- apply to all employers irrespective of size or industry sector

- apply to job applicants and existing workers of all ages

- use the same definitions of direct discrimination, indirect discrimination, victimisation and harassment as already exist in the other strands of anti-discrimination legislation (see Chapter 10)

- allow justification for age discrimination in certain circumstances

- ban age as a criterion in recruitment, selection and promotion unless it is objectively justified (for example, where a job requires a lengthy period of training)

- abolish compulsory retirement ages, or alternatively allow a default retirement age of 70, if this can be justified

- prohibit pay policies based on age (although pay based on length of service or experience will be potentially justifiable)

- remove the upper age limit for employees to bring unfair dismissal complaints and redundancy pay claims to tribunal

- alter the formula for calculating statutory redundancy pay (and the basic award for unfair dismissal) so that it no longer favours older employees or excludes service under the age of 18.

Until the implementation of age discrimination legislation, the only relevant guide to age in the context of employment is the Code of Practice on age diversity in employment, published initially in mid-1999. The Code recommends that employers should not use age as a criterion in recruitment, employment or redundancy decisions. The Code (like other Codes of Practice) is not legally binding on employers, but it is important to note that its provisions may be taken into account (where appropriate) by an employment tribunal. This means in effect that a failure to follow the Code's recommendations could go against an employer at tribunal.

Employers may wish also to bear in mind that applying an upper age limit on recruitment decisions may in certain circumstances discriminate indirectly against women (see Chapter 2 under 'Age discrimination in recruitment', page 41).

Myths and stereotypes based on age

There are many myths and negative stereotypes about people based on age. For example:

- Older people are incapable of learning new skills, especially technology (all individuals differ with regard to their willingness and ability to learn and change, and arguably older people will, provided they are given appropriate training, be just as capable of learning as younger people).

- Older people are 'past their best' (employers may wish to consider whether they have any direct evidence of any correlation between age and job performance).

- Younger people lack experience and therefore cannot be trusted with meaningful work (lack of experience does not mean an employee is not trustworthy).

- Younger people are unreliable (people of any age may be reliable or unreliable, depending on their personal attitudes to work).

- Older people are likely to have high levels of sickness absence (according to research, the opposite is true).

- If an older person is line-managed by a younger person, this will inevitably create conflict (conflicts arise all the time between managers and their staff, and an employee's attitude to management will depend on many factors other than age).

- An older person will not 'fit in' with a team of predominantly younger people (compatibility in working relationships is very important, but there is no evidence that older people have difficulty forming productive working relationships with younger people, or vice versa).

Practical issues associated with age

Given the rapidly changing demographic mix of people in the UK, employers who have in the past discriminated against people on grounds of age will lose out unless they change their attitudes and policies. It is estimated that by the year 2020, more than half the UK population will be over the age of 50, and that there will be two million fewer working people under the age of 50 than at present (*Equal Opportunities Review, No. 115*). People over the age of 50 represent a valuable source of experience and talent, and those organisations that fail to show enthusiasm towards the employment and retention of this group of workers are likely to face very severe skills shortages.

Checklist for age diversity in employment practices

In preparation for the forthcoming age discrimination legislation, and to promote diversity, employers should:

- audit all their policies, procedures and practices now to ensure they are age-neutral, and to identify and eliminate any age-based criteria or features

- review pay systems and criteria for bonuses etc to eliminate any age-based or age-related features

- review any service-based criteria (for example, extra holiday entitlement granted to employees after a specified number of years' service) to ensure that such criteria are justifiable. Adopting a policy or practice of requiring employees to achieve a minimum length of service in order to qualify for a benefit will in future be indirectly discriminatory against younger people and will therefore have to be based on a legitimate aim and be proportionate to the achievement of that aim (see Chapter 10 for an analysis of indirect discrimination, page 181).

- check to ensure that equal opportunities and harassment policies include age within their scope

- abolish age limits in recruitment, unless there are exceptional circumstances justifying an age criterion in a particular case

- ensure that no age restrictions or indications of age appear in job advertisements (for example, such wording as 'young, energetic person required')

Continued

Continued

- amend application forms so as to remove any requirements for job applicants to provide their age or date of birth

- review graduate recruitment schemes to ensure they do not apply any age criteria, and to establish whether they can be justified as a method of filling entry-level vacancies.

- ensure that employees are given access to promotion opportunities irrespective of age, and that promotion decisions are based on employees' skills and proven potential to do the job, irrespective of age

- amend any training and development policies to ensure that they afford equal opportunities to workers of all ages

- refrain from using age as a criterion in a redundancy selection exercise

- review retirement policies and prepare for the possibility that compulsory retirement ages will be abolished.

Further information about age discrimination in practice appears in Chapter 2 ('Age discrimination in recruitment', page 41) and Chapter 8 ('The implications of compulsory retirement ages', page 151).

Points to note

- Sex discrimination against both men and women is prohibited by the SDA 1975, which bans gender discrimination in recruitment, employment and termination of employment, and by the Equal Pay Act 1970, which covers pay and all other terms of employees' contracts of employment.

- The SDA 1975 (as amended) provides that it is discriminatory and unlawful to treat an employee or job applicant unfavourably on the grounds that they intend to undergo, are in the process of undergoing, or have undergone a sex change.

- The Employment Equality (Sexual Orientation) Regulations 2003 protect gay and lesbian people, bisexual people and heterosexuals against any form of detrimental treatment on grounds of their actual or perceived sexual orientation.

- The SDA 1975 states that married employees (of either sex) must not be treated less favourably than unmarried employees on grounds of their marital status.

- Any unfavourable treatment of a female job applicant, existing employee or ex-employee on the grounds that she is (or was) pregnant or took maternity leave will constitute direct sex discrimination.

- Discrimination against parents may occur if a valid request for flexible working is received and the employer either fails to follow the procedure prescribed for dealing with the request or refuses the request without having a valid business reason for doing so.

- Part-time workers are protected against all forms of discriminatory treatment on grounds of their part-time status, unless the treatment can be justified in the particular circumstances.

- Employees engaged on fixed-term contracts, ie contracts that are set up to last for a specified period, continue until a particular task or project is complete, or continue until the occurrence (or non-occurrence) of a specified event, must not without justification be treated less favourably than comparable permanent employees.

- The RRA 1976 prohibits discrimination in recruitment, employment and termination of employment on grounds of colour, race, nationality, ethnic origins and national origins.

- The Employment Equality (Religion or Belief) Regulations 2003 provide that unfavourable treatment on grounds of an individual's actual or perceived religion or belief during recruitment or employment, at termination of employment and post-employment will be unlawful.

- The DDA 1995 requires employers not to treat disabled workers or job applicants unfavourably for any reason related to disability, and to make reasonable adjustments to accommodate the needs of individuals who are disabled.

- The definition of 'disability' in the DDA 1995 is very wide and includes both physical and mental impairments, learning difficulties, and a wide range of illnesses and other conditions, including intermittently recurring conditions and conditions controlled by medication or support.

- Although there is no age discrimination legislation in the UK at present, the UK will be obliged to implement age discrimination legislation by October 2006 as a result of the EU Framework Directive which obliges all member states to introduce legislation banning direct and indirect age discrimination, victimisation and harassment.

Action points

- Allow any worker who is undergoing gender re-assignment a reasonable amount of time off work to undergo the necessary medical or surgical treatment, and ensure they are not penalised on account of taking time off work for this purpose.

- Be particularly alert to any instances of banter, taunts or jokes based on sexual orientation which could create an uncomfortable working environment for a particular employee (whatever their sexual orientation) and thus constitute unlawful harassment.

- Review carefully whether any policy or rule banning people in close relationships from working in the same department can be justified on business-related grounds, and if so, ensure it is applied both to married and unmarried partners and also to people in other close personal relationships.

- Ensure that no female employee is treated in any way unfavourably on grounds related to the fact that she is pregnant or plans to take maternity leave.

- Be aware of the requirement to conduct risk assessments in relation to pregnancy as soon as a woman of child-bearing age is employed.

- Put procedures in place to deal with requests for flexible working from employees who are the parents or carers of a child under 6, and train line managers to deal with such requests.

- Consult employees about their general needs in relation to religion and belief.

- Review policies on time off and holidays to ensure these are sufficiently flexible to allow employees of different faiths to be granted time off on days or dates that are significant to them on grounds of their religion or belief.

- Ensure that any discriminatory treatment of a disabled worker or job applicant can be justified on grounds that are material and substantial, and take such action only after all reasonable adjustments have been made.

- Seek to identify any measures that will assist or support a disabled employee in the workplace, and discuss with them what adjustments to working arrangements would help them overcome any difficulty that they may be experiencing.

- Audit all policies, procedures and practices, including pay systems, to ensure they are age-neutral, and to identify and eliminate any age-based criteria.

- Ensure that equal opportunities and anti-harassment policies and procedures include treatment on grounds of trans-gender status, sexual orientation, religion and age, as well as sex, marital status, race and disability.

Reference

IRS Equal Opportunities Review, No. 115.

Conclusion

Anyone who has read through this book will undoubtedly be firmly committed to the promotion of equality and diversity and the avoidance of all forms of discrimination and harassment in the workplace. Practising equality and diversity makes sense for organisations of all sizes, and in all sectors.

An employer who has implemented effective equal opportunities and anti-harassment measures and who is genuinely committed to making sure these measures work in practice will be one that can recruit, motivate and retain the best people and achieve the highest possible levels of performance and productivity. Equality and diversity are not only beneficial for employees, but are also essential if the organisation is to succeed in achieving high standards of service or productivity, and with it a reputation for excellence.

Useful Addresses and Websites

ACAS

Head Office

Brandon House
180 Borough High Street
London SE1 1LW

Tel: 020 7210 3000
Helpline: 020 7396 5100
Fax: 020 7210 3645
Website: www.acas.org.uk

Central Arbitration Committee

Brandon House
180 Borough High Street
London SE1 1LW

Tel: 020 7210 3000
Fax: 020 7210 3645

Chartered Institute of Personnel and Development

CIPD House
Camp Road
London SW19 4UX

Tel: 020 8971 9000
Website: www.cipd.co.uk

Commission for Racial Equality

St Dunstan's House
201-211 Borough High Street
London SE1 1GZ

Tel: 020 7939 0000
Fax: 020 7630 7605
Website: www.cre.gov.uk

Criminal Records Bureau

PO Box 91
Liverpool L69 2UH

Tel: 0870 909 0811
Website: www.crb.gov.uk

Department for Education and Skills

Head Office

Sanctuary Buildings
Great Smith Street
Westminster
London SW1P 3BT

Tel: 020 7925 5000/5555
Website: www.dfes.gov.uk

Department of Trade and Industry

Industrial Relations Division

1 Victoria Street
London SW1H 0ET

Tel: 020 7215 5000
Fax: 020 7222 0612
Website: www.dti.gov.uk

Disability Rights Commission

DRC Helpline
Freepost MID 02164
Stratford-upon-Avon CV37 9BR

Tel: 0845 762 2633
Fax: 0845 777 8878
Website: www.drc-gb.org

Employers' Forum on Disability

Nutmeg House
60 Gainsford Street
London SE1 2NY

Tel: 020 7403 3020
Website: www.employers-forum.co.uk

Employment Appeal Tribunal

Audit House
58 Victoria Embankment
London EC4Y 0DS

Tel: 020 7273 1041/2/3
Fax: 020 7273 1045
Website:
www.employmentappeals.gov.uk

(for Scotland)
52 Melville Street
Edinburgh EH3 7HF

Tel: 0131 225 3963
Fax: 0131 220 6694

Employment Service

Head Office

Rockingham House
123 West Street
Sheffield S1 4ER

Tel: 0870 001 0171
Website:
www.employmentservice.gov.uk

Equal Opportunities Commission

Arndale House
Arndale Centre
Manchester M4 3EQ

Tel: 0161 833 9244
Fax: 0161 838 8312
Website: www.eoc.org.uk

Health and Safety Executive

Rose Court
Southwark Bridge
London SE1 9HS

Tel: 020 7717 6000
Website: www.hse.gov.uk

HSE Infoline

Caerphilly Business Park
Caerphilly CF83 3GG

Tel: 0870 154 5500

Home Office

Integrated Casework Directorate
Lunar House
40 Wellesley Road
Croydon CR9 1AT

Tel: 0870 606 7766
Helpline for guidance on individuals'
right to work in the UK:
020 8649 7878
Website: www.ind.homeoffice.gov.uk

Information Commissioner

Wycliffe House,
Water Lane
Wilmslow SK9 5AX

Tel: 01625 545 745
Website: www.dataprotection.gov.uk

Redundancy Payments Offices

England and Wales

7th Floor
Hagley House
83–85 Hagley Road
Edgbaston
Birmingham B16 8QG

Tel: 0121 456 4411
Fax: 0121 454 951

(for Scotland)

Ladywell House
Ladywell Road
Edinburgh EH12 7UR

Tel: 0131 316 5600
Fax: 0131 334 8441

Trades Union Congress (TUC)

Congress House
Great Russell Street
London WC1B 3LS

Tel: 020 7636 4030
Website: www.tuc.org.uk

Work Permits

Customer Relations

Integrated Casework Directorate
North (Sheffield) Home Office
Level 5
Moorfoot
Sheffield S1 4PQ

Tel: 0114 259 4074
Website: www.workpermits.gov.uk

Work Permits

Business Teams (Croydon)

Home Office
Block B
Whitgift Centre
Wellesley Road
Croydon

Tel: 0208 760 4802/4805

Work Permits

Business Teams (Sheffield)

Home Office
Foundry House
Millsands
Bridge Street
Sheffield S3 8NH

Tel: 0114 279 3678

Index

Race Relations Act (Amendment)
Regulations 2003 6, 10, 216
Race Relations Amendment Act (RRAA)
2000 19, 216
racial harassment, definition of 119–20
recruitment of employees see employee
recruitment
recruitment procedures of an organisation
3
redundancy, and discrimination 1, 147–51
selection for 148–51
see also discrimination, at termination
of employment
references, and discrimination 153
religion, discrimination on grounds of 1,
3, 5, 10–11, 52–6, 120, 141–2, 153,
183, 193, 197, 217–21
GORs 10–11, 218
useful information on 221
religious harassment (harassment on a
religious pretext) 120, 125, 218, 219
requirements for a job see job
requirements
retention of employees see employee
retention
retirement age(s), compulsory 151–3
reverse discrimination see positive
discrimination on behalf of minority
groups
rights, conflicting see conflicting rights in
the workplace

selection of candidates for employment
27–50
avoiding discrimination in 27–48
criteria for 27
keeping records on 43
making the decision on 42–3
scoring systems 43
see also employee recruitment
sex discrimination, indirect 42, 90, 100,
110, 139–40, 198, 212
see also gender discrimination; sexual
harassment
Sex Discrimination Act 1975 6, 74, 80,
87, 111, 118, 121–2, 139, 152, 158,

172, 174, 179, 181, 187–8, 196, 198–9,
202–3, 204, 205
EC Code of Practice on the Protection
of the Dignity of Men and Women at
Work 121–2
EU law and 198–9
sexual harassment 121–2, 198
sexual orientation, discrimination on
grounds of 1, 3, 5, 11, 120–1, 183,
193, 196, 202–4
GORs 11, 203
harassment in relation to 120–1
see also Employment Equality (Sexual
Orientation) Regulations 2003
social events, and discrimination 63
stereotyping as discrimination 2, 24, 36,
108–9, 204, 228, 230–1
stress-related illness, and discrimination
137–9
Sunday working, and discrimination 52–4

team, recruitment/selection candidate's fit
with 36–7
time off for religious holidays (etc),
discrimination over 52–6, 84, 141–2
dismissal/discipline over 141–2
human rights implications of 55–6
time off to care for dependants,
discrimination over 51
training, access without discrimination to
100–4, 105–7
influence on employee outcomes of xi,
101
scheduling of 101–2
see also discrimination, in training
and development; induction training
trans-gender issues see gender re-
assignment
tribunal(s) see employment tribunal

valuing diversity see diversity, valuing by
an organisation of
victimisation, discriminatory 184–7

Working Time Regulations 1998 81, 83
work permits in the UK 48–9